Victorian Period Piece

Victorian Period Piece

Studies Occasioned by a Lancashire Church

J. Stanley Leatherbarrow

LONDON

S·P·C·K

1954

First published in 1954 by
S.P.C.K.
Northumberland Avenue, London, W.C.2
Made and printed in Great Britain by
William Clowes and Sons, Limited, London and Beccles

CONTENTS

ILLUSTRATIONS

AN ACKNOWLEDGEMENT

THE mid-Victorian period which this study makes some attempt to describe is as remote from our present way of life as the period of the Restoration. Its economic assumptions, its philosophical certainties—except amongst the erudite minority—its ways of building, its dress, its pleasures, are so different from the democratized set-up of a hundred years later that it can be studied with the detachment belonging to observers on a separate plane of existence. Yet most of us have known in our lifetime at least a few people who have so remarkably survived from that remote age as to make an acquaintance with them something akin to the turning of the pages of a living history book. Three such persons have inspired the writing of this book.

The first was Anna Maria Philips of the Park, Prestwich, who was born in 1857 and died in 1946. Until the end of her life she maintained that large house in a style practically unchanged from that of her father and her grandfather who built it in 1800. Dr G. M. Trevelyan in his life of Sir G. O. Trevelyan describes it as "a most interesting monument of the ways of life of Manchester merchant princes a century and more ago". Something of the manner of life lived by Miss Philips in the 1930's has been described in Chapter 1 of this book. During the time of its writing the mansion has been completely demolished by the Urban District of Whitefield and the Borough of Prestwich, who became the owners of the Park estate after Miss Philips's death and who, whilst exerting every effort to maintain the grounds in their beautiful condition, could find no use whatever for the Georgian house. So within the time of writing one more link with the Victorian epoch has been severed. The privilege of having known it towards the end of its remarkable life, therefore, becomes all the more precious, and the task of trying to recapture a little of its atmosphere and to set it down on paper, something of a duty.

Acknowledgement

The two other links with that epoch are the two sisters Isabel Mary and Mary Monica Heywood, daughters of Sir Thomas Percival Heywood, second baronet, of Doveleys, Staffs, and nieces of the Reverend Henry Robinson Heywood, builder of Swinton Church. Isabel died peacefully during Hitler's war, her sister in 1951. Whilst both the Philips and Heywood families derived from a dissenting tradition, these two ladies grew up in fortunate circumstances during the time when their father was taking his place as one of the lay leaders of the developing High Church movement. Through his friendships they became acquainted with some of the most eminent Churchmen of the day. The crucifix which hangs on the writer's study wall came to him from Miss Isabel Heywood after her death and was one which she especially valued as having been blessed by Dr Pusey himself.

The conversation of these two devout sisters, who were ever ready to talk about their earlier years to those who were really interested, was again a privileged glimpse into that delightful Victorian epoch. To those like the Heywood family who were well equipped with material possessions, the way of social life on that Staffordshire countryside was truly idyllic. Never were children reared in surroundings of greater devotion, beauty, and innocent pleasure. To recapture the relationships of their sanctified family life was to dispel many of the prejudices and illusions that one had held about the repressions and inhibitions of Victorian domesticity. "Were not your friendships and pastimes very sternly controlled in your home life?" I once asked one of the sisters. "Good gracious, no," she replied. "Father didn't mind how late we were out riding with the M. boys, so long as we were in good time for family prayers in the morning." Our notions of the sternness of Victorian family life would have to be a little revised if we could know more at first hand of what actually went on in families such as this.

That is all a long time ago, and there are not many who survive with minds sufficiently clear to tell us what life was like for them at the beginning of the second half of the nineteenth century. To have known two or three such people is perhaps one of the lasting privileges of a lifetime. Such mentors enable one to struggle towards the achievement of what thoughtful people in every age yearn to do, namely to disentangle the abiding from the passing in human experience. Because these three gracious ladies have helped at least one aspirant in that direction, he dedicates this study in their memory, with affection, gratitude, and deep respect.

I am grateful to Mr Cecil Stewart, Head of the School of Architecture in the Regional College of Art, Manchester, who has informed me that the church of St Thomas, Pendleton was described in the contemporary issue of the *Manchester Guardian* as "built after a design furnished by Mr F. Goodwin, of London, and Mr Lane, of this town." My ascription of the church, therefore, to Thomas Taylor of Leeds on page 143 is incorrect. It remains still to be discovered for which Manchester church Taylor was responsible.

I wish to thank Mr Roger Fulford, who has read my book in page proof and out of his encyclopaedic knowledge of the nineteenth century has made one or two suggestions which I have noted in the text. To Bishop B. O. F. Heywood and Miss Dorothy Heywood—present bearers of an honoured name—I extend my most cordial thanks for their permission to quote extensively from their father's private diary and to use certain family photographs. I wish to thank my friend Mr Robert Walmsley of John Dalton St, Manchester, for help in reading the manuscript and correcting the proofs; and my respected brethren of the Concord Club, who have given me much encouragement and advice after hearing substantial portions of some of the chapters read aloud to them at their meetings.

In conclusion, I wish to make grateful acknowledgement to the following publishers for permission to include quotations in this work: Longmans Green & Co., Ltd., *My Apprenticeship*, by Beatrice Webb; George G. Harrap & Co., Ltd., *A Norfolk Diary: The Reverend Benjamin J. Armstrong*, edited by H. B. J. Armstrong; and John Murray (Publishers) Ltd., *An Eighteenth Century Correspondence: to Sanderson Miller, Esq.*, edited by L. Dickins and M. Stanton.

J. S. L.

INTRODUCTION

ABOUT eighty years ago a faithful Lancashire priest commissioned one of the foremost architects in England to rebuild his parish church. There was nothing unique in this, for the Church revival of those days was producing a spate of church building and restoration in every part of the country. So it comes about that the spires and towers of the Gothic Revival stretch skywards in almost every other Anglican parish, sometimes to the admiration of the discerning; more often to their execration. The building of these Victorian churches has been frequently written about; pious pens have extolled their builders in a thousand parish magazines and jubilee handbooks. What has not been so frequently attempted is a sketch of the movements, social, religious, architectural, and even personal, in mid-Victorian England which led up to those buildings which are an inescapable feature of our contemporary landscape. Who were the folk who built these churches and what were the influences bearing upon their lives to make them the sort of people they were?

Victorian studies are having an increasing fascination for people in this troubled mid-twentieth century. To speak of an object as a Victorian period piece is not now to cover it with disparagement, as might have been the case before 1914. There appears to us to be a solidity, a settled quality of life about those Victorians which is reflected in their buildings and which is beginning to compel our admiration. So the Victorian period piece is now an object of interest, whether it be a piece of Staffordshire pottery or a church by Gilbert Scott. These studies converge upon Swinton Church in Lancashire: a building designed by George Edmund Street at the bidding of the Reverend Henry Robinson Heywood in 1869, to replace a Georgian chapel of 1791. Those are the bare facts of the matter. But so many approaches met at that one point in 1869 which produced the new church. It is a task of considerable interest to explore each of those approaches backwards to points very far removed from 1869. In the conviction that these avenues of social history and development meet in such churches, the making of Swinton Church is suggested as a representative essay. What has been attempted in this instance could be reproduced a thousand times elsewhere. Yet the study of this one will be worthwhile if it enables us to see in the many Victorian parish church spires and towers not the freakish fancy of some wealthy visionary, but the epitome of the social history of a fascinating era.

1

THE SOCIAL APPROACH

I

SWINTON Church was consecrated on 2 October 1869. It therefore stakes a claim to be very nearly mid-Victorian, for that date is almost a half-way mark in the Queen's reign. It was thirty-two years since the young girl first met her Council at Kensington Palace at 11 a.m. on 21 June 1837. Then, an observer could note, never was anything like the first impression she produced or the chorus of praise and admiration which was raised about her manner and behaviour. It was very extraordinary; something far beyond what was looked for. It augured better prospects for the future of the British Monarchy, which thoughtful men considered to be in a very precarious state after years of madness, badness, and downright foolish eccentricity. Nearly thirty-two more years were to elapse before the Queen Empress, slowly declining in the four years' afterglow of her Jubilee apotheosis, at last quitted the scene, and by her death brought an epoch to an end.

The period of social approach to the building of Swinton Church is really the first half of Queen Victoria's reign. A still more convenient division of time during which to study this approach might be achieved by pushing the earlier date back to 1832 and closing the period in 1868. This takes us from the first Reform Bill to the great Conservative adventure in enfranchisement, when some 1,080,000 persons were added to the Parliamentary Register. It is in fact the period during which the people of England were trying to assimilate the first measure of reform, to adjust themselves to the shift in the social centre of gravity which it involved, and to remedy its inadequacies by carrying through a second act which, so far at any rate as the towns were concerned, meant the adoption of household suffrage pure and simple. The period is one which has been called "The Transition from Aristocracy"; it covers the gradual transfer of the predominant power in the State from land to commerce, from the great peers, whether of Tory or Whig affiliation, to the new men, the bankers, the merchants, the shippers, and the factory owners. The transition was not a sudden one: it did not come overnight as a result of the passing of the first Reform Act. In spite of the prediction of dire catastrophe which had been made by the upholders of the old régime we find that, when the dust of battle had settled, the landed faction, perhaps a little to its own astonishment, still found itself to be pretty firmly entrenched in the Reformed Parliament, and throughout the period the personnel of the cabinets of succeeding governments was largely aristocratic.

Still, the landed faction could not really resist the pressure of economic forces which the Industrial Revolution and the upsurge of new money had brought into play. It took a hard knock at the repeal of the Corn Laws. Cheap bread for the masses in the new industrial towns prevailed against the proprietary rights of British agriculture, and the turn of the issue showed into what hands the bias of power in the legislature was falling.

But if the industrial middle classes were satisfied with the place in the sun which the new legislation had won for them, there was one section of the population which certainly was not. The condition of the working classes throughout this period was on the whole deplorable. The pictures of working-class life in Disraeli's novels, in such stories as Mrs Gaskell's *Mary Barton* and Kingsley's *Yeast* and *Alton Locke*, and in contemporary journals, reveal a state of society in which much of the new wealth was being concentrated in the hands of the privileged few, whilst the majority subsisted in abject poverty. The working classes had expected some alleviation of their lot from the first Reform Bill, and indeed the first Whig government which succeeded it was by no means devoid of legislation which at any rate touched the fringe of some of the social problems. But the pace of improvement was very slow; so slow that the working classes became quickly disillusioned with what had been accomplished in 1832. So this period sees the rise and fall of Chartism, a movement greatly feared by those in power, reaching a climax which turned out to be ridiculous rather than revolutionary in 1848, and yet, in spite of its apparent failure, achieving in the long run in a peculiarly English contradictory way most of what it wanted by the time the secret ballot was secured in 1872.

It is not an easy matter to survey this period concisely, for the student is almost overwhelmed by the richness of contemporary writing which illustrates the movements of the time. The contemporary letters and journals have been carefully worked over and embodied in many scholarly books describing the reign. Queen Victoria's own letters are the principal source of information, but in many other odd corners of literary lore it is possible to gain an exact knowledge of what men and women of the time were thinking about the problems of their own age. The journals of Charles Greville, Clerk to the Council, are one of the richest veins of ore of this sort of historical data. Intimately connected by family ties and by friendship with most of the leading personalities of the day, he was in a unique position to know exactly what was going on in the parliamentary world. He was frequently employed as a go-between when the most delicate negotiations were being transacted between the parties. He was an inveterate collector of political gossip, though he scorned to set down much of the private and scandalous *bavardage*, which probably would have been of more interest to the social historian of a hundred years later than ever he could have supposed possible. He was intensely self critical, and dubious as to the ultimate interest of his voluminous scribbling. He need not have worried, for no student of the first half of the reign would ever think of neglecting Charles Greville's diaries as one of his main sources of information.

The main alignment of the classes of society thus briefly sketched has been amply illustrated in many standard historical works on the Victorian era. We must now try to show how people in this part of Lancashire, where the Victorian period piece was to be built, were conscious of the movements in the social structure, and how they played their part in the shifting scene with its tensions as between crown, aristocracy, middle classes, and working proletariat. If the scene did shift and the social pattern change, the people of Lancashire had no small part in the movement of its various components. If the building of the church was in some part evidence of stirrings in the social order we may look at it as it now stands with a good deal of added interest; it is a tangible monument to new ideals and aspirations which rose from a period of social development, in which the aristocratic and the wealthy commercial classes were becoming more conscious of their responsibilities in the ownership and administration of the new wealth, and in which the working classes were learning to take a more intelligent interest in the creation and administration of the outward symbols of their community life.

II

The average Englishman loves domesticity and it was perhaps the ideal home life of the new Queen and her family which helped more than anything else to set the tottering throne upon firm foundations. The alliance between Victoria of England and Prince Albert of Saxe-Coburg was not in any sense a political *mariage de convenance*: it was a love match from start to finish, and the romantic Britisher gave the Queen credit for it. In November 1839 the Queen wrote to all her family and told them that she was soon to be married. Meeting the Duchess of Gloucester in town, she told her that she was to make her declaration the next day. The Duchess asked her if it was not a nervous thing to do. She said: "Yes; but I did a much more nervous thing a little while ago." "What was that?" said the Duchess. "I proposed to Prince Albert", replied the Queen.

The happy family life at Windsor was an astonishing change to the British public, who had been taught to think of the domestic intimacies of the Royal Family as they saw them portrayed in the salacious evidence produced at Queen Caroline's trial. Whether that picture was fair and true or not, it enabled the new Royal Family to stand out in heightened contrast. The shots fired at the Queen were fired by mad men. If the ruling classes found it hard to accept the foreign Consort in the scheme of things, and if British insularity was more than a little suspicious of the brisk efficiency of the Germanic mind, with its reports and schemes for improvement and reform, it was none the less appreciative of him as a faithful husband. In 1844 the Queen could report to King Leopold that the newspapers said that "*No* Sovereign was more loved than I am (I am bold enough to say) and *that*, from our *happy domestic home* . . . which gives such a good example." The coloured prints of the Queen, her husband, and the royal children which adorned cottage walls were evidence of popular affection even when the father of the family happened to be a Chartist. The aristocratic and middle classes began to come into line as to the ordering of their family life. Whig historians have commented upon the widespread illegitimacy in the great Whig families of the eighteenth century. A great brood of natural children, often accepted and acknowledged and living side by side with the legitimate offspring, was a customary feature of noblemen's households. The mistress was fairly commonly tolerated in almost every rank of respectable society. When " Mr Press Custance's *Lady*" went to church at Weston in 1780 she sent before to ask Parson Woodforde's leave to sit in his seat. The parson granted his permission, making only the difference that he desired his sister not to attend church on that occasion owing to the Lady sitting in the seat. It is a far cry from this to the happy domestic unity of Lord Francis Egerton and his wife at their aristocratic establishments at Worsley and Bridgewater House; or to the spectacle of the middle-class banking family of Heywood solemnly conducting family prayers before and after their holiday excursion to view the engineering wonders of the Menai tubular bridge. That unchastity was abolished in Victorian society from English life we shall not be so foolish as to suppose. But at any rate it was driven underground: the ideal became marital faithfulness, and

2

there is no reason to believe that it was not happily achieved in innumerable families. Infidelity was not pleasantly condoned by public opinion, and if its survival gives pretext to some modern writers to castigate the hypocrisy of Victorian society, there is no more reason to vilify the Victorians for their failure always to achieve their ideals than the aspiring idealists of any other age. That domestic fidelity did emerge as an ideal was largely due to the example set by the Queen's own family life and the happy marriages of such of her ministers as Gladstone and Disraeli. A felicitous domestic life is most often the fruit of a deeply felt family religion. Conversely, intense family sentiment will frequently produce the usual manifestations of the religious life. It is not, therefore, unreasonable to see in this new pattern of harmonious family life embedded in religious practices which was set by the Queen, a little of the impetus to the widely spreading religious movements of the middle of the century. Quite often a new church was the concerted enterprise of several devoted families in a neighbourhood. The appropriated pew which many clerical builders disliked for other obvious reasons was, at its best, the outward citadel of family religion. Family prayers and the family pew are a symbolic expression of the intense family spirit in Victorian religion. Without doubt that spirit emanated in a large part from the family sentiment of Victoria and Albert, and the happy family life which the Queen's subjects could see exemplified at Windsor.

Nor was it necessary to travel as far as London to see the Queen. When a glee club of Lancashire working men could sing madrigals under her bedroom window she must have seemed in very truth to belong to the people. Her many progresses up and down the country, staying at the great houses of noblemen, enabled the ordinary folk to feel very close to her whose picture in hideous coloured lithographs from Christmas almanacs looked down upon them from their kitchen walls, and whose name fell upon their ears Sunday by Sunday as they listened to the pompous state prayers of the Anglican liturgy. The Queen passed through Swinton in October 1851, eighteen years before the new church was built. Hundreds of village folk must have seen her in even closer proximity during her stay with the Earl and Countess of Ellesmere at Worsley Hall on the same occasion.

It was the first visit of Queen Victoria to Manchester. On 10 October, she and Prince Albert arrived at Patricroft Station and came to Worsley along the Duke of Bridgewater's canal by the Royal Barge. Heavy Lancashire rain fell and marred the effect of the pageant of barges and the decorated regatta boats which accompanied them. The progress of Her Majesty was loudly cheered at each bridge and along the banks of the canal by the crowds of sightseers. On the following day the royal party left Worsley about 10 a.m. and proceeded through Swinton, Irlams o' th' Height, and Pendleton to the boundary of Salford. At Swinton the scholars from the various schools were grouped in Moor Lane and sang the National Anthem as the Queen passed. Stands were also erected in the village, but the natural economy of the natives prevented them from paying to use them and financially they were a failure. A triumphal arch was erected near White's Farm in Moor Lane and special constables were appointed to keep the crowds in order.[1] They lined the route at intervals of about a hundred yards. Each constable held his baton erect and as soon as the royal party got in the carriages at Worsley Hall, the first constable brought his baton smartly down to his side, giving the cue to his neighbour to do likewise. Thus was the news of the approach of the *cortège* signalled by living telegraph all along the route.

As a guard of honour the Queen was accompanied by a large number of Yeomanry Cavalry. These rode with her as far as Cross Lane in Salford but were not allowed to proceed farther. Yeomanry Cavalry were a little too reminiscent of Peterloo; the memory of that murderous dash into the crowd was still a sore point with Lancashire people. Thus the royal party came to Manchester. There were five carriages containing the Queen,

---

[1] The author's great-grandfather was amongst the estate tenants enrolled as a special constable. My great uncle took my grandmother, then eight years of age, to see the procession. A family tradition relates that he said to her, "Look out for t' mon wi' t' big nose." For the rest of her life her recollections of the day centred rather round the Duke of Wellington than Queen Victoria.—*J. S. L.*

Prince Albert, the Prince of Wales, the Princess Royal, the Duke of Wellington, the Duke of Norfolk, the Marquis of Westminster, the Earl and Countess of Ellesmere, Earl Grey, Viscountess Brackley, Viscountess Canning, the Honourable Captain Egerton, the Ladies Alice and Blanche Egerton, the Honourable Beatrice Byng, Colonel Phipps, Colonel Gordon, Sir James Clark, and the Reverend H. M. Birch. The last named had been tutor to the Prince of Wales; as he looked out of his carriage to the left when the procession reached Irlams o' th' Height he no doubt saw on the opposite side of the Irwell Valley the ancient tower of the parish church of Prestwich, to which opulent living he was to be presented as rector by the Earl of Wilton in the following year. The visitors were conducted from Worsley to Salford by the High Sheriff, Mr Thomas Percival Heywood, elder brother of the future builder of Swinton Church. He rode in his state chariot with the Earl of Carlisle and his sister-in-law, Mrs Oliver Heywood.

At Windsor Bridge, the Mayor of Salford, Mr Thomas Agnew, was presented to the Queen by Earl Grey, and then led the way into Peel Park where an address, engrossed on vellum, was read and presented to Her Majesty. Seventy thousand scholars then sang the National Anthem, including a new verse written for the occasion by Mr Charles Swain, a local poet. So out of the Park and along Chapel Street the procession passed into Manchester, which was reached at 11.45 a.m. At Victoria Bridge the Mayor of Salford handed over to the Mayor of Manchester, Mr John Potter, who after being received by the Queen presented a bouquet to her. The procession then passed along Victoria Street, Market Street, High Street, Shudehill, Swan Street, and Oldham Street to Piccadilly. The great central space of Manchester was gay with ornamental fountains, decorated arches, illuminated scrolls, lamps, and the usual paraphernalia for the reception of royalty. The destination of the cavalcade was the Exchange, which was densely crowded, in spite of the high price of admission at 20s. each person. Here the Mayor and Corporation received the royal party, and an address was read by the Recorder of the City. The national anthem was sung by the choristers of the cathedral and the Mayor was knighted. The ceremonies in the Exchange took about half an hour, and the party then returned to Worsley. Shortly after the royal visit the Exchange received the title of "Royal", and a marble statue of the Queen was erected in Peel Park.

On the following day at 8 a.m. a deputation of workmen from Manchester arrived at Worsley Hall to sing under the Queen's window. They were then invited into the house and entertained the company with two pieces entitled, "Lo! the early beams of morning" and "Now pray we for our country". They were followed by fourteen hundred scholars from the Earl of Ellesmere's estate who gathered in the Hall grounds with clergy and teachers. There were flags, banners, bands, and even another loyal address to be presented. Finally the scholars watched the royal party embark on the state barges to be taken to Patricroft Station for the return journey. The Earl and Countess of Derby and the Earl and Countess of Wilton were also in attendance. Thus did the Lords and Commons of Lancashire assemble to do honour to the Queen. The royal lady and her party reached Windsor Castle about 8 p.m. the same evening, no doubt suitably exhausted by the vociferous protests of Lancashire loyalty.

There is a suggestion that her subsequent gratification in the memory of the Manchester expedition was tempered by the rather mortifying information in the following month that the Hungarian patriot Kossuth had also been received in the same city with enthusiastic demonstrations as great as had attended her own visit.

It is not difficult to imagine what an impression such a gala day must have made upon the working classes of Lancashire. The Queen and her lords and ladies supplied for our ancestors just that touch of glamour which in this more celluloid age is made so easily accessible to us by the scintillating confraternity of Hollywood. Certainly her visit was talked about until recent years by the elderly folk who had survived with 11 October 1851 as one of the memorable days of their lives. Their existence was sufficiently drab, hedged round with monotonous and low-paid jobs in the mines and factories. Life was static to an extent which it is hard now to visualize. Holidays were short and infrequent, confined to a day or two at Blackpool each year or a short school excursion to a near-by beauty spot. Their imagination lacked the wider vistas which have been supplied in our day by cinemas and easier opportunities for travel. The colour and excitement and pageantry of that day must have made it outstanding in their grey existences. Above all, it was centred upon a person, and it requires no great stretch of the imagination to see how the colourful enthusiasm of that exciting day would be transferred to the person of the royal lady who had made it possible. Such gala occasions were subtle propaganda for the monarchical idea. There was little anti-royalist sentiment amongst the Commons of Lancashire, and the apex of the social pyramid against which Swinton Church was built was firmly loyalist. The splendours of the procession which passed down Moor Lane in 1851, the cheering school children *en route*, the glee club beneath the Queen's window at Worsley Hall, these details of the social background of the middle part of the reign are not to be forgotten as planks in the solid foundation of that settled order of society which exhibited itself, amongst other ways, in the mid-Victorian churches.

III

Whilst Swinton Church was being built, the builders could see from their scaffolds, two miles away to the southwest, the spire of a singularly correct imitation of a thirteenth-century church. Twenty-three years previously Lord Francis Egerton had set Gilbert Scott to do his painstaking best, and Worsley Church was the by no means unimpressive result. But more lay behind this church than a successful essay in geometrical Gothic; it was a symbol that aristocracy had taken a turn for the better.

The bulk of the aristocracy had contemplated the 1832 Reform Bill with fear and anger. They regarded it quite rightly as an assault upon their entrenched privileges exercised throughout the eighteenth century by means of pocket boroughs, placemen, and patronage. The middle classes had now become too powerful to suffer this monopoly of government any longer, and, after fighting the struggle to the last ditch, aristocracy had at last to succumb to the inevitable and to accept a legislature which they considered would be composed of

. . . mob orators, men who are willing to pay the basest court to the multitude; . . . low, fierce, desperate men, who will turn the House into a bear-garden, and will turn the monarchy into a republic, mere agitators, without honour, without sense, without education, without the feelings or manners of gentlemen.

But really, it did not turn out to be anything like so lurid as these lugubrious predictors had anticipated. Greville described the opening of the first session of the Reformed Parliament in 1833. He commented upon its inferiority in point of composition to preceding Houses of Commons, and the presumption, impertinence, and self-sufficiency of the new members who behaved as if they had taken it by storm and might riot in all the insolence of victory. But the story was very different at the end of the session.

Let the praise rest where it may, whether it be due to the wisdom of men or the result of that disposition to right itself which has always appeared inherent in the British Commonwealth . . . a Reform Parliament turns out to be very much like every other Parliament except that it is rather differently and somewhat less ably composed than its predecessors.

There had been no sign of tumbrils bowling along Whitehall; the great aristocrats were safely in their shoes, and Trollope's Duke of Omnium was very willing that the Queen should be queen so long as he was allowed to be Duke of Omnium. . . . Their revenues were about the same. The Duke of Bedford still ruled with semi-regal grandeur and more than common efficiency from his palace at Woburn. Greville said that he never saw such an abode of luxury and enjoyment, one so full of resources for all tastes. The management of the Duke's estate was like the

administration of a little kingdom. He had four hundred and
fifty people in his employment on the Bedfordshire property
alone, not counting domestic servants. His pensions amounted to
£2,000 a year. There was order, economy, grandeur, comfort,
and general content. In 1848 Greville found equal satisfaction
when he stayed at Endsleigh, the Duke of Bedford's residence in
Devonshire. Like the country around, it was exquisitely beautiful.
The house, which was a cottage, cost between £70,000 and
£80,000, and the grounds with their sixty miles of grass rides
and gravel walks, thousands more. This was a property which had
come to the Bedfords as monastic spoils; the family had been
gorged with abbey lands both here and at Woburn.

Commerce was invading this domain in the shape of a great
copper mine, the best and most profitable in the West of England.
Fortunes had been made in the mine, the shares at one time having
been worth £70 apiece. Yet, although the whole countryside was
rich in copper, the Duke told his visitor that he was not going to
grant any more leases to mine it, though he could have made a
great deal of money by them. He professed not to want the money,
and declined to promote the spirit of gambling which followed on
such commercial speculations. Agriculture was his chief concern,
and the copper mining was detrimental to agriculture. Farmers
let their carts and horses to the miners instead of using them on
their own farms, and, though mining was both profitable and
popular employment, the Duke considered it mischievous and
would not allow any more of his ground to be broken up for the
chance of finding the copper. The first great Reform Bill had
come and gone, the Corn Duties had been abolished, but 1848,
the year of Revolution, found the great territorial magnates still
firmly fixed in the saddle.

Yet there was some stirring in the tree-tops of the aristocratic
mind. It was beginning to develop a sense of responsibility, to
perceive that the ownership of vast wealth, often immensely increased by the discovery of minerals underneath the land, demanded the display of benevolent duty towards the people who
lived upon it. If wealth and territorial possessions no longer conveyed the absolute right to determine the character of the

legislature and by influence and patronage to direct the country's policy, it still required its owner to have a care for the well-being of the humbler folk who farmed the land and the toilers who created the wealth. The era which followed the Reform Bill saw some change of heart in the landowning aristocrats; that change of heart could not be more vividly illustrated than in a brief sketch of the difference between the characters of the third Marquis of Hertford, who died in 1842, and Lord Francis Egerton, afterwards Earl of Ellesmere.

There must have been infinite gradations of character between the worst and the best which are exemplified in these two noblemen, but the personality of each is so striking in its own way that we may offset them against each other so as to show how the latter exhibited the finest ideals of aristocracy which the other had no scruple in dragging through the dirt. It may be doubted whether aristocracy could have survived had there been many more extreme examples like the Marquis of Hertford. Francis Egerton did a good deal to re-establish the confidence of ordinary people in his order and to show that mid-Victorian aristocracy was still as capable of moral leadership as in the finest days of feudalism. Francis Charles, third Marquis of Hertford, generally supposed to be the model for the Marquis of Steyne in *Vanity Fair*, was born on 11 March 1777 and died on 1 March 1842. Greville, whose obituary notices are fair and concise summaries of some of the leading figures of his day, described his life and death as equally disgusting and revolting to every good and moral feeling. In his youth, as the favourite of George IV when his mother was the Prince's mistress, he was known as a sharp, cunning, luxurious, and avaricious man of the world. An inveterate and successful gambler, he supported himself by the cunning shrewdness of his play, and when he succeeded to his title as Lord Hertford with an enormous property, he delighted in vulgar pomp and ceremony and could only endure those who paid him court and homage. In his moral life he appears to have touched the depths, and the chronicler declares that no example of undisguised debauchery was ever exhibited to the world like that of Lord Hertford. He travelled about with a company of prostitutes who were his principal associates, was lifted by two footmen from his carriage into the brothel and openly flaunted his immorality before the town. He died without a serious thought or kindly feeling, never doing a generous or a charitable action and surrounded to the last by a venal harem who pandered to his disgusting pleasures. Men of the world were nauseated by the sight of innumerable carriages of private individuals who followed his pompous funeral from Dorchester House, pretending to show respect which none of them felt. Even Sir Robert Peel's carriage followed in the procession, greatly to the disgust of the Duke of Bedford, who wrote: "What is the use of character and conduct in this world, if after such a life and death and will as Lord Hertford's, such a mark of respect is paid to his memory by the First Minister of this great country . . .?" Here was aristocracy at its lowest ebb.[1]

It was a fortunate thing for Swinton that its local aristocrat was Lord Ellesmere and not Lord Hertford; it was equally fortunate for Lord Ellesmere that the property which he had inherited lay in such a rich neighbourhood as Worsley and Swinton. The mineral which had added superfluous wealth to the Duke of Bedford's Devonshire estate was copper; Ellesmere's good fortune lay in coal. The piling up of the "Bridgewater Millions" is as romantic a story as any in the whole tale of the Industrial Revolution. The Duke of Bridgewater, disappointed in his suit with a famous London beauty, retired to his Lancashire estates, six miles from Manchester, lived more or less a recluse's life at the old half-timbered Worsley Hall, and devoted his whole interest to the exploitation of the mineral resources which lay underneath his land. The problem of cheap transport of his coal to Manchester led to his discovery of the engineer Brindley, who devised the remarkable canal with its famous Barton Aqueduct which was regarded as one of the wonders of the engineering world. As a pioneer of inland waterways, the Duke built up a prodigious

---

[1] Mr Roger Fulford has pointed out to me that a more favourable picture of Lord Hertford is derived from the *D. N. B.* or from the pages of Croker. He was very reactionary: hence some of the obloquy. He was quite a success as ambassador to Russia in the 1820's.—*J. S. L.*

fortune, and the canal continued to earn large dividends until the coming of cheap railway transport. Greville tells something of this story because Lord Ellesmere married his sister and he visited Worsley from time to time. He speaks of the immense population which came together in this neighbourhood to obtain employment in the Duke's concerns, but he gives the impression that the Duke enjoyed the financial profits of his commercial enterprises and never troubled himself about the source from which he derived them. Here it seems that Greville was telling less than the truth; his information regarding the "old Duke" was inadequate, for Bridgewater certainly resided at the old Hall for the greater part of his time, took the closest interest in the progress of his commercial adventures, particularly the canal, and built a certain amount of property to accommodate his workpeople. Compared with the philanthropy of Ellesmere, of course, his sense of social responsibility was small, but it is unfair to judge him, an essentially eighteenth-century man, by the enlightened standards which were exemplified in his heir.

Lord Francis Leveson Gower, later Egerton, succeeded on the death of his father, the Duke of Sutherland, to the immense fortune entailed upon him by his great-uncle, the Duke of Bridgewater. He found himself the possessor of vast wealth and surrounded by a population which Greville describes as sunk in ignorance and vice. There were various difficulties in regard to the trust under his great-uncle's will with which Egerton had to contend when he inherited the property. The canal and collieries had been left in trust to the Duke's agent, Bradshaw, with unlimited power of management, and Egerton's first task was to get this agent, a dissolute fellow, as Greville describes him, out of the trust. A man named Sotherton was appointed when Bradshaw had been removed by a bargain, but Sotherton was no sooner in power than he began to demonstrate his independence in a way that was refractory and displeasing to the new owner. Egerton went to law with Sotherton, but found him so firmly established by law as a trustee that he ended by compounding with him in a sum of £45,000 to relinquish the trust and to appoint a nominee of Egerton's in his place.

Legal difficulties having now been removed, and a new and satisfactory trustee having been found in the person of James Loch, Egerton and his wife set about with fierce energy to reform the condition of the people amongst whom they were to live. They found it very bad, with the mass of the people in the lowest state of ignorance and degradation. They entered upon their task entirely from a sense of duty, from fully recognizing the authority of the maxim that "property has its duties as well as its rights". It was not a maxim that Lord Hertford would have agreed with; nor perhaps the Duke of Bridgewater himself. But the age of seriousness had arrived and the Bridgewater Millions were a very useful asset in promoting its fruits.

The first thing was to live amongst the people, and, as the old half-timbered Hall was not consonant with mid-Victorian ideas of social elegance, a new palace had to be built in which Queen Victoria was to be entertained in 1851. Greville stayed there for the first time in November 1845 and described the fine new house which his brother-in-law had built. It was, he said, a very handsome specimen of Blore's architecture, rather spoilt by alterations made while the building was in progress; comfortable enough, but with many faults. In parenthesis we may mention that the reign of this house was not a long one as such houses go. The Ellesmere family never lived in it after its occupation as a military hospital in the First World War. When the estates were sold to the Bridgewater Trust soon afterwards, no adequate use could be found for this pretentious structure. It fell more or less into decay, at last came into the hands of the demolishers, and at the time of writing all that remains of the palace that entertained Victoria is one ruined corner. The old Hall, by a strange turn of chance, has met a happier fate; it is now one of the offices of the National Coal Board, and the home of the great Duke who created the Bridgewater fortune by excavating and transporting the coal beneath it now becomes one of the administrative centres from which coal from the same seams is mined and distributed not for private but for national benefit.

Greville in 1848 took a poor view of the neighbourhood. He called it a miserable place; no place at all; no trees worth looking at, and a wet clay soil; no extent and everything to make. The house stood on an eminence, commanding a very extensive prospect of a rich flat country, the canal running beneath, not a quarter of a mile off, while farther off the railroad crossed Chat Moss, and all day long the barges were visible on the one, and continuous trains snorted and smoked along the other, presenting a lively exhibition of activity and progress. But it was a miserable country to live in; so wet and deep that the roads all about were paved, and the air eternally murky with the fire and smoke vomited forth from hundreds of chimneys and furnaces in every direction; no resources, such as hunting and shooting, and no society but the rare visitants from distant parts. We who now live in this once unhappy land are, however, gratified to observe that when on 29 July 1849 Greville again visited Worsley he described it as "a place I found immensely improved." The improvement was entirely due to the Ellesmeres' stern sense of duty, to the conception of a responsibility owed by a landowner to his tenants. The landowner's first duty was to live amongst his people, and therefore they had spent £100,000 in this fine house with all the appendages of gardens, etc. A singular change had overtaken the aristocratic outlook since the passing of the Reform Bill.

But the benevolence of this reformed aristocracy did not stop with the building of expensive mansions in order to live amongst their people. They built churches, including the Gilbert Scott creation near their new home, schools and reading rooms, spared neither pains nor money to civilize and improve the population, to spread education and to encourage habits of thrift, sobriety, and intellectual progress. Their efforts were not unrewarded; as years went by, the condition of the tenantry improved beyond all measure, and during the second half of the century the community life of Worsley with its church, school, and recreational facilities established its reputation far and wide as a model village. The Ellesmere family were truly respected and loved by those amongst whom they lived, and the foundations of many characters conspicuous for both personal goodness and material enterprise were laid during these formative years in the minds of hundreds of ordinary folk who came under the influence of this remarkable family.

Greville's brother-in-law, Lord Ellesmere, died on 18 February 1857, and the diarist's eulogy stands in interesting contrast to what he had written when Lord Hertford died. The sketch of his activities in public life does not overrate his abilities, which were not of a very high order, but he had a good understanding, a cultivated mind, and a superficial acquaintance with a wide variety of subjects over which his reading had roamed at will. The reproduction of all his merits as detailed by Greville would be tedious and disproportionate in a short sketch, but his public life may be summed up by saying that he stood nearly alone in the station he occupied, with vast wealth, unblemished character, esteemed by people of all parties, without an enemy in the world, and at all times ready to exert his best energies in the public service or to promote the benefit and happiness of his fellow creatures.

Something should be said of his private life, for his position as the great local aristocrat near Swinton is not without bearing on our theme; the influence of the powerful magnate was not lost upon the rising commercial middle classes. If his example had been bad, the story of the development of spiritual life in the neighbourhood might have been very different. But it was wholly good, for he was sincerely religious, without intolerance and austerity or the slightest particle of ostentatious or spiritual pride. From the moment of his succession to the property he considered himself in the light of a trustee for working out the moral and spiritual improvement of the people committed to his charge. Yet it was in his intimate family life that those who were privileged to gain admittance to that fortunate circle saw him at his best. He lived in and for his family without any thought of worldly and political advancement, unsurpassed as a husband, father, brother, or friend. The epithets of Greville seem to us too often to touch the superlative, for we perhaps are not accustomed in these days to write of our departed in such rhapsodical terms; yet Greville was his brother-in-law and at close family quarters had the best opportunities of judging the real merits of the man. Nor need we rely upon Greville's evidence alone; the family traditions of numerous Worsley people to-day enshrine the memory of Francis Egerton as a man greatly beloved.

We have noted the serene family life of the Royal Family at Windsor; we have seen it illustrated in one of the wealthiest aristocrats of Victorian England who happened also to be a near neighbour to the people of Swinton. Whether the aristocracy took its cue from the Queen or not, it cannot be doubted that the commercial middle classes were influenced in every manner and habit of their lives by what they saw of the class immediately above them, an order of society to which they themselves were often struggling to attain. Where that influence was wholly good, as it was on this piece of the Lancashire countryside, it is not to be wondered at that religion, works of philanthropy, and social amelioration began to spread widely around this centre. Francis Egerton, opulent aristocrat, set a striking example in the steward-ship and right use of the new wealth; we are not surprised to find that the mill-owners, the smaller colliery proprietors, the engineers, and the bankers followed in his wake. The middle classes were becoming increasingly conscious of their power and opportunity; slowly they were wresting the reins of government from the great families who had held them so long. But their newly found wealth and power was not to be used only in the promotion of middle-class government. Religious, educational, and cultural fields lay within their grasp to conquer; if one opulent aristocrat could accomplish so much there could surely be no limit to the influence for good which lay within the power of so much wealth concentrated in the hands of the middle classes. So the ball now passes to them; if in this story we have seen how the neighbouring village of Worsley benefited by a strong sense of aristocratic stewardship, we must go on now to see that it was to consecrated middle-class wealth that Swinton owed so much.

IV

Our study is so predominantly one of the influence of middle-class family life and the consecration of its money to spiritual ends that this part of the subject must have a later chapter to itself. In the particular devotion of one rich family Swinton Church took its origin, and we must study the early history and rise of that family very carefully if we are to understand our subject. Nevertheless, at this point something needs to be said about this new and powerful element in Victorian society.

Contemporary observers were even more impressed than we could be at the change which had come over Lancashire life as a result of the Industrial Revolution. Edwin Waugh mused on the subject as he performed his walks of naturalist and antiquarian observation over the Lancashire countryside. "I saw", he says "the country that was once thick with trees that canopied herds of wild quadrupeds, and thinnest of people, now bare of trees, and thickest of population; the land which was of least account of any in the kingdom in the last century, now most sought after; and those rude elements which were looked upon as 'the riddlings of creation', more productive of riches than all the Sacramento's gold, and ministers to a spirit which is destined to change the social aspect of Britain. . . . A great fusion of thought and sentiment springs up, and Old England is in hysterics about its ancient opinions. A new aristocracy rises from the prudent, persevering working people of the district, and threatens to push the old one from its stool. What is to be the upshot of it all? The senses are stunned by the din of toil, and the view obscured by the dust of bargain-making."

A hundred years have elapsed since Waugh uttered his plaintive question, and still we have not seen the upshot of it all. It has taken a century to reach the time when the ownership of the means of production and the production itself is passing from the hands of the prudent and persevering and perhaps lucky few into the possession of the whole community. Waugh was impressed by the rise of the new aristocracy, who were, in fact, the successful minority who rose from the ranks of labouring people or from families of yeoman stock, and who, by the possession of a little capital and much capacity for shrewd business dealing and hard work, created for themselves vast private fortunes.

The Heywood family, who are the subject of our immediate study, appear to have been small yeoman farmers in the neighbourhood of Bolton who established themselves in banking in Manchester and Liverpool and built up a great fortune by helping to finance industrial enterprises in the business world of Lancashire. No better illustration of their method could be found than in the chapter in Disraeli's *Coningsby* where the hero visits Lancashire to see at first hand something of that industrial progress which is introducing a new factor into the fine balance of parties in the political world. It is a fascinating picture of the rapid growth of the textile trade helped along by ready banking facilities. He saw all; they were kind and hospitable to the young stranger, whose thought, and earnestness, and gentle manner attracted them. From every morn to the late twilight, we are told, Coningsby for several days devoted himself to the comprehension of Manchester. He noted the unprecedented partnership between capital and science working on a spot which nature had indicated as the fitting theatre of their exploits. More important still, he noted, and Disraeli was also noting through his eyes, with a shrewdness which was of incalculable importance to the future of the Tory party and the government of England, that the new wealth was rapidly developing classes whose power was imperfectly recognized in the constitutional scheme, and whose duties in the social system seemed altogether omitted.

We are intended to smile at the naïve enthusiasm of Mr G. O. A. Head of Stalybridge with whom Coningsby entered into discussion in the coffee-room of the Adelphi Hotel after dinner one night. This typical provincial industrialist affected even to think little of Manchester:

"Why, in the way of machinery, you know," said the stranger, very quietly, "Manchester is a dead letter."

"A dead letter!" said Coningsby.

"Dead and buried," said the stranger ... "and no mistake. We

3

have all of us a very great respect for Manchester, in course; look upon her as a sort of mother, and all that sort of thing. But she is behind the times, sir, and that won't do in this age. The long and short of it is, Manchester is gone by." . . .

"If you want to see life," said the stranger, "go to Staleybridge or Bolton. There's high pressure."

"But the population of Manchester is increasing," said Coningsby.

"Why yes; not a doubt. You see we have all of us a great respect for the town. It is a sort of metropolis of this district, and there is a good deal of capital in the place. And it has some first rate institutions. There's the Manchester Bank. That's a noble institution, full of commercial enterprise; understands the age, sir; high-pressure to the backbone. I came up to town to see the manager to-day. I am building a new mill now myself at Staley-bridge, and mean to open it by January, and when I do, I'll give you leave to pay another visit to Mr. Birley's weaving-room, with my compliments."

Disraeli preserves the proper names in one or two instances here: the first bank to be established in Manchester and called by its founders the "Manchester Bank" was that of Byrom, Allen, Sedgwick, and Place. It was opened in 1771 and when it failed in 1788 its premises were bought by the Heywoods. It is not, therefore, fantastic to see in Disraeli's nomenclature a passing reference to the business of the family which claims our principal interest in this study. It is even more absorbing to follow Con-ingsby into the next chapter and to accompany him to the prin-cipal factory and home of Oswald Millbank, father of his school friend. The date of the visit is 1836, and here we see not only the industrial outfit but also something of the home-life of the new commercial aristocracy. The mill itself stands on the banks of a powerful stream, ornamented by some old elm-trees; it is " a vast deep red brick pile, which, though formal and monotonous in its general character, is not without a certain beauty of proportion and an artist-like finish in its occasional masonry." A little farther down the stream are two other smaller mills and a quarter of a mile farther on appears the village, " of not inconsiderable size, and remarkable from the neatness and even picturesque character of its architecture, and the gay gardens" that surround it. A reference to the church is not forgotten, " in the best style of Christian architecture" with its parsonage and school. The village also boasts another public building, an institute with its library, lecture-room, and reading-hall. This is a somewhat different picture from what is often drawn of the sordid horrors and slavery of the conditions of the workers in the Industrial Revolution: it is to be remembered that the date is a fairly early date, 1836, and the picture is a contemporary one.

But the illustration is not complete without some glance at the headpiece of this community, Mr Millbank, whose son Oswald had been at Eton with Coningsby. Meeting the traveller at the works, he instructed Mr Benson, his clerk, to show him everything.

Coningsby beheld in this great factory the last and the most refined inventions of mechanical genius. The building had been fitted up by a capitalist as anxious to raise a monument of the skill and power of his order, as to obtain a return for the great investment.

"It is the glory of Lancashire!" exclaimed the enthusiastic Mr Benson.

Mr Millbank's house was on the other side of the principal factory, half a mile up the valley, " surrounded by beautiful meadows and built on an agreeable and well-wooded elevation." It was "a commodious and not inconsiderable dwelling-house, built in what is called a villa style with a variety of gardens and conservatories." Coningsby accompanies the factory-owner to dinner at his home: they enter the gardens at 5 p.m. and the visitor lingers a moment

. . . to admire the beauty and gay profusion of the flowers.

"Your situation", said Coningsby, looking up the green and silent valley, "is absolutely poetic."

"I try sometimes to fancy", said Mr Millbank, with a rather fierce smile, "that I am in the New World."

They enter the house with its " capacious and classic hall, at the end a staircase in the Italian fashion." At dinner the meal is "plain but perfect of its kind." Chicken, sherry, the dessert classed as " . . . remarkable. Millbank was proud of his fruit." Grapes, peaches, figs encourage reminiscences of Eton and how greatly Coningsby and young Millbank would have enjoyed them there. The dining-room walls are " covered with pictures of great merit ; all of the modern English school "; landscape by Lee, a group of animals by Landseer, " household humour and homely pathos " by Wilkie. Etty contributes specimens "worthy of Venice when it was alive ", Danby " the twilight ruins of ancient cities", and Uwins a Neapolitan festival. There is tea in the drawing-room after the meal and a suggestion of music on the guitar. But Miss Millbank, with the becoming modesty of the maiden of the time, evades the task of performing. However, she has made her entrance into the story and time will develop the incipient romance which we obviously perceive between her and young Coningsby.

Such glimpses of the social scene are valuable in our under-standing of the Victorian commercial aristocracy because they have been drawn with the master touch of a great novelist. But an understanding of that social background is not necessarily confined to a recourse to contemporary literature. It survived in many places until comparatively recent times and may still sur-vive in a few isolated instances, though the high taxation of the Second World War has for the most part dealt it a death-blow. Those who had the privilege of knowing Miss Anna Philips of the Park, Prestwich, Lancashire, and of visiting her home, were introduced to a scene not vastly different from the social environ-ment described in this passage of *Coningsby*.

Anna Maria Philips was born at the Park in 1857 of a family which illustrates pre-eminently the rise of the commercial aristo-cracy. The Philips family originated in Staffordshire in the parish of Checkley, but, further back than that, it is possible that they were Flemish weavers who escaped from religious persecution. In 1659, Nathaniel Philips bought the Heath House at Tean and the family became established as small landowners and merchants in small-wares and textiles. In the early eighteenth century some of them migrated to Manchester and in 1747 opened a warehouse at 35 Church Street, which remains to-day as the headquarters of the well-known firm of J. & N. Philips and Co. In the middle of the century we find various members of the family living in and around Manchester, at King Street, St James's Square, and at Sedgley, but in 1780 a move was made to the country village of Stand in the parish of Radcliffe, about six miles from Manchester. At this period the merchanting business began to prosper greatly, and in 1798 when Robert Philips married Anne Needham he decided to buy the Park, a property of 126 acres surrounded, like an island, by an extensive sea of the Earl of Derby's estates. Here he built his house, demolished in 1950, in the style of an Italian villa, of large proportions, bearing a remarkable similarity to the warehouse in Church Street. It had the formal and symmetrical dignity of the style, but its most attractive feature was perhaps the beauty of its setting amidst luxuriant gardens and lawns and steeply rising banks of choice rhododendrons. The development of this family of commercial aristocracy was thus running to type, for having secured its vast fortune by merchandise it established itself socially by the purchase of land and was now prepared to embark upon political adventures.

The next stage in the saga had to wait for the next generation, and Robert's eldest son, Mark, was born in 1800, the year of the purchase of the land. He was educated at York and Glasgow University, since Oxford and Cambridge were barred to Dissenters, and the Philips family, characteristically, were staunch Unitarians. Mark had ambitious plans as regards land and building; he erected a house for himself on the Park estate called Outwood Lodge, but his notions expanded with age, and later came the erection of the gigantic pile at Welcombe near Stratford-on-Avon, one of the largest houses in the Midlands. It was finished only a little before he died in 1873, was used by his younger brother in which to dispense the well-regulated family hospitality of mid-Victorian times, and in these latter days has passed into the glamour of a luxury railway hotel.

In 1832 Mark Philips entered Parliament as one of the first two members for Manchester after the passing of the Reform Bill, occupying what would no doubt have been the place of Sir

Benjamin Heywood, had indifferent health not forced him to
resign a brief parliamentary career. Mark Philips's work in Parliament was principally the piloting of a Bill levying a penny rate
for the provision of parks and open spaces in Manchester: Philips
Park in the Bradford district of the city remains as a memorial
to his name.

Robert Needham Philips, father of Anna Maria Philips, succeeded his elder brother Mark as head of the family. In 1877 he
was High Sheriff of Lancashire and in the same year was elected
Liberal member for Bury. He represented the town until 1885,
when he retired owing to ill health, and the Park in this period
was one of the typical political country houses of the time in the
Liberal interest. He inherited Welcombe after his brother's death,
spent a large part of his retirement there, and died in 1890.

It was this mid-Victorian atmosphere which was so remarkably
preserved by Miss Anna Philips at the Park until her death in
1946. Little was altered there from the time of her grandfather,
who, as she would remind her friends with pride, was born in the
last year of George II's reign. The hospitality of the house was
dispensed with an old-world dignity and courtesy. Occasionally,
in the lamp-lit drawing-room—electricity never sullied those
prim rooms—Miss Philips might be encouraged to speak of early
days when she went, sternly guarded, with her sister, who married George Otto Trevelyan, to Ireland, in his delicate work
after the Phoenix Park murders, or of the grandeur of a London
Season when she accompanied her father on his social functions
from their town house in Berkeley Square. They heard the original
performances of the Gilbert and Sullivan operas at the Savoy,
drove together in the Sunday morning Parades in Hyde Park, and
she would wait with the groom in the courtyard of the House of
Commons for her father. The year followed a fixed routine for
these commercial aristocrats. Welcombe in October, Berkeley
Square for the Parliamentary Session in January with the ladies
following to town in May. Then in mid-July there was the seaside
or holidays abroad and a return to the Park from August till
October. In London there were dinner-parties of sixteen to
eighteen people twice a week, with footmen in black plush knee-

breeches and flesh-pink silk stockings and pumps with gilt buttons. In Berkeley Square, near by, lived Lord Mildmay, Lord Powys, Lord Dorchester, the Marquis of Bath, Lord Rosebery, and the Tecks. The commercial aristocracy of Lancashire had thus become closely assimilated to the older landowning families, but on one point the independent, dissenting Philipses were adamant. They would not accept a title; Lord Melbourne offered Robert Philips a baronetcy and is reputed to have called him a sensible fellow when he declined it. Mr Gladstone offered a baronetcy to Robert Needham Philips, but that also was refused.

The Victorian age with its merchant princes and commercial aristocracy has long passed away, but the Park, Prestwich, remained for some of us in the 1930's and 1940's as tangible proof that it really existed, and as a unique token of the ways of life of the former century for the delight of the social historian. But that came to an end with the death of Miss Anna Philips in 1946. This is not an account of the excellencies of that remarkable woman, one of the last of the eminent Victorians, but a brief sketch of how she survived into a different world as a continuing symbol of a vanished order. Came the note on grey paper written in characteristic pointed hand: "Pray walk across about four o'clock on Tuesday next and see these gardens which are now at their best and meet so-and-so with whom, I think, you may have some common interest"—as though she could not imagine that you would ever wish to walk across for the pleasure of seeing her alone. Then there was the long walk from the nearest bus route on the Bury New Road, the nearer approach through part of the garden, and Frankton, the gracious butler and friend opening the front door which led into the chilly hall with its groups of white marble statuary. Then would come Miss Philips to conduct you solemnly around the gardens, to point out a choice flower here and there, or perhaps to be drawn into some family reminiscence. "Yes, poor dears"—stopping before some monument to some departed member of the family—"died of a decline: so many of them did in those days. So little idea about fresh air." Then a return to the house, a tea on the solid mahogany of the dining-room table; none of your finicking handing round in drawing-rooms

with plates and cups balanced precariously on knees. Perhaps
a Unitarian minister was your neighbour on your left or
a newly arrived local clergyman on your right—"with whom, I
think, you may have some common interest". Robert and Mark
and Robert Needham Philips looked down at you from the walls
in portraits something more than life-sized, but "The Cherry
Girl" by Cuyp was an even greater attraction. The next room was
a smaller room where Miss Philips worked or read, and here was
the bookcase containing many of the latest published books;
seldom did you come away without the loan of two or three of
the best, neatly tied up in a brown-paper parcel. If you were invited to dinner, which was a rare privilege reserved for special
occasions, you sat after the meal in the drawing-room, which was
a very grand double room, each half with a large and intricate
crystal chandelier. There was an enormous picture by Pyne of
Pallanza and a marble group of Lady Trevelyan and Mrs Price,
daughters of Robert Needham Philips, as little girls, and there
were chairs and little sofas of shining woodwork and green or
red plush. Beyond the drawing-room was the West Room or
library in which Mr Philips had worked, and still containing his
flat-topped double desk. Bookshelves and Victorian oil-paintings
lined the walls, but one masterpiece also hung there, "The Lady
with the Fan", by H. Bol (1611–81). Upstairs, a region to which
you never penetrated if you were only a tea visitor, there were
ten bedrooms, and on the top floor other rooms for the servants,
some without windows. In subterraneous depths there were
cellars, some for boilers, some for wine. Sherry and Madeira were
the fashionable drinks in Mr Philips's time, and forty dozen
sherry at one time lay there.

Such was the domestic Victorian period piece which so
strangely had survived, and some of us were able to see, as we
drew near the middle of the twentieth century. All of a piece it
was, for when Robert Philips built the house he had it furnished
throughout by Waring and Gillow of Lancaster, and so the whole
outfit presented a unity of period until the very end; no Jacobean
court cupboards or interesting dower chests; no priceless bits of
Chippendale or Sheraton, but all Waring and Gillow, 1800 solid

mahogany throughout. Shades of the commercial aristocracy brooded over its dissolution soon after Hitler's war had come to an end. (Could it have been true that that solemn and impressive dining-room sideboard "went for" £6?) We had not known that commercial aristocracy in its heyday, that had been a hundred years ago, but we had known that wonderfully gracious, welcoming, and hospitable lady who for so long had preserved something of its atmosphere and who perhaps felt—though she would never have said so—that she was compensating for the great wealth that her forbears had amassed in private hands by distributing its privileges amongst a wider public in the subsequent era when democracy had succeeded the merchant princes. "I drove to our polling booth in the Ringley Road", she wrote after the General Election of 1945, "and voted for the Labour candidate, Tomlinson, as no Liberal was standing." Her family had grown up and grown rich, in spite of the landed aristocracy and their Toryism. The Park itself was always an independent enclave, a gesture of defiance, as it were, flung at the surrounding and overweening encroachments of the great Lancashire peer. At the end of a long life it would have been too great a break with tradition, too sore a departure from the sturdy industrial independence of a father and a grandfather who scorned to accept a baronetcy, to vote for the Tory candidate. Perhaps it was a shrewd bit of insight on the part of her who had enjoyed all the best that commercial aristocracy could give in this world, that the future lay rather with the proletariat. There is grandeur in the spectacle of the old lady, last of the hundred-years line of merchant princes, nimbly driving off to vote for the Labour candidate. It is the game and spirited salute of the old order, graciously striking its colours and making way for the new.

V

Thus arose with the Industrial Revolution a new class, whose power, as Disraeli noted, was at first imperfectly recognized in the constitutional scheme and whose duties in the social system seemed altogether omitted. Political recognition came with the first Reform Bill; increasing political power showed itself in the abolition of the Corn Laws. The new men, such as Cobden and Bright, who spoke for the influential commercial classes, were strong personalities who could turn a fiscal issue when all the prestige of the older landowning aristocratic order was marshalled against them. As for its duties in the social system, that omission could soon be rectified once the new commercial class had secured its place in the parliamentary system. Millbank was soon building his model village with church and school and institute, Mark Philips was promoting bills for the provision of open spaces in crowded industrial areas, and the Heywood family were sponsoring Mechanics' Institutes, building churches and schools, and deepening their philanthropy by exemplary devotion to religious ideals and practices.

The Industrial Revolution had established itself with such widespread rapidity in Lancashire that even by 1836, Mr G. O. A. Head of Stalybridge could speak of Manchester as a back number. Countless textile manufacturers had built up rich businesses with the help of the inventions of Kay, Crompton, and Arkwright. Merchants like J. and N. Philips were merchanting their goods and finding a ready market for Lancashire products throughout the world. Nasmyth and others like him had brought engineering to the county, the Duke of Bridgewater had shown how the earth could be exploited for the needful coal on a big scale and how that coal could be transported cheaply by the development of inland waterways. Yet another fillip was given to the mobility of goods and a fresh impetus to the expansion of commerce by the coming of railways, though this meant a serious blow to the Duke's canal and to many other canals throughout the country.

The coming of the railways to Lancashire had been marked by a sad tragedy which occurred so near to Swinton that some particular notice of it may be made. In 1830 Swinton was a recently created chapelry in the ancient parish of Eccles, and it was at Eccles, two miles away, that the opening of the Liverpool and Manchester railway was marred by the death of the Rt Hon.

William Huskisson, one of the country's leading statesmen, who had already served as President of the Board of Trade and Colonial Secretary, and who was described by Lord Melbourne as the greatest practical statesman he had known, the one who most closely united theory with practice. Eyewitness accounts of the tragedy, which deprived England of a stateman whose ability would have been of undoubted value in the coming years, were handed down in Swinton until late in the century. A contemporary description speaks of the ceremony as of the most brilliant, with a splendid state carriage prepared for the illustrious passengers who took part in the event. The trains were crowded to excess, some paying as high as five guineas for the passage. The train which contained the state carriage was started on the second line, and stopped at Parkside to take in water. Many of the passengers took this opportunity of alighting. All seemed delighted, and seemed to enjoy this novel mode of travelling. Here, however, happened an awful calamity, which cast a gloom over the whole proceedings. The Duke of Wellington, who stood in front of the car, recognized Mr Huskisson and cordially shook hands with him. Mr Huskisson then alighted from the carriage in which he sat, but on returning to speak to Mrs Huskisson he stood on the step holding the door in his hand. At this moment the bugle of the "Rocket" announced the approach of that engine. All the gentlemen succeeded in getting into their carriages with the exception of Mr Huskisson, who, being nervous from illness, became flurried and lost his presence of mind. He fell, or as it has been asserted, threw himself off the step to avoid the danger. The driver being unable to stop the engine, it came on with terrific speed and passed over Mr Huskisson's leg and thigh. A scream from Mrs Huskisson, and a sorrowful murmur which ran through the company announced to those behind that some untoward event had occurred. Mr Littleton, M.P. for Staffordshire, raised the unfortunate gentleman from the ground, who exclaimed, "This is the death of me." A board was then procured on which the hapless gentleman was placed, and he was then conveyed in the musicians' carriage to a convenient house, which was the Eccles vicarage. Here it was that Mrs Blackburne, the wife of the vicar of Eccles, who was alone at the time, displayed outstanding qualities of resource. Never for a moment losing her presence of mind, she took charge of the injured gentleman, rendered him every assistance and kindly nursed him until his death which took place at 9 p.m., about nine hours after the accident. Greville, in his account of the accident, says that it was the Earl of Wilton, at whose house at Heaton Park about six miles away some of the party had been staying, who helped to convey Huskisson to the vicarage and who saved his life for a few hours by knowing how to tie up the artery. Amputation was not possible and Huskisson died nine hours later, Wilton, Granville, and Littleton being with him to the last. Benjamin Heywood, who was present at the scene, lent his horse to carry the news back to Liverpool. The Duke of Wellington was deeply affected and could hardly be persuaded to continue the journey to Manchester. It was represented to him that the mob might be dangerous if he did not appear. Greville says that there were perhaps 500,000 people present on this occasion and only one man was killed—he the Duke of Wellington's most dangerous political opponent and the one from whom he had most to fear.

Thus did the railway come near to Swinton, bringing death at its first appearance. It was the final achievement of the Industrial Revolution, which, as Waugh had observed, had so markedly changed the face of Lancashire, and which had produced changes in the social and political order no less remarkable than those on the surface of the land. Wealth there was in abundance, but the bulk of it was concentrated in the hands of the capable and fortunate few :

We only know the last sad squires ride slowly towards the sea
And a new people takes the land and STILL IT IS NOT WE.

There was precious little of the new wealth distributed amongst the masses who earned it with their incredibly long hours of dreary work. It had gone to create a new class of industrial plutocrats, and much of the future social history of England was to depend upon the way in which this commercial aristocracy would use its new wealth. Was that class soulless, uncultivated, provincial, Philistine, as Matthew Arnold believed? We wonder at his invective expressed in a letter addressed to "My Countrymen" and dated "Grub Street, 19th March, 1866". He covers them with scorn; attacks their self-satisfaction; accuses them of having no ideal beyond that of doing "a roaring trade"; declares their religion to be "narrow, unintelligent, repulsive"; makes them responsible through their influence on the foreign policy of the government for the Crimean War, the desertion of Denmark in her dispute with Germany; and sums them up as being "testy, absolute, ill-acquainted with foreign matters, a little ignoble, very dull to perceive when [the rich middle class] is making itself ridiculous". "The provincial narrowness and vulgarity" is another phrase with which he vilifies them. Bagehot assails them as being out of the current of common European causes and affairs, a race contemptuous of others, with no special education or culture as to the modern world, and too often despising such culture.

One cannot help feeling, in trying to assess the justice of these attacks, that the real cause of annoyance to these critics was the Nonconformity of the middle classes. "An *insula in insula*" is Bagehot's description of a Nonconformist; as compared with a Churchman, he was as an ordinary Englishman to a cultivated European. It was certainly true that large numbers of the industrial middle class were Nonconformist; the two families who have so far been particularly noticed, the Philipses of the Park, Prestwich, and the Heywoods of Manchester, were both staunchly Unitarian in the early part of the nineteenth century. There was perhaps good reason for this, for Nonconformity gave the middle class a place in the ecclesiastical sun which was denied to them where an old landed family seemed to possess a proprietary right in the parish church. But it is a gross overstatement to say that this middle-class influence was entirely outside the confines of the Established Church. A great deal of it was within the Church, and many of the rebuilt churches of the middle of the century bore witness to the munificence of the rich local manufacturer.

What is much more important is that both Churchmen and Nonconformists manifested the increasing seriousness of the age. It was presumably at this time that the famous Nonconformist conscience began to assume importance as a political factor, and John Bright was being no more than honest in expressing Nonconformity's opinion of itself when he said that "if a good measure is to be carried in this House, it must be by men who are sent hither by the Nonconformists of Great Britain". Many statesmen noted that the strength of the Liberal party lay in Dissent, yet social and political historians cannot fail to marvel that the so-called political party of Dissent was led by one of the most conspicuous High Church laymen of the country. Still, perhaps it is no more remarkable that Mr Gladstone should have captained the Liberal-Nonconformist phalanx than that the proud ranks of territorial aristocracy should have been marshalled by a free-thinking Jew with a thin veneer of Erastian Christianity. It was even necessary to purchase a small landed estate for Disraeli at Hughenden in order to cloak this legal fiction with some semblance of squirearchical propriety.

But the real clue to this tangle of political allegiances lies rather in the all-prevailing "seriousness", the high sense of moral earnestness and responsibility which roused thoughtful men of all traditions than in mere questions of denominational difference. The whole answer to this phenomenon lies in the two great religious reawakenings of the eighteenth and nineteenth centuries which must be considered later. They were both manifestations of the recrudescence of the religious spirit, and though their doctrinal forms may have been different they succeeded in producing that same seriousness which was differently manifested in such personalities as Lord Shaftesbury, Richard Cobden, John Bright, William Gladstone, and, for the purposes of our particular study, the Heywood family. It was not Nonconformity nor a sense of what was expected of him as the leader of the great political party of Nonconformity which made Mr Gladstone speak as he did, but a profound sense of moral obligation consequent upon the religious sanctions of human life. It was this stern sense of spiritual responsibility which made him breathe an unspoken prayer to his God every time he rose to his feet in the House of Commons, which made him write in his diary in 1865 when he was defeated in the Oxford University election:

And they shall fight against thee, but they shall not prevail against thee, for I am with thee, saith the Lord, to deliver thee.

There was the deep feeling in his mind that he was a chosen instrument of the Almighty, a feeling which he was not ashamed to entrust to the privacy of his diary:

The Almighty seems to sustain and spare me for some purpose of His own, deeply unworthy as I know myself to be. Glory be to His name.

There is nothing specifically Nonconformist about this; it is the mystical assurance of all devout souls throughout the ages who have felt their lives to be directed by some higher power than that of their own human reason. When the Prime Minister of England could think and speak with such religious conviction it is no wonder that the rich manufacturers whom he led should consider that their own affairs and not least their commercial prosperity were ordered by God himself. Nonconformist and Anglican alike could not escape from the seriousness of the age.

When James Schofield of Milnrow near Rochdale, a pious and orthodox Anglican, signified his intention of financing the rebuilding of his parish church soon to be undertaken by the energetic leadership of Canon Raines, his vicar, and with George Street as architect, he gave formal expression to this conviction that the prosperity of the rich manufacturing classes was a thing ordained by God. On 21 November 1863 he gave a promissory note to the value of £3,000 towards the "rebuilding of the Church of Milnrow", wishing that "this gift be regarded as a thank-offering to Almighty God for my worldly prosperity and for the many mercies which have been vouchsafed to me". It was in this spirit that the commercial aristocracy contributed substantially to the building of many of these architectural Victorian period pieces. God had been very good to James Schofield and his like: whether he had been equally good to the operatives who worked his textile machinery, and the colliers who provided the coal which kept the mill wheels turning, is not recorded in this particular instance. But we are not entirely without information as to the view which those workers elsewhere took on such questions. Our Victorian churches owe largely to the new-found seriousness of the commercial aristocracy: but what was the lot of the working classes at this time and had they any share in the enterprise?

VI

"Still it is not we"; so much new wealth produced by the Industrial Revolution, yet so much of it concentrated in the hands of the few and so little spread amongst the masses for a general improvement of the standard of life. This period of social preparation for our Victorian period piece was one in which economic conditions ran to extremes—extremes of wealth and luxury for the new commercial magnates, who began to approximate their mode of living to that of the old territorial aristocracy, and extremes of poverty and wretchedness for the low-paid and overworked denizens of the mills and the mines. "See how every successful trader buys an estate", writes Cobden to John Bright. The Philips family were adding the gargantuan Welcombe to their large property at Stand, and the eldest son of Sir Benjamin Heywood was now well established at a very pretty country place on the banks of the Dove in Staffordshire. "The sons of weavers", wrote John Morley in the *Fortnightly Review* in 1868, "are hunting up genealogies and spreading their wings for sublime apotheosis among the county families." The assimilation between the older aristocracy and the rich middle classes might be furthered by a marriage here and there; there was no insuperable objection to the daughter of a Lancashire earl of ancient lineage marrying the son of a prosperous woollen manufacturer or banker. As ever, in the constant flux of English society, the Victorian aristocracy was enriching its blood and strengthening its ranks by alliance with the new men—providing that their substance was sufficiently impressive. Yet there was the ever-present poverty and degradation of many of the working class amidst so much new wealth. It was a fact which did not fail to impress and even puzzle some of the most thoughtful contemporary social observers.

Greville relates a conversation in 1834 with William Ponsonby who had just returned from the assizes at Dorchester. There were two cases which impressed him sufficiently to mention them; one was a conviction of a number of men for illegal association, the other was for a child murder, during the investigations into which it had been discovered that there was a woman whose trade was to get rid of bastard children, either by procuring abortions, or destroying them when born, and that she had a regular price for either operation. Political discontent and moral depravity are significant notes of the social life of this period. In that part of the country, Dorsetshire, Ponsonby professed to find principally a recklessness, a moral obtuseness, exceedingly disgusting. Greville was led to marvel at the fact that, while education had been more widely diffused and a strong Puritanical spirit at work and vast talk about religious observances, there should be such a brutish manifestation of the moral condition of the lower classes, and that they should be apparently so little humanized and reclaimed by either education or religion. There comes a reference to that startling contrast which he mentions again and again—in this country all is contrast, contrast between wealth, the most enormous, and poverty, the most wretched, between an excess of sanctity and an atrocity of crime.

In 1842 the situation was no better. Lord Wharncliffe, a Yorkshire man, and Kay-Shuttleworth, a Lancastrian, gave Greville an account of the state of the country and of the people which was perfectly appalling. There was an immense and continually increasing population, deep distress and privation, no adequate demand for labour, no demand for anything, no confidence, but a universal alarm, disquietude, and discontent. Nobody could sell anything. Somebody had said, speaking of some part of Yorkshire, "This is certainly the happiest country in the world, for *nobody wants anything*." Kay-Shuttleworth said that nobody could conceive the state of demoralization of the people, of the

4

masses, and that the only thing which restrained them from acts
of violence against property was a sort of instinctive conscious-
ness that, bad as things were, their own existence depended upon
the security of property *in the long run*. Whilst the situation might
be worse in the north, there were similar indications all over the
country, and Greville was certain that he had never seen in the
course of his life so serious a state of things. He found it incredible after thirty years of uninterrupted peace when altering,
amending, and improving had been going on wherever the
government could find anything to work upon. The strange
thing was that nobody could point out any remedy; those who
clamoured for the repeal of the Corn Laws did not really believe
that repeal would supply the cure. It was a dismal reflection that
with such a Constitution and with all the country's wealth,
ingenuity, peace, and supposed virtue, it could not prevent the
existence of a huge mountain of human misery, or find security
against evils and mischiefs so great as to threaten revolution.

There were those, of course, who thought that solutions were
possible along the lines of parliamentary and economic reform,
and by the combination of workmen to protect their own interests.
The condition of the workpeople and the various agitations for
reform have been drawn in great detail by the Hammonds in
their *Town Labourer*, and a good many of their illustrations are
taken from Lancashire sources. Their study ends where it has
been suggested ours should begin, namely in 1832, but no study
of social conditions in Lancashire in the first half of Victoria's
reign could omit to mention the so-called Peterloo massacre.
The memory of that piece of tragic and stupid bungling went very
deep into Lancashire minds: it has been noted that in 1851 when
the Queen was making her royal progress from Worsley to Manchester the Yeomanry Cavalry were not allowed to accompany
her into the town itself; for the Yeomanry Cavalry were the
villains of the Peterloo piece.

On 16 August 1819 a great meeting was planned to take place
in St Peter's Fields, then on the outskirts of Manchester, now the
site of the Free Trade Hall. Henry Hunt, the chief orator, passed
through Pendlebury, the next village to Swinton, on the night

before the meeting. The horses were taken out of his carriage, and men and women drew the carriage with its occupants at a great speed along the road to Manchester. Eighty thousand people marched peaceably towards St Peter's Fields on the following day. The folk were in their Sunday clothes, bands played "God save the King", and one out of every three persons was a woman. Three thousand men came from Middleton led by Samuel Bamford, who ordered his following not even to carry sticks unless they were old and infirm. Three thousand more came from Rochdale, and at last the whole assembly reached the Fields to demand universal suffrage, vote by ballot, annual parliaments, and the repeal of the Corn Laws. There is little doubt but that the magistrates lost their heads. It is easy to vilify them, and without doubt their conduct was inexcusable, but it is at any rate only fair to these men to realize that most of them must have lived through the horrors of the French Revolution, and they had a desperate fear of the scenes of the Terror being repeated here. We know now that the bulk of the assembly were honest law-abiding Lancashire folk; we know that their very modest demands for enfranchisement were as far removed as could be from red terror. But we refuse to see the situation through the panic-stricken mentalities of the local authorities in those days. After all, their fear and consequent conduct was not more absurd than the heresy hunts and Communist trials of this later enlightened century. Panic there certainly was, but it was the panic of men who had lived through times when the streets of the French capital had literally run with blood, and the earliest stages of that Revolution had seemed peaceable enough and not greatly dissimilar from the scene now being enacted in St Peter's Fields.

When Hunt began to speak, the magistrates gave the order to disperse the crowds. The Yeomanry Cavalry advanced, brandishing their sabres, rode into the cheering crowd which gave way to receive them, and arrested Hunt. Then came the mad tragedy: the Yeomanry cried, "Have at their flags", and began striking wildly all round them. It has been said that they were drunk. They slashed away with their sabres right and left. Eleven people died, two of them women, one a child, and over 400 were wounded, 113 being women. One woman from Swinton had her breast cut off. More than a quarter of the wounded were wounded by the sword. Bitterness and hatred rankled in the minds of Lancashire working-class people at the memory of this tragic event for years to come. It was said afterwards in Swinton that some of the magistrates who gave the order to the Yeomanry to scatter the crowd lived in Swinton Park and the neighbourhood of the village.

The Peterloo incident had some small repercussion during the brief parliamentary career of Sir Benjamin Heywood; it is a curious piece of evidence as to the way in which the soreness was still rankling in 1832. On 15 March Mr Henry Hunt, who had been sent to prison for two and a half years as a result of his part in the unlawful assembly in St Peter's Fields, but who had now reached the Reform Parliament as member for Preston, moved for an inquiry into the affray at Manchester in August 1819. Mr Heywood—as he was then—was too cautious to be caught in this fashion, and opposed the motion, being convinced that no good could result from further inquiry. A subsequent speaker commended Mr Heywood's caution; he asked whether there was any member more freely returned and by a more independent and manufacturing constituency than the honourable gentleman who now with so much honour to himself sat for the County of Lancaster. That honourable gentleman, he said, might be taken as a fair representative of what was to be expected from a manufacturing constituency, and his opinion might be taken as the voice of the great manufacturing and commercial interests of the County of Lancaster. That opinion was that it would be better now not to interfere with this subject, and not to hazard ill consequences by reviving the recollection of events which had much better be forgotten.

It was all very well for honourable gentlemen in Parliament to try to hush up the memory of that tragic bungling as an event much better forgotten. In that place Mr Hunt's reminder could easily be quashed: it was not so easy to excise it from the memory of Lancashire folk, and the spirit which was prepared so peaceably to demonstrate for the rights of man in St Peter's Fields in 1819 might easily display a much more sinister attitude in the recollection of the brutal force which had been used against women and children to suppress it. Force could be met by force if the Reformed Parliament turned out to be a failure in righting some of these human wrongs. The spirit of the Peterloo demonstration lived on in Chartism, of which the authorities were so justifiably afraid in the 1830's and 1840's.

Chartism pursued Mr Heywood into Parliament again in the person of the indefatigable Mr Hunt, but again the member for Lancashire was successful in evading the suggestion that he should be its protagonist. On 18 July 1831 Mr Hunt presented a petition from the working classes of Manchester, signed by 19,400 persons, in favour of universal suffrage, annual parliaments, and vote by ballot. He said that he had deferred the presentation of it until he saw the honourable member for Lancashire, Mr Heywood, in his place, as he felt it his duty to call upon that honourable member to support the prayer of the petition. He reminded Mr Heywood that when he entered Manchester in triumph after his election, some of the flags carried before him on that occasion had mottoes on them, bearing such inscriptions as "No Corn Laws", "Annual Parliaments", "Universal Suffrage", "Vote by Ballot". He suggested that Mr Heywood was therefore in some degree bound to support the prayer of a petition which prayed for these things.

Mr Heywood repudiated such responsibility by declaring his complete ignorance of the inscriptions on the banners and went on in a somewhat patronizing tone to say that he was sorry to see petitions of that description coming from the working classes of Manchester. He had, he said, some intercourse with the working classes there, and he had their real benefit at heart, but he had told the delegates who had brought up the petition that he sincerely believed that annual parliaments and universal suffrage would, if obtained, effect the destruction and starvation of the working classes themselves. Mr Heywood did not make it clear exactly why this awful doom should be consequent upon such an apparently innocent adventure in enfranchisement, but he was strongly supported by the next two speakers, Mr Warre and Lord Stanley, who indignantly protested against the doctrine that parliamentary members or candidates should be responsible for their supporters' election slogans.

On 15 September 1831 Mr Hunt was again trying to rouse Mr Heywood, this time on the subject of the Corn Laws, moving that the House should resolve itself into a Committee to consider that thorny problem. He referred to the fact that the working classes of Lancashire had subscribed £400 towards Mr Heywood's election expenses in consideration of a pledge that their representative should oppose the Corn Laws. Mr Heywood again succeeded in being evasive. He admitted that he felt strongly with respect to the impropriety of continuing the present restrictions on the import of corn, but he thought that the honourable member for Preston had chosen a most unfortunate period for discussing the question. He felt grateful for the support offered him at his election by the working classes of Lancashire, but he was happy to say that their pecuniary assistance was not needed, and that all the money which they had subscribed had been returned to them.

Mr Heywood escaped the importunities of Mr Hunt by resigning his seat when the Reform Parliament was dissolved in 1832, but Manchester continued to be one of the storm centres of Chartism for the next sixteen years. In 1839 Greville notes that the accounts of the Chartists at and about Manchester represented them to be collected in vast bodies, collecting arms, constantly practising marksmanship with their firearms, and threatening that if their demands were not complied with they would enforce them by violence. Risings took place at Birmingham and Newport; at the latter place the magistrate Frost himself headed a riot and was sentenced to death by a special commission at Monmouth, though the sentence was afterwards commuted. Stephens, the great Chartist orator, formerly a Wesleyan preacher, was arrested at Ashton-under-Lyne on 27 December, 1838, and charged with "attending an unlawful meeting at Hyde" on 14 November; for this, in the following August, he was tried and sentenced to eighteen months imprisonment. Greville admits that the magistrates completely lost their heads and blundered between fear and folly, leaving the honours of the day with the mob agitator.

During this period great meetings were held, in support of the Charter and its six points, in the neighbourhood of Swinton. Orators of the Stephens stamp fanned the excitement of the people into a mad blaze. Force was suggested as the only means of obtaining social justice, torchlight meetings were held all over the country, and the leaders of the people recommended every-body who had any money in the banks to take it out, to abstain from eating and drinking anything upon which duty had to be paid, so as to cripple the Government. Public meetings were for-bidden. Middle-class folk were sworn as special constables with powers of "Watch and ward" to disperse or arrest any groups of two or three people or more.

1842 was another critical year. On 18 August Sir James Graham reported to the Queen the state of the country and measures taken for its pacification. At Preston vigorous measures had been taken to suppress strikes, and strong resistance was offered to Chartist mobs entering cities. On the following day he reported that the accounts from the North were satisfactory, five of the principal Delegates at Manchester having been arrested, warrants issued for four others, and important papers having been seized which disclosed a conspiracy going back to July 1841. It had been the anniversary of Peterloo, "a conflict which took place in Manchester in the year 1819 between the Yeomanry Cavalry and the populace, and it is feared that there may be a great assemblage of persons riotously disposed on that day". So wrote Sir Robert Peel to Her Majesty. Major-General Sir William Warre, in command of the Northern District, was reinforced by 1,400 men, a sufficient force to preserve order, but there was little cause for anxiety, and Peel informed the Queen on 18 August that reports from Manchester, Preston, and Wigan were very good. The movement, he wrote, was not one caused by distress. Demand for employment had increased and the price of provisions had fallen; the riots were a political agitation, a demand for the People's Charter, but the sternest measures would be put into force against the Delegates, and they would be arrested the very moment they transgressed the law. Manchester was the centre of unrest, and disorderly scenes appearing in more remote places were inspired from Manchester: when peace and confidence was restored in the centre, the example would quickly tell in the circumjacent districts.

In 1842, there was mobbing and rioting in a great many places in Swinton. The mob marched six or eight deep through the lanes between the workers' cottages. They meant to draw the plugs of the boilers of the "New Engine" and "Red Cat" Coal Pits and other works. Strikes, they believed, would bring the Government to its knees. A detachment of cavalry dashed down what is now Station Road towards the marching Chartists, with swords drawn. An old village worthy who saw the incident and committed his recollections to paper later in life, says that some of the agitators, seeing the cavalry approaching, threw off their jackets and caps and flung them into the first house they came to. Then, with pipes in mouths, they stood smoking, as though civil disturbance had been the thought farthest from their minds. One man ran upstairs in a cottage and crept under the bed, but a soldier followed him and made him a prisoner. Others ran into the fields, threw off their coats and began working; others escaped to the moss where the soldiers could not follow: horses that attempted it sank up to the flank in the bog. The fugitives had to be pressed into service to help to rescue the horses, on the promise of their liberty; but many were nevertheless taken prisoners and severely dealt with. A prominent Chartist named Wood of Patricroft, who had led a number of rioters and done much damage at Astley, found sanctuary at Swinton. Search was made for him all over the country, but he hid quietly at a cottage in Long Fold until the excitement of the year had quietened down.

Chartism in this country reached its climax in 1848, the year of European revolution; yet, in contrast with the toppling of crowns in less favoured countries, the dreaded climax turned out to be a very tame affair. On 9 April Lord John Russell informed Prince Albert of the plans which had been made to deal with the situation. The mammoth procession which was to present the petition for the Charter was to be allowed to proceed as far as Westminster Bridge, and was to be stopped there. If the Chartists showed fight, the military would be called out, and Lord John had no doubt of their easy triumph over a London mob. He was nervous and apprehensive of the loss of life and trusted that all might pass off quietly. The Prince, replying to him from Osborne on the following day, had no doubt who would be found the stronger in the event of an armed clash, but he, too, hoped that commotion might be avoided for the sake of the example of stability which he desired that the country might display to the rest of Europe. Unemployment was increasing, and his own investigations had proved that the Government was to some extent responsible, having, in face of a parliamentary clamour for economy, reduced the number of workmen employed upon public works. It was not the moment, he thought, for the taxpayers to economize upon the working classes.

On the same day at 2.0 p.m. Lord John Russell sent a reassuring dispatch to the Queen. The Kennington Common meeting had proved a complete failure: about 12,000 or 15,000 persons had met in good order. Their leader, Feargus O'Connor, appeared to be nervous when confronted by the determination of Mr Richard Mayne, Commissioner of Police, and upon being told that the meeting would not be prevented, but that no procession would be allowed to pass the bridges, he expressed the utmost thanks and shook Mr Mayne by the hand. He then addressed the crowd and advised them to disperse and went off to the Home Office to repeat his assurances of good behaviour to Sir George Grey. The mob was in good humour and dispersed without any untoward incidents.

Greville gives a graphic account of the curious collapse of what the authorities had feared might have been the climax of a revolutionary movement. On 9 April he and his clerks were all sworn as special constables: in fact, he says, every gentleman in London became a constable, guns were prepared, and the forces of law and order were ready to adopt a warlike attitude. This determined demonstration of defence gave a memorable lesson which would not be lost either on the disaffected and mischievous or on the loyal and peaceful. It was a salutary object lesson for foreign countries of the essential stability of England. Greville characterizes the Chartist movement as to the last degree contemptible. Certainly O'Connor's attitude seems to have been pusillanimous in the extreme. He was terribly frightened on meeting Mayne and thought that he was going to be arrested. His relief on being assured otherwise was so great that he insisted on shaking hands, swore he was his best of friends, and then harangued the demonstrators to disperse quietly. After the interview at the Home Office, Grey asked him if he was going back to the meeting. He said that he was not. He had had his toes trodden on till he was lame and his pocket picked, and he was having no more to do with it. The demonstration collapsed in ridicule. The petition turned out to be signed by less than two million people instead of six as O'Connor had stated. It contained fictitious names together with the insertion of every species of ribaldry, indecency, and impertinence. It was a curious termination to the supposed English Victorian Revolution.

Lord John Russell ended his dispatch to the Queen with a report that accounts from the rest of the country were good. At Manchester, however, the Chartists were armed and had bad designs: but there, likewise, the designs came to nothing. Manchester folk were waiting with trepidation for the upshot of the London demonstration. Sir Benjamin Heywood, who was staying at Hyde Park Gardens at the time, wrote to his son Oliver some account of the London situation on 10 April. Everything was suspended on that day, both business and pleasure; the parks were closed, the streets cleared. The middle classes were determined to offer the utmost demonstration of strength to the Chartists and Repealers. Sir Benjamin pointed out that the underlings of the Home Office and Downing Street received the Chartist delegates roughly and discourteously, which they ought not to have done. Lord Morpeth and Lord John behaved differently and gave up a day to discuss the petition. No doubt it was this combination of politeness and firmness which disarmed the Chartist aggression. Sir Benjamin professed so much confidence in the intelligence and good feeling of the people that he did not fear any dangerous outbreak, though disturbance was possible. He regarded it as a great point, when opportunity offered, quietly and kindly to help them to see the danger to themselves of universal suffrage: he had apparently not changed his mind on this point after sixteen years. He advised Oliver to let his mind turn itself in that direction and he would feel a power grow up. The people must be treated with more consideration. It was likely enough that they themselves might be Chartists in their circumstances of privation and disappointment and ignorance. "We must sympathize with them and try to enlighten them."

Sympathy and enlightenment, such were the sovereign remedies which these commercial aristocrats proposed for the solution of the mid-Victorian social problem. Such men had a touching faith in the efficacy of educational and cultural processes to solve the problems which had given rise to Chartism. Greville was tremendously impressed with the educational experiments of his friend Dr Kay, later Kay-Shuttleworth, a Lancashire man, in Norwood. It was a well-managed and successful Poor Law School, with urchins from about eight to twelve years old; when Greville visited them in 1839 he thought he had never seen a congregation of more unpromising and ungainly heads. He described them as the worst and lowest specimens of humanity, starved ill-used children of poor and vicious parents, generally arriving at the school weak and squalid, with a tendency to every vice and without having received any moral or intellectual cultivation whatever. Yet the educational system at the school was such that intelligence soon began to develop and moral faculties to improve. It gave the diarist opportunity for another of those contrasts in the state of England which he dearly loved, the contrast between the imperfect and defective education given to the highest and richest class of society who were brought up stupidly at an enormous expense, and the spectacle of what was accomplished in the Poor Law School by such small means. When he saw what was done there, it made him think what ought to be done elsewhere and then contrast the possible with the actual state of the case.

It must have been an alarming experience for the children of the Battersea Schools, Robert Eden's and Dr Kay's, when Lord and Lady John Russell, Charles Howard, Macaulay, and Greville visited in 1842. Macaulay was put up to examine the boys in history and geography, Lord John and Greville following with a few other questions. The lads apparently rose to the occasion: they answered, said Greville, in a way that would have put to shame most of the fine people's children. The schools were admirable, well managed at small expense. It was a wonder that educationists did not turn their thoughts to a similar scheme for the upper classes who went through a certain process miscalled education, which left boys at the end of it nearly as ignorant as at the beginning, with the exception of the rudiments of Greek and Latin. At Eden's school they learnt reading, writing, arithmetic, drawing, history, geography, and certain matters connected with statistics. At Dr Kay's, the same things were taught, with higher branches of mechanics and especially music, in which they were very proficient. Greville discovered yet another contrast between the boys at Eden's school and the aristocratic schoolboys: while the latter considered learning as an irksome employment, going to school an event full of misery and woe, never thinking of anything but how to shirk their lessons and find time for play and idleness, the poor boys rejoiced in their school, loving the instruction they received, and no punishment being so great to them as exclusion from the schoolroom.

Sympathy and enlightenment: enlightenment through the Poor Law Schools, through the National Schools, which Churchmen were running up in such numbers all over the country, through the British Schools with which the Dissenters implemented the voluntary schemes for their own children; enlightenment through the Mechanics' Institutes which strove to meet the problem of adult education and which Sir Benjamin Heywood was sponsoring with such enthusiasm in Manchester. Was this an adequate answer to the threat of industrial unrest and political agitation which troubled the authorities in the most ominous days of Chartism? But to many earnest men enlightenment could not stop short at intellectual enlightenment; it must go hand in hand with spiritual enlightenment. Thus it was that in 1852 Sir Benjamin

gladly promised his *only front* piece of land in Miles Platting
when the Diocesan Church Building Society applied to him for
land on which to build a church. Gladly would he give it to them
for the enlightenment of that sordid area in which he was a
property owner with a sense of social responsibility, and, said he,
"I must think of a handsome money donation also. I have long
wished this to be done; with a church, bath and washhouses,
schools, mechanics institution, we shall surely make some impression." That was the beginning of the, afterwards, notorious
ritualistic church of St John, Miles Platting. Twelve years later,
his son Henry was appointed to the incumbency of Swinton. In
March 1864, before his induction to the new task, he was seeing
the gentlemen of Swinton who were welcoming him so cordially
to tell them that he must be certain as to their intentions about
providing a new church. Henry Robinson Heywood had learnt
his lesson well from his father. A new church was to be not only
the interesting architectural hobby of a rich family of the commercial aristocracy. It was to be the instrument and expression of
sympathy and enlightenment in a growing industrial community,
the symbol of one answer of the middle classes to the problem of
working-class wretchedness. There were many more features
than one to the Victorian period piece.

VII

It remains now to give a more particular historical and topographical sketch of the neighbourhood in which the period piece
was to be built. From the historical point of view that need not be
a lengthy task, for the district of Swinton is almost devoid of any
traditional or antiquarian interest. It was nothing more than a
barren piece of moorland about five miles west of Manchester.
There are traces of Danish occupation in the district, and the
place may have taken its name from a Danish chieftain Sweyn
who settled in the locality. Swynton, an early spelling of the name,

may rather suggest a place of extensive pig rearing. Other occur-
rences of both "Dane" and "Swine" in local names gave colour
to both views. The place is mentioned in deeds of land tenure in
the Middle Ages as pasture land, and ownership of lands in
Swinton by the lords of Worsley indicates the close connection
between the two localities. The lords of Worsley received lands
in Swinton on condition that they paid an annual sum of three
silver halfpennies to the Hospital of St John of Jerusalem and
four silver pennies to the Monks of Stanlaw. The Abbey of
Whalley, which succeeded Stanlaw, and Eccles Parish Church both
held land at Swinton, and the tenants of the Abbey at Monton and
Swinton had common land on Swinton Moor. At the dissolution
of Whalley Abbey, Henry VIII granted to Thurstan Tyldesley,
lord of Worsley, "all our messuages, lands, tenements, and other
hereditaments with all and singular their appurtenances in
Swynton . . . which were lately of John Paslawe, last Abbot of
Whalley, *in capite* by military service for the tenth part of a
Knight's fee at an annual payment of 35s. 2d.". Hollingworth,
in his *History of Manchester*, speaks of the royalist armies being
encamped on Swinton Moor during the "Great Rebellion" in
preparation for an assault on Manchester which, in fact, was never
made.

These sparse gleanings seem to be the only mention of Swinton
until the time of the Industrial Revolution and the expansion of
Manchester. It is late in the eighteenth century before the place
begins to take shape as a local community, and its true civic
ancestors are the groups of hand-loom weavers, whose cottages
began to spring up at the cross-roads between the route which
ran from Manchester to the Lancashire coast, and the direct road
from the ancient parish church of Eccles by way of some of the
outlying hamlets of that wide parish at Clifton and Pendlebury to
the ford across the Irwell, leading to the other side of the valley
and the ancient parish church of Prestwich. The growth of
Swinton began with the erection of more cottages for hand-loom
weaving. One block was known as the "Barracks" and was quite
different from previous labourers' cottages, being built for hand-
loom weaving as well as for domestic purposes. Each house had

its large cellar capable of holding the hand-loom. The living-room was a large kitchen which could also, if necessary, be used to accommodate a loom. An elderly inhabitant remembers these cottages, now demolished, and describes them as very comfortable but built without much regard for privacy, back to back, and with limited communal lavatory accommodation. Another reminiscence speaks of two, three, and four looms, and sometimes more, fixed in the bedrooms and a great many in the cellars. In the cellar there was always an earth floor, or, as the local inhabitants called it, a "clay floor". Some of the living-rooms had earth floors which had become as hard as bricks and as black as coal with constant use and could be mopped and washed like a flag floor.

When work was brisk the rattle of the machinery could be heard punctuated by the weavers' whistle or the snatch of a favourite hymn or song. The old women wound the bobbins or "pins" as they were called: silk and cotton goods were woven and then carried in a "piece-poke" or "wallet" across the shoulder to the markets of near-by towns. It was a near step from this to the assembly of the machines under one roof and the beginnings of the factory system. Elkanah Armitage, the great Pendleton manufacturer, began business in a room over a stable behind the White Lion in Moor Lane, Swinton. From there he removed to the Old Mill in Moor Lane, and from that headquarters gave out work to weavers which could be done in their own homes. A good deal of harshness was often associated with these early factory masters who gave out work for home industry. Heavy fines were inflicted for the least defect in the cloth and an ill-tempered master would sometimes send a weaver home to re-pick the cloth when there was practically no fault in it. Dishonest "putters-out" would cheat the weavers in a variety of unscrupulous ways. A penny and upwards a yard was the wage rate for weaving, and sometimes a shilling a hole would be the fine imposed for the slightest fault in the cloth. Weavers occasionally struck for more pay, and mass meetings were held at central points to air their grievances. Such meetings were a fruitful field for the rise of Chartism.

The coming of power-looms gradually put an end to the domestic hand-loom weaving, and the factory system was introduced early in the century with its long hours of labour and dreary surroundings. It has been pointed out that though home industry was hard and long it was psychologically less oppressive than the factory conditions where workers were crowded closely together and regimented by the hours imposed by the factory bell. Something of the joy of work passed from the labourers' lives with the coming of factory conditions. Herded together in low ceilinged and dimly lit weaving sheds, resentment at slave-like conditions quickly produced the industrial unrest amongst the workers which found an outlet in Chartist agitation. Whilst the new commercial aristocracy built up great fortunes from the factory system, their employees earned hardly enough to keep themselves alive with the plainest of food. Most of them had porridge three times a day, for breakfast, dinner, and tea. The porridge was sometimes poured into a big dish and placed in the centre of the table; when the father of the family gave the sign by rapping on the table with the spoon, the children went for the porridge like wild animals. The porridge might be eaten with buttermilk, or with treacle and water. The bread was a peculiar Lancashire variety called "Jannock", or barley bread, and oat cake. White bread was a luxury and very scarce, so that poor people hardly ever tasted it. Much depended on the local harvest for, before the abolition of the Corn Laws, little foreign wheat was imported; if the harvest was a failure, the only bread procurable was made from barley flour, which, when kneaded and ready for baking, looked very dark. When it was placed in the oven it took two or three people to keep it in, for it ran out in a thick paste. When baked it was as solid as a swede turnip and if broken and put into milk it would sink to the bottom like lead. These "barley-times" as they were popularly called were times of great hardship to the poor. Flour was also needed by the weavers for sizing their warps and the flour had to be of good quality. In times of bad harvests the price of flour would rise to the almost prohibitive price of sixpence a pound.

These were the local conditions which produced the political agitations which have already been referred to. In the early part of the century the people were crying out for reforms. Rioting, plundering, and mobbing were frequent in the district, and farmhouses would be ransacked by infuriated crowds in search of food. In 1817 a detachment of "Blanketeers" set out from Swinton and were joined by bands of discontented workers from other neighbouring villages who intended to march to London and lay their grievances before the Prince Regent in person. They left Swinton on 24 March and reached Macclesfield in Cheshire on the same evening. But hearing that the military and the Lancashire and Cheshire Yeomanry had dispersed and arrested many of the leaders of similar detachments, they returned the next day.

The abolition of the corn duties did a good deal to ameliorate the living conditions of the working classes, and in the 1850's Edwin Waugh in his rural rambles found a great fear amongst them that the duties might be replaced. He records it in a "ramble from Bury to Rochdale", a quaint conversation printed *in extenso* in the local vernacular in a little roadside inn with old Sam the landlord and Mary his wife. Politics enters the discussion, and Jone O'Jeffry's, a newcomer, begins to inquire of this learned stranger from Manchester about the parliamentary crisis, in which Lord John Russell had resigned as head of the Government and the likelihood there seemed to be of a protectionist party obtaining power:

Jone: Han yo yerd aught abeawt Lord Stanley puttin' th' Corn Laws on again? There was some rickin' abeawt it i' Bury teawn, when aw coom off wi' th' cart to neet.

Sam: They'n never do't, mon! They cannot do! An' its very well, for aw dunnut know what mut become o' poor folk iv they did'n do. What thin'n yo, measther?

Waugh explains to them the unsettled state of parliamentary affairs and gives them his firm belief that the Corn Laws had been abolished once for all in this country, and that there was no political party in England, who wished to restore them, who would ever have the power to do so:

Jone: Dun yo think so? Aw'm proud to yer it!

5

Sam: An' so am aw too, Jone. But what, aw know'd it well enough. Eh, mon; there's a dhyel moor crussuz o' brade lying abeawt i' odd nooks an' corners, nor there were once't ov a day. Aw've sin th' time when thi'd ha bin cleeked up like lumps o' gowd.

There was great rejoicing in Swinton in 1846 when Sir Robert Peel brought his famous Bill into Parliament for the total repeal of the Corn Laws, and at last there were "a deal more crusts of bread lying about". One village worthy collected all the children together and made them sit on the kerb stones while he served them with cheese and bread and beer from a wagon. The children brought their own drinking mugs which were filled as often as required from a huge barrel; the older folk had celebrations of like kind. Before the repeal, when the harvests were poor and the people almost in a state of famine, days of fasting and prayer were observed, when the folk flocked to their churches and chapels to supplicate for better harvests. These "fast days" came to an end after the Corn Laws were repealed, but the same idea was revived in recent critical times of war in the "National Days of Prayer".

The American Civil War brought acute distress to this as to every cotton manufacturing district of Lancashire. In 1863 supplies of raw cotton were blockaded in the American ports and most of the mills came to a standstill. The only mill to run in Swinton was Mr Stuttard's "Albert Mill" which was run principally on Indian cotton called "Surat". Poverty and distress were widespread amongst the people, and more fortunate villagers opened soup kitchens to avert starvation. The Unitarian School was opened to provide occupation for the people, and a teacher was employed to give lessons in elementary subjects. Some of the willing pupils improved their scanty education in this way and later on became mill managers. Cast-off clothing was sent from different parts of the country, and the gentry took an active part in organizing relief. When the first load of cotton reached the village after the "cotton panic", the people went wild with rejoicing, running out of their houses to see it pass, with tears of joy streaming down their faces. The lean period ended with a time of unusual prosperity for the cotton operatives. The markets had become depleted with the long stoppage, work was in arrears, and there was a great demand for cotton goods. Trade improved, and everyone had more work than they could do. In this period of prosperity following the American Cotton famine, the idea of a new Swinton Church began to take shape, and six years after the war broke out the church was finished and consecrated.

The Volunteer movement was a prominent feature of the social life of the community in these ten years preceding the building of the church. It arose as a response to the threat of a war with France. The supposed imperialistic ambitions of Napoleon III sent stolid middle-class Englishmen into uniform, much to the merriment of *Punch*, and, in company with similar detachments all over the country, the Swinton Volunteers were sworn in, Mr James Aspinall Turner, M.P., and other gentlemen taking a prominent part in the movement. It was said that Swinton supplied more men for the Army than any other town or village of its size in the United Kingdom.

The Franco-German War which came soon after the consecration of the church brought a further encouragement to English trade. The price of manufactured goods increased, coal advanced to enormous prices, and colliers' wages advanced proportionately. Unused to large supplies of ready money, the new wealth was often recklessly spent, and colliers were known to indulge their inveterate gambling habits by the unusual experience of "tossing" with gold sovereigns.

One final glimpse of social conditions in the area may be taken, this time again from the pages of Greville's diary. When Greville visited his brother-in-law, Francis Egerton, at Worsley in 1845 he took the opportunity of making a short social survey in the Manchester district. He inspected the marvellous canal and the yard which was a sort of dockyard and manufactory for the canal's requirements. Then he was taken for a sail in the Trust boat, a luxurious barge, fitted up with every contrivance and comfort even to a fireplace and a kitchen. The boat was drawn by two horses with postilions in livery and all the craft, with small exceptions, had to give way to the Trust boat. He went also through the subterranean canal, about a mile and a half long, into the coal pit, saw the men working in the mine and came up by the shaft. It was a black and dirty expedition, scarcely worth the trouble, but he was glad to have made it. He considered the colliers a very coarse set, but they were not hard worked, and, in fact, did no more than they chose to. There are many miles of this underground canal. Greville does not mention the fact, well known in the neighbourhood, that it was necessary for the colliers to lie on their backs on the heaped up coal of the barges and propel them along by pushing on the roofs of the passages with their feet.

On the following day he went to Manchester and saw one of the great cotton and one of the great silk manufactories. Very curious it was to him, ignorant as he was of mechanics. He could only stare and wonder without being able to understand the niceties of the beautiful and complicated machinery by which all the operations of those trades were performed. The heat of the rooms in the cotton mill was intense, but the man who showed them told them it was caused by the prodigious friction. The room might be cooler, but the people liked the heat!

Greville also visted at Worsley the infant school, which was admirably managed, and the recreation ground of the colliers and other employees on the estate. It was a large piece of ground, planted and levelled round what was called the paying-house where the men were paid their wages once a fortnight. The object was to encourage sports and occupations in the open air, and to induce the employees not to go to the alehouse. There were cricket, quoits, and football: ginger beer and coffee were sold to the people, but no beer or spirits. Regretfully, Greville notes that this had only a partial success; the thirst generated by the subterranean propulsion of the coal barges was not one to be slaked by ginger beer.

Another visit was paid to Patricroft to see Messrs Nasmyth's great establishment for making locomotive engines. He inquired at all the places he visited about the wages and habits of the workpeople. In Birley's cotton factory, which, it may be remembered, had earlier been mentioned by Mr Head to Coningsby, he found

1,200 employed, the majority being girls who earned from ten to fourteen shillings a week. At Nasmyth's the men made from twenty to thirty-two shillings a week. They loved to change about and seldom stayed very long at one place; some would go away in a week and some after a day. In the hot factory rooms the women looked very wan, very tired, and, one might guess, very miserable. They worked eleven hours generally, but though it might be thought that domestic service must be preferable, there was the greatest difficulty in procuring women servants. All the girls went to the factory, in spite of the confinement, labour, close atmosphere, dirt, and moral danger which awaited them. The parents made them go because they earned money which they brought home, and they liked the independence and the hours of freedom in the evenings and at weekends.

Greville also visited the Manchester Collegiate Church, soon to become Manchester Cathedral, and found good singing and an excellent reader there. He visited the Athenaeum (or the Institute) and saw Dr Dalton's statue, a good work by Chantrey. Then he went to Messrs Hoyle's calico-printing establishment, which he recorded was extremely well worth seeing and interesting, the more because it was intelligible. People knew very little about the many processes the calico they wore so cheaply went through, and what a mighty business its preparation was. The visitors were told that 800 men were employed there and that the highest wages were two guineas a week. The room containing the copper cylinders had in it a capital of £100,000, the cost of the cylinders. He was surprised to hear that the price of labour (the wages) was not affected by the more or less irksome nature of the employment. The workman at the calico printing, which was much more agreeable than the cotton-weaving business, was as highly paid as the latter, perhaps more highly; indeed, the lowest rate of wages seemed to be at the mill. However, the astonishing news of the death of Lady Holland and the consequent termination of the pleasant activities of the Holland House set now usurped Greville's interest and put an end to his Lancashire sociological investigations for the time being. We cannot but be grateful for the data which he has given us.

This sketch of the social background of the period piece has taken us from the years of dire hardship which followed the Napoleonic Wars, through the period of agitation for Reform and the Chartist movement which succeeded it; we have glanced at conditions in Lancashire at the time of the Corn Law repeal and the American Civil War, and our survey has brought us to the more properous years of the 1850's and 1860's. The working classes were realizing something of the strength of combination, and the years of exploitation lay behind. Power had passed from the aristocratic landowning classes to the wealthy industrial middle class, and Gladstone's first government in 1868, the year during which Swinton Church was being built, ushered in the triumph of liberalism. But there were indications of this power of the rising working class which was soon to bring to birth new political parties then unknown. Mr Street, the architect of the Milnrow Church, was informing Canon Raines, the vicar, in 1868 that Messrs Ellis and Hinchcliffe, contractors, had told him that Rochdale was by no means a cheap place to build at; the trade unions, they said, had great power there and made rules as to hours of labour, etc., which were very much to the prejudice of the contractors. The rule of organized labour was looming on the horizon though it was yet to be many years before it could assume the responsibility of government.

Was the organized labour of the coming age to be a purely political and economic power? This was a question which the enlightened members of the rich middle class had to face. They were not blind to the new forces that were stirring and they had a shrewd idea what the future might hold. "The time may come", wrote Sir Benjamin Heywood to his son Oliver in 1854, "when the working people will get the upper hand; but I hope it will not be yet." Could not the working people be trained in some way to exercise that power judiciously when it should come into their hands? And how better could they be trained for this responsibility than by being invited to take a leading part in these enterprises of church building which were going on all over the the country in the middle part of Victoria's reign? Mechanics' Institutes and the like would see to their further secular education, but to help to build a great church and to have a share in managing its affairs, this indeed was a real training in the responsibility of administration. It has frequently been contended that the Socialist party learned both its social idealism and its business method within the community of the nonconformist chapel. There is equal evidence to suggest that in the building and management of these new Victorian churches and in the routine business of the Sunday-school, and particularly in the discussions in the Mens' Classes of those days, the Established Church was not by any means behind in providing scope for an apprenticeship in community management. There is a significant note by the Reverend H. R. Heywood in the February Parish Magazine of 1868. He says: "It is not fathers and heads of families only who must build the church, but sons and daughters, children and servants. . . . If all will do something, the result is certain." The Heywood family and the rich parishioners, the bankers and the cotton spinners, were providing the bulk of the money but the *little people* must do their part as well. The response of the *little people* was not inconsiderable.

Perhaps the success of the Established Church in the second part of Victoria's reign—and it was successful, more successful, it may be contended, than in any other period of its history—was because so much of the Church expansion of that era of rapidly increasing population was regarded as being a community effort. The rich gave after their means, the poor after theirs; but in the planning of the new parish churches each had his share and each counted for something in the running of the machine which was for so many people the sole preoccupation of their lives. To many it was not only the spiritual focus of the community, but also the intellectual and recreational. They had built it and they maintained it in good working order. So, at last, it is not unreasonable to see our Victorian period piece in the light of a great experiment initiated by wealthy men of vision for the training of a new generation of the working class in the adventure of community leadership. Whether having tasted a little power and learned their lesson they would then desert their teacher for the more exciting and possibly more profitable adventures in political fields was something that was hardly visualized in 1869. Beatrice

Webb was perplexed as to what would lie ahead for the common people when the purely religious urge began to grow dim within them. But in 1869 the building of the church might appear a great spiritual adventure, an attempt to soften the harshness of the industrial system and to capture the working classes, thus rapidly becoming emancipated and enfranchised, for the service and glory of the sort of God whom the rich middle classes understood.

2

THE RELIGIOUS APPROACH

I

WE are now to consider the kind of religion which was presented in these new Anglican churches of the Victorian period; how did the rich middle classes visualize the God for whom they erected such elaborate places of worship? The development of the Anglican idea of God is a lengthy study to which scant justice can be done within the scope of such a brief essay as this. Nevertheless some attempt must be made to sketch the growth of religious ideals and the shaping of the inspiration which impelled so many Victorian capitalists to devote so much of their time and to pour out so much of their money to rebuild the ancient churches and chapels of the Established Church and to erect new buildings in the recent agglomerations of industrial population.

The student of ecclesiastical history may well complain that the protagonists of the Evangelical and Tractarian Revivals have done some disservice to the true picture of the Anglican development by a conspiracy to denigrate the state of the Church in the years which preceded the dawn of their own particular enthusiasm. It is easy to assemble evidence of neglect and decay in selected parishes or to draw lurid pictures of corruption in contemporary manners and morals. It would not be impossible to produce similar pictures in this enlightened century. Not before time there have been some recent attempts to redress the balance and to demonstrate that the stream of Anglican piety, whilst not perhaps spectacular and boisterous, was flowing pretty strongly and deeply through the eighteenth century. The picture of clerical life which is given us in the Woodforde diaries is not one that would appeal to the sort of fervent soul who enjoyed the emotional pyrotechnics of George Whitefield or the titillating ritualism of a High Mass marshalled by a Mackonochie at St Alban's, Holborn. Nevertheless it is the not unimpressive record of an Anglican pastor, living constantly upon his glebe, reading his prayers, baptizing his infants, visiting his sick, and burying his dead. Woodforde's career may not be soul-shattering or epoch-making, but it is of the very stuff and substance of the Anglican pastoral tradition. As John Beresford so finely described it in the introduction to the first volume of the diaries, it "is like embarking on a long voyage down a very tranquil stream. There is no grand or exciting scenery: there are no rapids, nor is there any ultimate expectation of the sea. But there are green fields on either side, and trees, and a very pleasant murmuring of water; there is the harmony which comes only from controlled movement, and there is peace."

Much has been written about the wonders which were done when John Wesley, disdaining the humdrum duties and petty squabbles of the average parochial cure, took the world for his parish and set out on his horse to proclaim the gospel of personal salvation in the parishes of a large number of his clerical brethren who may or may not have been doing the job adequately for themselves. Methodist historians have naturally not had as much to say of the Wesley of the "pre-conversion" days; the disciplines of the Anglican system and the rigours of the Holy Club are not perhaps so congenial to those who have found emancipation from them in a less legalistic system. Yet it should not be forgotten that it was the Church of England as it was in the early part of the eighteenth century which produced the early John Wesley. It was the parsonage at Epworth and the devoted parents who inculcated the notion of the fear of God as the chief end of man in the mind of the future world-conscious evangelist, and whilst his candent personality set in motion certain forces in English religious life which resulted eventually in large numbers of Englishmen separating themselves from the State Church, many another who had been suckled in similar nurseries to that of Wesley remained, like Samuel Johnson, life-long devotees of their Anglican inheritance.

VICTORIAN PERIOD PIECE—SWINTON CHURCH, LANCASHIRE

[*Facing page* 62

STREET'S TOWN IDIOM

Swinton Church as completed by Street in 1869

STREET'S COUNTRY IDIOM

Denstone Church, Staffordshire.   Built by Sir T. Percival Heywood, Bart., 1862

[*Facing page 63*

That inheritance was producing unmistakable fruits of the spiritual life throughout the century which owed nothing to the revived evangelical conscience of the Wesleys. They may be studied in such books as W. K. Lowther Clarke's *Eighteenth Century Piety*, Canon Smyth's *Simeon and Church Order*, and Miss M. G. Jones's *The Charity School Movement*. The widespread activities of S.P.C.K. and S.P.G. are sufficient evidence that the Spirit of God was not quenched in this much-maligned century; the immense literary and missionary output of the societies may be studied as tangible proof of what was being attempted and accomplished within the strict confines of the Anglican Church.

Nor has sufficient credit been given to the actual amount of church-building that went on throughout the century. The immense outcrop of Methodist chapels and Victorian parish churches which covered the country in the following century of leaping population has tended to obscure the substantial achievement of the Georgian builders. But we are learning to appreciate Georgian churches in these days when so many beautiful things have been filched from us by the iconoclasm of speculative builders and the indiscriminate destruction of Hitler's bombs. We are beginning to study them as some of the finest gems in the crown of our architectural tradition; it may shortly dawn upon us that these lovely buildings were not erected simply to give connoisseurs of two hundred years afterwards the opportunity of producing nicely illustrated books on the fine arts, but that they were an earnest attempt on the part of sincerely religious men to bring the knowledge of God to expanding populations who could find no room within the cramped walls of the medieval parish churches.[1]

The work of Wren and his early eighteenth-century disciples in the metropolis is sufficiently well known, and the fate of their bombed churches is now being so urgently canvassed that no one can doubt that the Church in London was alive to its responsibilities

[1] In 1851 an ecclesiastical census showed that there were ten million places of church accommodation of which just over half were in Church of England buildings.

of providing opportunities of worship for the population in late Stuart and early Georgian times. But the enterprise of building churches not only in the capital but also in the provinces went on steadily throughout the century. Huge churches, capable of holding 2,000 people, were built in the new industrial towns, and zealous squires in outlandish country villages were also caught up in the craze for rebuilding. The Georgian churches of both town and country are worthy of comparison both in grandeur of conception and in perfection of decorative detail with the great palaces conceived in the Burlington and Adam periods of the Whig hegemony. A good deal of the story of this valiant attempt of religious men to keep up with the spiritual requirements of an increasing population may be read between the lines in Mr Marcus Whiffen's *Stuart and Georgian Churches outside London*. Whilst the primary interest of such a book is of course architectural, no discerning reader can fail to appreciate that the whole architectural structure rests upon an intensely religious foundation.

The list of churches given at the end of the book, whilst making no pretence to completeness, is an impressively long list of what was accomplished by religious enterprise throughout the century. The great towns naturally provide the greater number, seven in Bristol, four in Liverpool, four in Manchester, three in Shrewsbury, eight in Birmingham, four in Worcester, six in Leeds, two in Sheffield. We cannot charge the Established Church with complete indolence when we survey the new accommodations which were provided for rising populations in such churches as St Philip's, Birmingham, St Chad's, Shrewsbury, St Luke's, Liverpool, St John's, Manchester, and Holy Trinity, Leeds. Nor shall we overlook the spiritual enterprise which is implied by the building of large country churches in comparatively small villages like Ombersley and Hartlebury in Worcestershire and Shobdon in Herefordshire. These are names taken at random from a long list. They could be multiplied many times in evidence that individual landowners in the country, and corporate bodies such as vestries in the towns, were eager that Church life should keep pace with rising populations. It was an unequal struggle as far as the Church of England alone was concerned. Churches were costly structures, and it would have been an impossibility in the towns to provide sufficient new seats for all those, still perhaps only a fraction of an industrial population, who wished to worship God on Sundays. Here was part of Wesley's problem; the shortage of accommodation impelled his followers to build their own chapels for the overplus of population who could not find room in their parish churches. The existence of sets of buildings alongside the parish churches was a powerful factor in hastening the inevitable schism, though it has been pointed out, almost *ad nauseam*, that the Wesleys were loyal sons of the Church of England, bitterly regretted any organized dissent from it, and, as long as they were able, did their best to apply the brake upon the fissiparous tendencies of their enthusiastic converts.

This building of churches and chapels throughout the century is good evidence that religion was not at such a low ebb as the Victorians would have had us believe. Moreover, the buildings were filled with people who had some sort of recognition of a duty to worship God. When the Wesleys proclaimed their message to the overplus of population who were not regular worshippers simply because there was no room for them in the existing buildings, their words were not falling, as in these days, upon a mental soil which has become almost impermeable by the hardening processes of excessive materialism and frantic pleasure-seeking, but upon minds which had already certain well-defined convictions about such eternal verities as heaven and hell, and death and judgement. The intense emotionalism of the early Methodist preachers was applying a torch to material which was already ripe for the burning. It is not altogether to the discredit of what the Church of England had been doing quietly for a couple of centuries that the Wesleys found souls which could so easily be enkindled. The tragedy is that the enlivened consciences which this movement produced, with its insistence upon personal conversion and the quest for holiness, could not be retained within the economy of the Anglican system. The story of early Evangelicalism, with the wonderful crop of philanthropical fruits which it produced, testifies to the extent to which the Methodist revival permeated the Church of England. It will ever remain a matter for speculation, whether the main body of Methodism could have been absorbed within the Church of England if it had been more tactfully handled by Bishop Butler and if John Wesley could have a little restrained the enthusiastic pull of his converts away from what was established and institutional towards what was merely novel and sectarian.

Perhaps the real trouble was that Anglicanism itself had not sufficient faith in the divine sanction of its own institutionalism, and, to give it that, it needed the impetus of a new vision which was not to dawn upon a second little group of Oxford scholars until a hundred or more years after the Holy Club, which, while beginning to grope a little in the same direction, finally reached a conclusion so vastly different from that of the Tractarians. It is in the interplay and the tension between the heirs of these two movements that we must look for the real significance of the Victorian religious situation. Too often they have been studied in antithesis; less than justice has been done to the extent to which one owed to the other.

The early life of John Henry Newman clearly demonstrates the power of a scrupulous Evangelicalism in shaping the later career of the great Catholic apologist. The Reverend Walter Mayers of Pembroke College, Oxford, had much to answer for when he placed in the hands of that sensitive boy the books of Calvinist writers. Romaine and Scott ("to whom, humanly speaking, I almost owe my soul") were fortified by Law's *Serious Call to a Devout and Holy Life*; Milner's *Church History* gave him his first taste of the Fathers, and Newton, *On the Prophecies*, early inculcated a lively belief that the Pope was Antichrist. This youthful indoctrination brought Newman to the thought of "two and two only supreme and luminously self-evident beings, myself and my Creator . . . the fact of heaven and hell, divine favour and divine wrath of the justified and the unjustified". Who can believe that this intense preoccupation in the business of personal salvation—so characteristic of the Evangelicals—could have been lessened in later days when influences, equally strong, had taught him the stupendous grandeur of the conception of the Catholic Church and of the absolute necessity of finding salvation in and through the Divine Society.

It is the conception of the awe and majesty of offended Godhead and the penitent's response of "What shall I do to be saved" which eighteenth-century Evangelicalism passes over into the nineteenth century, to be incorporated into that strange amalgam of mid-Victorian piety which inspired the nineteenth-century church builders. What an awe-inspiring spectacle is that of the Reverend Patrick Brontë, A.B., incumbent of Haworth, near Keighley, preaching a sermon in the church of Haworth on Sunday, 12 September 1824, "in reference to an Earthquake and Extraordinary Eruption of Mud and Water that had taken place ten days before in the Moors of that Chapelry". How sternly he points the moral to his light-hearted parishioners who had taken the opportunity to make a day's picnic of going to view this curious natural phenomenon!

As I proceeded up to the channel, along which the overwhelming and ruinous flood had lately passed, I heard some, whilst surveying the ruins of overthrown bridges and walls, lament in pathetic terms the great expense that must be incurred by the different townships.

Others, I observed, were absorbed in matters still nearer home; whose sorrows were confined within the narrow limits of their own fields of corn, so lately their hope, but now laid prostrate and ruined. But the greater part, by far, I could perceive, rushed on, impelled by mere idle curiosity.

Here and there, however, I was able to discern one in deep contemplative mood, who saw by faith through nature to nature's God. . . .

Several graceless persons wrangled and disputed with each other, even in the very bottom of the cavities, and on their edges; utterly regardless of the warning voice of Providence, that so lately spoke to them in thunder, and seemed even yet to give a tongue and utterance to every chasm that yawned around them.

Many, I perceived, on their return home, who in all the giddy frivolity of thoughtless youth, talked and acted as if they dreamed not either of heaven or hell, death or judgement.

Let us pray earnestly for divine grace, that we may be enabled to act differently, and to walk by faith in Christ Jesus. We have just seen something of the mighty power of God; He has unsheathed His sword and brandished it over our heads, but still the blow is suspended in mercy—it has not yet fallen upon us. As well might He have shaken and sunk all Haworth as those parts of the uninhabited moors on which the bolts of His vengeance have fallen.

Be thankful that you are spared—Despise not this merciful, but monitory voice of Divine Wisdom—Hear, and learn to be spiritually wise, lest the day come suddenly upon you. . . .

It is not without interest to know something of the kind of oratory which fulminated from the top deck of the pulpit of old Haworth Church to fall upon the ears of the young women who were to be amongst the most conspicuous female adornments of nineteenth-century literature. It is a good specimen of the minatory preaching beloved of Church of England Evangelicals of the first part of the nineteenth century, and many Church of England folk who afterwards embraced the tenets of the Tractarians had been nourished on such preaching as this. It laid the foundations of a wholesome belief in the terror of offended Godhead who could even manifest his displeasure by engineering uncomfortable topographical disturbances such as the "extraordinary disruption of a bog", and in whom it behoved all right thinking and prudent persons to find salvation.

With the rediscovery of a forgotten article of the Creed which dealt with "the Holy Catholic Church", we find ourselves in the fourth decade of the century in an entirely new climate of thought. One can feel in the writings of the early Tractarians the pulsating excitement of the discovery of strange truths, of the setting out on a most delightful voyage of adventure in which the consequences of these amazing new premises were only dimly discerned. How disconcerting must have been the irruption of gay young souls like Hurrell Froude into the preserves of high-and-dry Church and State Toryism and into the strongholds of popular Evangelicalism. In some of the controversial pamphlets of the late 1830's one traces the flight of this incautious propagandist of the new Catholic truth, sailing in like some mischievous mosquito to sting some easily shockable don and then buzzing away in gay abandon to survey the fun whilst grave John Henry Newman tries to apply healing salve to the aching donnish wound. Regard this indignant sermon preached by Dr Godfrey Fausset, the Lady Margaret Professor of Divinity, before the University of Oxford, at St Mary's, on Sunday 20 May 1838. It is barely five years since John Keble launched this strange new doctrine in his Assize Sermon from the same pulpit, but events have marched so rapidly that Dr Fausset can entitle his sermon "The Revival of Popery".

It is young Mr Froude who is at the bottom of it all. What singular talk is this, "that the power of *making* the body and blood of Christ is vested in the successors of the Apostles . . ."; that "our present Communion service is a judgement on the Church and could with advantage be replaced by a good translation of the liturgy of St. Peter". He has even spoken against "the *so-called* Reformers" and reproached the orthodox for their "odious Protestantism" and for "regarding the Papacy as a devastating phenomenon". He has suggested that we are "a Reformed, not a Protestant Church" and expressed the eager desire to "un-protestantize" us. The preacher thunders his tremendous warning against such dangerous talk. "Let us not", he says "incautiously entangle ourselves in those mysteries of iniquity from which God's mercy has once granted us so signal a deliverance." In a letter in reply on "certain points of Faith and Practice" the Reverend J. H. Newman, B.D., Fellow of Oriel College, attempts to explain away the harsher expressions in his friend Froude's *Remains* and to meet the Lady Margaret Professor's wrathful denunciations with sweet reasonableness. Nevertheless we are aware that things cannot be as they were before; there are new ways of thinking here, new ideas and suggestions introduced by these tracts. Sincere men are going to hold ideas about interpretations of formularies of the Church of England which to them seem mutually incompatible. The war is on, and henceforward there is such talk of parties within the Church as was never heard so rancorously before.

In 1841, Walter Farquhar Hook, D.D., vicar of Leeds, wrote

6

a letter to the Bishop of Ripon on the state of parties in the
Church of England. At a meeting of the district committee of the
S.P.C.K., which had been held in Hook's parish of Leeds on
31 March, the bishop had interrupted a statement which the vicar
had begun to make with reference to the condition of parties in
the Church. In obedience to his lordship's command, Hook did
not continue, but he intended to have his say now and proposed
to publish his remarks in a letter. He stated what must by now
have been evident to all thoughtful men—that the Church of
England was a divided body. The unhappy determination of the
Hebdomadal Board at Oxford to censure Mr Newman had proclaimed this from one end of the country to the other. So, after
setting forth the tenets of the High Church party and the Low
Church party and pointing out the vices to which each might
tend by pushing their principles to the extreme, he pleaded that, in
all the controversies in which the two parties may be engaged, it
might be remembered that they were brethren; he hoped that
while they contended for the truth they would contend as brethren amicably discussing, not as foes engaged in deadly feud. The
interrupted address had intended to point out how, in a variety of
ways, the S.P.C.K. might be calculated to afford common ground
on which both parties might meet. But concession might be
carried too far; and if the consciences of High Churchmen were
violated and they were compelled to withdraw from the Society,
he did not doubt of their being able to form a new Society more
efficient than the old one.

It is against this background of developed partisanship, so far
removed from the normal tranquility of eighteenth-century parish
life, that the building of Victorian churches must be set. Zealous
partisanship may have generated enthusiasm, but there is the note
of suspicion and sometimes of strife and distress running through
many of the parochial records of the second half of the nineteenth
century. Theological disputation there certainly was in the
erudite University circles of the eighteenth century, with their
Deist and Socinian and Trinitarian controversies, but it is hard
to imagine those controversies rippling the even surface of parish
life. There is not the slightest indication, for example, in the

Woodforde diaries that the rector even knew of the existence of such diversities of opinion. If, as an educated man, he must have been aware of them, he left them well behind in his New College days and henceforward devoted himself to the less exacting task of farming his glebe and supping with incredible appetite in the company of his squire or clerical neighbours. Not until after his death is there the tiniest tremor upon the surface of Church life in the parish of Weston Longeville. It was only in 1803 that one of his parishioners could write that "our new parson Mr Dell has made the tythe double what it was. . . . We are to have singing at Church." There were many other less innocuous freaks of ritualistic fancy in store for the Churchfolk of the new century once the Oxford Movement got under way.

Nor can one discern any theological or ritualistic diversity in the pages of the diary of the Reverend William Jones, curate and vicar of Broxbourne and the hamlet of Hoddesdon from 1781 to 1821. He was a far too thorough-going Calvinist ever to admit that he could be troubled by the notion that any other explanation of the mysteries of life could be tenable than that which gave him complete satisfaction in his morbid philosophy.

It is far different when we move into the Victorian era, spread out so vividly before our eyes in the diaries of such men as Francis Kilvert of Clyro and Langley Burrell, and Benjamin Armstrong of East Dereham. The Tractarian movement has emerged from its Oxford cloisters, and the perils, which such men as Godfrey Fausset perceived when it was in its purely academic stage, have been enhanced a hundredfold now that the revived Catholic doctrines have clothed themselves in strange new garments in the parish churches. Kilvert was no bigot, neither Calvinist nor Catholic, but rather a follower of that even middle way of Prayer-Book Churchmanship which is a little reminiscent of Woodforde, plus a more highly developed sense of vocation and ministerial duty. Yet Kilvert cannot but stand amazed when he visits St Barnabas, Oxford, to hear Father Stanton preach in May 1876. There is the full paraphernalia of incense, processional cross, thurifers, acolytes, vestments, and so on; and there is Stanton preaching from the text, "He is altogether lovely" and repeating his text constantly, "in a very low die-away tone". Kilvert was disappointed in it, and so, he thinks, were many more. As for the Evensong, reaching its climax in the censing of the altar at the Magnificat, it appeared to him to be pure Mariolatry. His last comment on the proceedings is rather delightful. "As we came out of Church, Mayhew said to me, 'Well, did you ever see such a function as that?' 'No, I never did and I don't care if I never do again.' This was the grand function of the Ascension at St Barnabas, Oxford. The poor humble Roman Church hard by it is quite plain, simple and Low Church compared with St Barnabas in its festal dress on high days and holidays."

Armstrong's diary is nearly all a record of the advance of the Tractarian movement in the Norfolk villages, with a particular emphasis on church building and restoration, by one who is in complete sympathy with the movement. Over and over again we find him visiting neighbouring parishes where some dilapidated church has been restored, and marvelling at what can be accomplished by the co-operation of an energetic incumbent and a sympathetic squire. This second half of the nineteenth century is the very heyday of church-building and church-going. On 24 August 1862 he is at Yarmouth where the congregation in the vast parish church is as large as ever. In the evening the new Wherryman's Church near the station is crowded "with the class for whom it was built. . . . The thousands of people pouring out of the different places of worship and promenading afterwards was quite a sight." In 1870 he is able to contemplate in amazement all that he has been able to do by way of church restoration in twenty years. He preaches "on retrospection, drawing a comparison between the state of things now and twenty years ago. Nothing could be worse than the state of the Church in 1850. Then, the altar was a miserable mahogany table with a covering fifty years old; there was a vile yellow carpet; a Grecian reredos with daubs of Moses and Aaron; no painted glass, and the rail for the communicants intersecting the sedilia. Look at it now—an altar and super-altar of full dimensions, with flower vases always replenished with flowers; candlesticks and candles (now introduced); three altar-cloths changed at the seasons; the windows painted; a stone reredos highly painted and with a central cross; rich carpet; credence table; Bishop's chair etc., etc." Still the end of Mr Armstrong's restorations was not yet; he was still at the job towards the end of the diary in 1885 when, on 9 December, the nave of the parish church was reopened after the removal of the galleries and the substitution of a handsome wagon roof for the old ceiling.

Such visible contrasts are, of course, the stock-in-trade of the Tractarian writers for their frequent accusations of deadness in Church life in the previous century. But does the evidence really warrant that conclusion? The eighteenth-century churches were primarily regarded as preaching houses where salvation through Christ was proclaimed by a principal emphasis on the ministry of the Word. The splendid three-decker pulpit is really the significant focus of worship and not the altar, whilst Justification by Faith pays little heed to the material or decoration of the buildings in which it is proclaimed. The Holy Communion is an optional extra provided at festivals and other rare occasions for the pious few who did in fact leave their box pews in the nave and "draw near with faith" past the towering pulpit into the chancel, which was in reality a second room in which the sacramental service was conducted. Addleshaw and Etchells, in their illuminating book *The Architectural Setting of Anglican Worship*, have made it sufficiently clear that it was a difference of doctrinal emphasis which was responsible for the arrangement of the furnishing of the eighteenth century. The inferior position and possible neglect of the altar is due to the inadequacies of the Eucharistic theology of the period, and when Armstrong and many like him demonstrate with pride the difference they have made in the outward appearance of their churches, what they are testifying to is not necessarily the moribund state of the Anglican Church in the previous century, but the shifting of emphasis over the hundred years from the preaching of the Word to the frequent and decent administering of the sacraments.

This shifting of emphasis was the contribution of the Tractarian revival, and it is the measure of its success that there were probably few churches in the whole of the country, even those which were in the hands of clergy who were least in sympathy with its doctrinal presuppositions, which did not show some effects of the sacramental revival. Even Kilvert, who as we have seen, was by no means in sympathy with the advanced ritualism which was characteristic of the later stages of the movement, could note with gratification the change for the better which had come over the methods of sacramental administration during the previous half century. In 1874 he reports that the vicar of Fordingham told him that, when he came to that parish in the 1820's, no man had ever been known to receive the Holy Communion except the parson, the clerk, and the sexton. There were sixteen women communicants and most of them went away when he refused to pay them for coming. They had been accustomed to pass the cup to each other with a nod of the head. At one church there were two male communicants. When the cup was given to the first he touched his forelock and said, "Here's your good health, Sir." The other said, "Here's the good health of our Lord Jesus Christ." One day there was a christening and no water in the font. "Water, Sir!" said the clerk in astonishment. "The last parson never used no water. He spit into his hand."

These are extreme and lurid examples of the neglect of sacramental administration before the coming of the Tractarian revival; but those who had not suffered to the same extent were conscious of the inadequacies of their eighteenth-century buildings for presenting the fullness of the Anglican theological system which they had now been taught, with its nice balance between the preaching of the Word and the ministering of the sacraments. A desire to present the full Faith in dignified and adequate surroundings is clearly in the mind of the Reverend H. R. Heywood when, in his last sermon in the old Swinton Church in 1868, he sets forth some of the reasons which prompted him to undertake the rebuilding. Heywood inherited a plain brick Georgian structure which had been erected in 1791 when the Swinton chapelry was first created in the ancient parish of Eccles. No photographs survive of the interior, but recollections of old inhabitants lead one to suppose that it was typical of other buildings of its time which have come down to us with high box pews, galleries, three-decker pulpit, and an insignificant holy table. It was not of the classic period of eighteenth-century church building, and there is little to regret in its passing. Heywood spoke very scathingly about it when he referred to the building in the last sermon which he preached within its walls:

I was looking over this old church, this last week [he said] and in one part of it I couldn't help stopping and saying to myself, "I'll speak about this on Sunday. I'll ask if there are any that think this old church good enough for its purpose and I'll ask such, if they do to come over it with me this next week." Some of you may know your way from the gate to your sitting and no more. The Scholars' Gallery, or the Free Seats or certain of the entrances or many parts of the church furniture and so forth, perhaps you never have noticed or thought about; but to me it did (going over it) seem so sad that this should be God's house—from the poverty of it—that really, I mean what I say, that if any of you would like to be persuaded that we *ought* to have that new church and will come over the church with me and let me point out to you what I like, I do think you will go somewhat more willingly and cheerfully and thoughtfully to Church next Sunday than might be otherwise. . . . But when you think of the unscriptural arrangement of this church, when you think of the poorness and shabbiness of this church, then on these accounts . . . you will think that (if we can help it) God, and the presence of God, should not be treated thus. . . .

The gist of the argument here lies in the words *poorness, shabbiness,* and *unscriptural.* The ritualistic implications of Tractarian doctrines had introduced a desire for more beautiful buildings and more dignified ceremonial in the ordering of public worship, but when the preacher refers to the old arrangements as being unscriptural, he is obviously implying that the eucharistic teaching of Holy Scripture has not received proper acknowledgement under the old order and that a developed sacramental system requires its proper structural setting with chancel, sanctuary, and altar of imposing dimensions.

Thus it is that the sacramental revival in the theology of the

Church of England begins to make its mark upon the new parish churches and the ceremonial of public worship performed within them. But the change is accompanied by the developed partisanship sometimes resulting in open legal warfare which we have previously noted. The most extreme example of this warfare touched Heywood closely when his assistant curate, Sidney Faithorn Green, who had helped him in the Swinton rebuilding and had later become rector of Sir Benjamin Heywood's new church at Miles Platting, found himself, as a result of an action for contempt of court in connection with the working of the Public Worship Regulation Act, incarcerated for a lengthy period in Lancaster Gaol. Green's ceremonial practices were not greatly in advance of what was being done in many churches in the 1870's, but the Church Association fastened upon him as a test case and the Bishop of Manchester, Dr Fraser, declined to veto the legal proceedings. This *cause célèbre* produced a national sensation, and H. R. Heywood was active in every way in defence of his former curate. But whilst matters were pushed to this tragic extreme in the case of only a very few clergymen, there were not many who did not suffer from opposition and minor persecution as a result of their high sacramental and ceremonial ideas. Armstrong of East Dereham, as we are told by his grandson in the foreword to *A Norfolk Diary*, ministered to his people for thirty-eight years in an exacting and difficult parish with undeniable diligence, but he received no honourable recognition from the diocesan authorities, by whom he was regarded as a dangerous man. He accomplished much, as we have seen, in the way of church building and embellishment, but throughout the diary we discern an undercurrent of doubt and suspicion in some quarters of his parish which might have flared up into active and bitter opposition.

Armstrong interpreted the formularies of the Church of England according to what he had learnt from his Tractarian teachers, but he endeavoured to conform to the law in an entirely submissive spirit. He was bitterly disappointed in February 1871 by "a very discouraging and adverse judgement for the High Church party ... condemning the Eucharistic vestments as illegal, and also the eastward position of the priest at the altar". Yet he says, "With heavy heart and very unpleasant feelings I thought it best to yield a loyal and ready (though very unwilling) compliance to the above. But to my mind we are bound to obey the law, and I know that there was at least *one* present who would only be too happy to catch me tripping." In 1863 he refused to allow Brother Ignatius to lecture in Dereham on monks and monasteries, for though respecting his character and principles, he objected "to the enthusiastic monk throwing the apple of discord among us and entering upon an argument which would never be appreciated". His scrupulous loyalty and carefulness afforded him an immunity from his theological opponents, and when in 1875 the Church Association held a meeting in the town at which "Sacerdotalism" was fiercely assailed, the vicar attended the meeting and was allowed to make a spirited reply to the lecturer, ascending the platform amid loud cries of "Fair play". "The meeting agreed, nevertheless, that there should be a branch of the Church Association in Dereham, and the proceedings ended with the singing of the Doxology, these Protestants invoking the Angelic Host!!!" In 1880 he and his son were attacked in a Norwich weekly paper for "Romish" proceedings, and an interview with the editor only elicited the conviction that, "It is clear that I have an enemy, and also, judging by internal evidence, that he is a regular attendant at Church!"

This undercurrent of suspicion was the price which had to be paid in Victorian parish life by those who were attempting to present the fullness of Church of England theology as it had been derived from the two great revivals of the previous hundred years. Yet most of these earnest clergy were the product of a synthesis between Evangelicalism and Tractarianism. From the former they had learnt the necessity and urgency of personal salvation; from the latter, the conception of the Catholic Church as God's social instrument of salvation in the world, with its sacramental system as the surest way of procuring it. Fear of Romanism underlay the opposition that they encountered, and the controversy which raged round the Ecclesiastical Titles Bill of 1851 added much fuel to these flames. Something of the passions which it reawakened may be seen in Greville's journal, where that somewhat cynical observer of men and movements was so greatly disgusted by the spectacle of animosities displayed that he was provoked to present his reasonable view of the question in a long letter which he addressed to *The Times* over the signature "Carolus", 9 December 1850.

The opening of Street's two Lancashire churches in the same year, 1869, was somewhat marred by two anti-ritualist incidents which are so similar as to make us wonder whether there must have been a deliberate connection between them. On 15 March Mr J. P. Thomson, who was the clerk of works for the building which was rapidly reaching completion at Milnrow, wrote to Mr Street, "I am required by Capt. Schofield to state that at a meeting of the executors this day it was definitely resolved to dispense with the cross in the reredos and to substitute arched panels in Caen stone to coincide with those already shown on each side of the proposed cross. I have not yet seen the Rev. Canon Raines but don't think he will very much like the alteration." Canon Raines certainly did not like it, but he had no other course but to accept it, for he had received from Captain Schofield, who had sub-scribed already about £4,000 to the cost of the work, a letter, suitably written on a broad-edged mourning paper in a pen-manship of deep broad strokes, cutting incisively into the paper, the following categorical challenge:

Greenroyd, Rochdale. You are well aware how opposed my grandmother and self are to any ritualistic notions. By my orders Mr. Thomson wrote to Mr. Street to say I did not at all approve of the red Maltese cross on the white ground over the Com-munion Table. On making enquiries this morning I find the work is still going on. I have written to Mr. Street to instruct Rogers and Booth at once to stop it being made. Unless my wishes are carried out with regards to this church I shall not attend it at all neither shall I take any interest in it or its schools.

Canon Raines, like a wise man, knuckled under in this plaintive note to Street on 19 March: "I have no sympathy with the spirit which prompts the removal of the small cross from the reredos but I decline to interfere as the subject has not been named to me by any one and as the Capt., has just announced his intention to provide bells, pulpit, lectern, and, in short, all that is required to finish the church. He *allows* Mrs. M. to give the font." The power of the purse was thus successful in this instance in balking the spread of ritualism; Street removed the cross and substituted on the central panel of the Milnrow reredos a design incorporating a bleeding heart which apparently was satisfactory to Captain Schofield, but which in our day conveys a much more definite flavour of Romanism in its *motif* than a simple cross would have done.

Swinton Church was consecrated on 2 October 1869. During the previous week the vicar received the following note which is preserved among the many papers relating to the building of the church: "At a meeting of the Swinton New Church Building Committee held this 27th, of September, 1869, it was resolved (William Longshaw, Esq., being in the chair) that the Cross now being erected on the Reredos be removed, as it was decided that in its present position it was objectionable." The connection between the Milnrow and Swinton incidents is perhaps not very hard to find when we note that Captain Schofield had married at Eccles Church on 28 March 1867, Fanny, the elder daughter of William Longshaw of Swinton. It looks as though the two families had met in solemn conclave on this dangerous subject of Tractarian builders incorporating a cross in the reredos. It is evident that this unexpected declaration was something of a stab in the back to Heywood, and caused him considerable grief and disappointment. He refers to it at some length in the first sermon that he preaches in the new church; the typical reaction of a Tractarian clergyman to such opposition is perhaps worth quoting at length:

I come now to say a few words on a matter which I think I have no right to be silent upon, and which has caused others beside myself much sorrow this last week; in fact I do not deny that it has qualified (for *some* amongst us) in a material way, the rejoicing we had anticipated at this time. You will know to what I allude. The removal (by order of the Building Committee) of the Cross which formed part of the Reredos behind the Communion Table, which Reredos is a gift to the Church.

The vicar then quotes the terms of the notice he was served with, and goes on:

The Cross *has* been removed. It is not in the reredos, anybody can see it is not, and they can see now (even in an artistic point of view) the Reredos is spoilt without it, for the Cross was and is a very beautiful one, of marble and alabaster, a real work of art designed by Mr. Street, but this is not what makes the removal of the Cross (to many of us) so disappointing. It is not the mere absence of taste, or the lack of appreciation of what (in its way) is a little art treasure—no it is that any here could ever feel the Cross in any position objectionable. It is this which grieves some of us, that any of us members of the Church of Christ should ever object to any emblem of the Cross of Christ anywhere, at any time, in any place. St. Paul said "God forbid that I should glory, save in the Cross of our Lord Jesus Christ." Do you think, after he had said that, he would have been afraid of the sign of the Cross? My Brethren, please not to misunderstand my object in now speaking. I am not speaking in order to persuade any of you to take action to have the Cross put up again at present—a plain marble slab is ordered to supply its place. I am not speaking against anybody; the members of the Committee and myself are all at one and with an entirely good understanding between us. . . .

So it goes on, over seven more pages of faded sermon paper, the preacher obviously deeply disappointed and fearful of a cleavage on this issue within the parish:

It stands to reason we cannot all agree on everything, but we can all work and pray and strive to be (ever more and more) *at one*. Oh! we *must* do so, for my Brethren, say you what you will, and say *I* to myself what *I* will, it does open a gulph between us— between minister and people—when one (in his heart) so loves the sign of his salvation and the other (thro' a weak fear of Romanism, or Ritualism, or something of that sort) cannot endure it. . . .

Heywood's fears were fortunately not realized. His sincerity and goodness were sufficiently appreciated, and his power as a wealthy squire-parson was sufficiently influential to prevent any such considerable schism developing within his flock. It was not long before Mr Street's "little art treasure" was occupying its rightful place at the centre of the reredos, and the vicar was happy again. The difference was transitory, but it is indicative of the background of suspicion and fear against which the mid-Victorian clergyman ministered and built his churches. Wisdom, tact, and strategic withdrawals were often able to resolve a difficult situation. Sometimes, when pushed to extremes, as in Faithorn Green's case, there were painful and tragic consequences. Within the Church, men felt strongly upon these issues of doctrine and ceremonial. To those outside it the issues probably seemed as trifling in those days of high moral earnestness as they do to-day.

Let us now see something of the impact of the Church with its two developed doctrinal streams upon the general society of the day. If it was the good example of the Court which was influencing the aristocracy, the commercial middle classes, and the proletariat in turn, let us see how the Court was touched by the prevailing moral seriousness and the religious sources from which it derived. Then let us turn again to Greville's journals and see how the whole situation appeared to the social observer who stood outside the scene and who described it with a good deal of cynical detachment.

II

It might be a matter of whimsical speculation whether Victoria had within herself the capacity of following in the track of her wicked uncles. These who were responsible for her upbringing were quite determined that she should not. George IV passed from this life in an aura of sanctity such as becomes the deathbed of kings. The Bishop of Chichester, with the King's permission, repeated on his knees at his bedside a prayer which had been appointed for public use during his illness. At the close of it, His Majesty, having listened to it with the utmost attention, three times repeated "Amen" with the greatest fervour and devotion. His Majesty, we are told, was aware of his situation, and exerted himself as far as possible to profit by the season of reflection and self-examination then afforded to him. The contemporary writer believed that he was earnest in his religious feelings, and that he had been allowed the benefit from which the humblest sinner is not excluded. Nevertheless, in spite of this improving end, Victoria was brought up to believe in the wickedness of her relations of the previous generation, and the utmost care was taken that no taint of their dubious morality should be allowed to descend to her.

This conditioning of Victoria for respectability was something in which several people had a hand, but the seal of completion was set upon all their work by Prince Albert of Saxe-Coburg. His influence, and that of Leopold, King of the Belgians, who was also responsible for a good deal of the Queen's right thinking, can be clearly traced in the voluminous correspondence edited in those three indispensable books by Arthur Christopher Benson and Viscount Esher. For the earliest influences we must go to the first three chapters and trace the hands of Queen Adelaide and Baroness Lehzen and Baron Stockmar. It is interesting to reflect that the moral influences which had, through the force of their example upon the aristocratic and middle classes, some remote connection with the building of Swinton and similar churches, emanated to a large extent from continental and, more particularly, German Lutheran sources. There was, however, the Reverend George Davys, the Princess's instructor, who afterwards was rewarded for his responsible care with the Deanery of Chester and the Bishopric of Peterborough. This clergyman had been charged by the Duchess of Kent to see that the future Queen should be properly drilled to fulfil her vocation of Defender of the Faith and Supreme Governor of the Church of England as by Law Established. So, at an early age she began to attend Divine Service regularly with her mother, who professed a feeling to the Anglican bishops that the child had religion at her heart, that she was morally impressed with it to that degree, that she was less liable to error by its application to her feelings as a child capable of reflection. Her adherence to truth was, so her mother affirmed, of so marked a character that the Duchess felt no apprehension of that bulwark being broken down by any circumstance.

The Bishops of London and Lincoln were invited to conduct a personal examination of the Princess's religious knowledge and reported themselves as being highly satisfied with the result. The important features of scriptural history, of the leading truths and precepts of the Christian religion as taught by the Church of England, seemed to have been fully grasped: when to this moral equipment was added a remarkable facility with chronology, the principal facts of English history, geography, arithmetic, Latin grammar, and the use of globes it could scarcely be doubted that Victoria was well on her way to acquiring the intellectual resources suitable to a most Christian monarch, and that the baleful shades of the convivial but wicked uncles could be thereby dispelled as readily as the machinations of the demon king at the pantomime. In spite of this favourable episcopal school-leaving certificate, however, Victoria had to confess in later life that her earliest impressions of bishops were not happy ones; her feeling amounted in fact to one of *great horror* on account of their wigs and aprons. The Bishop of Salisbury, Dr Fisher, who having been tutor to the Princess Charlotte, "Daughter of England", might have supposed himself to be "good with children", managed to ingratiate himself a little by kneeling down and letting her play with his badge of Chancellor of the Order of the Garter, but the efforts of another bishop to win favour by admiring her "pretty shoes" were unavailing.

At an early stage in the long series of letters which Leopold of Belgium addressed to his niece he neglects no opportunity of moral caution; the child of thirteen is reminded that by the dispensation of Providence she is destined to fill a most eminent station, and that to fill it *well* must be her study. At fourteen she is exhorted to give some little time to reflection and self-examination. Vanity is to be carefully disciplined, for since the horrid head of revolution had reared itself in Europe, the position of "great people" has become extremely difficult. The transition from sovereign power to absolute want has been as frequent as sudden, and the character must be so formed as not to be intoxicated by greatness and success nor cast down by misfortune. Let trifling matters, then, be relegated to their proper place, and good sense show itself by distinguishing what is and what is not important.

The Princess was confirmed at the Chapel Royal on 30 July 1835, and the occasion elicited a suitable letter from her good uncle who, by reason of his situation in the camp of Beverloo when he wrote it, compared himself, perhaps a little doubtfully, to "those old camp preachers who held forth to many thousand people on some heath in Scotland". The 16,000 men who surrounded him were not, he hastened to add, very like the stern old Covenanters. His environment, however, was sufficiently similar to suggest some strictures upon the English episcopal religion. Humility was a particularly Christian virtue, but hypocrisy was a besetting sin of all times. He was sorry to say, with all his affection for old England, that the very state of its society and politics rendered many in that country essentially humbugs and deceivers. Let Victoria's character always be true and loyal; though, to be sure, that did not exclude prudence: worldly concerns demanded caution, which some might regard as the near relation to hypocrisy. Truth was the important virtue which from her earliest childhood her uncle had been most anxious to see saved and developed. In case of any doubt on the subject, governess Lehzen would be able to supply confirmation of his anxiety. So, metaphorically pressing the future Queen of England against his heart, Leopold R., her sincerely devoted camp preacher and uncle, drew this touching little confirmation address to its close.

On 17 June 1837 it was obvious that King William IV was nearing his end. It was therefore not inappropriate that so close a counsellor as her uncle Leopold should in his letter of that date enter on the subject of what was to be done when the King ceased to live. In the forefront of his advice stood the necessity of maintaining the influence of conservative principles and of protecting the Church. The new Queen must show herself attached to the English Protestant Church as it existed in the State; she was particularly where she was, because she was a Protestant. Whilst being averse to persecution she must miss no opportunity of showing her sincere feeling for the existing Church; it was right and meet that she should do so. Six days later, after the accession, he returned to the same charge: "The Established Church, I also recommend strongly; you cannot, without pledging yourself to do anything particular, say too much on the subject"—no doubt an exercise in truth, restrained by prudence and caution, such as he had previously inculcated.

To the general indoctrination of Leopold, the Duchess of Kent, Baroness Lehzen, and Baron Stockmar, therefore, as well as to the more specific teaching of her Anglican tutor and the bishops, we owe the grounding of Queen Victoria in a certain sort of Anglicanism. That it was primarily Erastian, soundly Protestant, and largely this-worldly, we are not surprised. These early influences were wholly lacking in sympathy with the mystical pietism which was to be found in some circles of Lutheranism, and which had, for example, so strongly influenced the religious development of John Wesley. Leopold's reminder that she was where she was because she was a Protestant was sufficient to preclude any active sympathy with Catholicism, especially when it presented itself quite shamelessly and inexcusably at her own front door within the familiar framework of the Establishment. Tractarians, Puseyites or whatever these dishonest innovators were called, were traitors to be resisted, certainly to be debarred from promotion, and, if possible, to be removed from the national Church. Yet there is not much evidence that Victoria had any sympathy with the extremes of popular Evangelicalism such as the Methodist movement had set going both within the Established Church and outside it. Indeed, extremes of any sort were abhorrent in her choice of bishops. In 1857 she was careful to make inquiries of Palmerston about the appointment of Mr Alford of Quebec Chapel to the Deanery of Canterbury. Was he a very Low Churchman? Lord Palmerston would remember that he agreed that it would be advisable in appointing bishops to choose those who were of moderate opinions—not leaning too much to either side. Extreme opinions led to mischief in the end and produced much discord in the Church which it was advisable to avoid.

7

In the third volume of Queen Victoria's letters there is an interesting correspondence between her and Viscount Palmerston on the question of appointing bishops. It arose from the suggested appointment of the Reverend Emilius Bayley, rector of St George's, Bloomsbury, to the See of Worcester, vacant by the death of Bishop Henry Pepys. Mr Bayley was not, in fact, appointed; the diocese received Canon Henry Philpott of Norwich, who entered in 1861 upon a really great tenure of office, and whose episcopate is still remembered with thankfulness by very old people in Worcestershire to this day. In connection with the suggestion of Mr Bayley, the Queen was anxious that the Prime Minister should bear in mind that the Bench of Bishops should include not only respectable parish priests but also University men of acknowledged standing and theological learning. In doctrinal controversies which agitated the Church there was need for skill and erudition amongst those who governed it. Viscount Palmerston took up this point in a long letter in which he compared the duties of bishops in the Church to those of generals of districts in the Army. The duties consisted in watching over the clergy of their dioceses, seeing that they performed their parochial duties properly, preserving harmony between clergy and laity, and softening the asperities between the Established Church and the Dissenters. Practical parochial knowledge was necessary to carry out these functions properly. A bishop must not be of an overbearing and intolerant temperament, and the less he engaged in theological disputes the better. Instances are then given of "theological bishops" and men chosen merely for their learning, who have been failures at the job. High Church bishops have exasperated the Dissenters and some Churchmen by their intolerance, particularly in the matter of refusing to consecrate burial grounds unless a wall of separation were built between the Churchmen's and Dissenters' portions. Palmerston then submitted a justification of the men whose names he had submitted to the Queen for episcopal office—Baring, Longley, Tait, Wigram, Waldegrave—and contended that though the High Church, Puseyite, and semi-Catholic Party had found fault with his choices, they had given great satisfaction to the nation at large. The people of the country, he declared, were essentially Protestant, and felt the deepest aversion to Catholicism; they saw that High Church, Tractarian, and Puseyite doctrines led men to the Church of Rome. The disgraceful scenes in the previous year at St George-in-the-East, where brawling had taken place as a protest against the High Church practices of the rector, the Reverend Bryan King, were only an exaggerated outburst of a very general and deep-rooted feeling. The clergy of the Established Church were, so Palmerston believed, never more exemplary in the performance of their duties, more respected by the laity and, generally speaking, on better terms with the Nonconformist body than at that time.

There is no doubt that the Queen was, from the start, deeply suspicious of and hostile towards the Tractarian movement, and she was well coached in this disposition by her earliest advisers. When godparents were being considered for the christening of the heir to the throne, Lord Melbourne expressed his approval of the choice of King Frederick William IV of Prussia. That choice, he said, gave great satisfaction, and would do so with all but Puseyites—one of the earliest mentions of that afterwards celebrated title—and Newmanites and those who leaned to the Roman Catholic faith. His strong Protestant feelings and his co-operation in the matter of the Syrian bishop had made the King of Prussia, so Melbourne said, highly popular in the country, and particularly with the more religious part of the community. The co-operation was in the matter of the setting up of the joint Jerusalem bishopric, an essay in Anglican and Lutheran joint action which was one of the contributory causes of Newman's final despair of the Church of England. There was further coaching of the Queen by Melbourne in a letter of 12 January 1842 when the Prime Minister attempted some explanation of the new life which was surging up within the Church. With respect to the Oxford affair, Melbourne said, her Majesty was aware that for a long time a serious difference had been fermenting and showing itself in the Church, one party leaning back towards Popery, and the other either wishing to keep doctrines as they were, or, perhaps, to approach somewhat nearer to the dissenting Churches.

That difference had particularly manifested itself in a publication, then discontinued, but which had been long going on at Oxford, entitled *Tracts for the Times* and generally called the Oxford Tracts. The Professorship of Poetry was then vacant at Oxford, and two candidates had been put forward, the one Mr Williams, who was the author of one or two of the most questionable of the Oxford Tracts, and the other Mr Garbett, a representative of the opposite party. The result of the election which was made by the Masters of Arts of the University was looked to with much interest and anxiety as likely to afford no unequivocal sign of which was the strongest party in the University and amongst the clergy generally. It was expected that Mr Garbett would be chosen by a large majority. This, in fact turned out to be the case; the election was fought with all the acrimony of religious partisanship, and the Tractarian candidate was beaten.

Victoria's hatred of Tractarianism, which was induced by the conviction which Leopold had planted in her that she was where she was in order to defend the Protestant settlement and which was encouraged in these ways by the tuition of her political advisers, persisted in the Queen's mind throughout her life. Lord John Russell, in writing to her in 1850 about the so-called Papal aggression, when the Roman Catholic hierarchy was re-established in this country, professed to believe that it was not a matter to be alarmed at. The real matter for alarm was the growth of Roman Catholic doctrines and practices within the Established Church. Dr Arnold had said, very truly, "I look upon a Roman Catholic as an enemy in his uniform; I look upon a Tractarian as an enemy disguised as a spy." It would be very wrong to do as the Bishop of Oxford had proposed, and confer the patronage of the Crown on any of those Tractarians. But, on the other hand, to treat them with severity would give the whole party vigour and union. The Queen reiterated the same sentiments in a letter about the same time to the Duchess of Norfolk. The real danger to be apprehended, she said, and what she was certain had led to those proceedings on the part of the Pope, lay in their own divisions, and in the extraordinary conduct of the Puseyites. She trusted that the eyes of many might have been opened. She would, however, much regret to see any acts of intolerance towards the many innocent people who, she believed, entirely disapproved the injudicious conduct of their clergy.

It was a wonder that, against this solemn and regal weight of opposition, the Tractarian movement was able to make any headway in the Church. Yet progress was made of such substantial sort that within fifty years Tractarianism had altered the face of the Church of England and had brought about the widespread Church revival of which the building and rebuilding of many parish churches was the tangible evidence. The influence of King Leopold and her early mentors and Prime Ministers upon the Queen was completed when she married the eminently suitable and conspicuously talented Prince Albert of Saxe-Coburg. History has magnanimously redressed the unfavourable balance of public opinion which greeted the arrival of this amazing character on the English scene. At first no vilification was cruel enough to level at the young prince. In 1839 the Tories were making a great disturbance, saying that Albert was a Papist, because the words "A Protestant Prince" had not been put into the Declaration. Suspicion of possible interference in British political affairs by this privileged foreigner at times reached a fever heat of absurdity. But maturer reflection has done justice to the stabilizing influence which Albert exerted on the young Queen, to the intellectual brilliance which he imported into the Royal circle and to the truly wise statesmanship with which from his unobtrusive position behind the throne he was able to soften the asperities of many a private and political situation. The measure of his vision of England's greatness took shape in the Great Exhibition of 1851, which was largely his conception; it is useless to speculate whether he would have played an increasingly powerful part in national affairs if an early death had not deprived the country of his brilliant talents. Certainly in her ecstasies of grief the widow of Windsor showed how completely her affection for Prince Albert continued to dominate her life, and how the example of his rectitude had fastened down for ever the main direction of her life. If Victoria had married a libertine and a wastrel, the course of English history, and particularly of ecclesiastical history, might have shaped itself very differently. Because Albert was the model of God-fearing propriety, and the home life of the Royal couple a model of domestic bliss, the whole tenor of society changed for the better. Aristocracy and middle classes followed suit, and the age of seriousness was ushered in. That Albert was equally interested in the affairs of the Established Church we cannot doubt, though a High Churchman like Armstrong of East Dereham regarded him with suspicion. It may have been no more than a piece of clerical gossip, but on 23 March 1862 Armstrong was told that the late Prince Consort had compiled, and actually printed, a new version of the Book of Common Prayer, from which every Catholic landmark had been carefully expunged. It was hoped, said Armstrong, that this precious production would supersede, gradually, the book at present in use. However, at the earnest remonstrance of his friends, the Prince had the good sense to order in the whole edition, though some few copies had fallen into private hands. In 1863 Armstrong reported that the Bishop of Oxford was said to be out of favour at Court and to have lost the Archbishopric of York for insisting on the consecration of Prince Albert's "wretched Mausoleum" in the gardens of Frogmore. Armstrong greatly feared that the tendencies of the Court were rationalistic through the influence of the late Prince Consort.

One may believe that his contemporaries were pushing matters a little far in such an accusation, though the High Churchmen may have had good grounds for their suspicions. There is an interesting memorandum of 27 February 1852, compiled by the Prince, in which he describes an audience which Lord Derby had with the Queen to explain what he intended to state in Parliament that evening as the programme of his ministerial policy. When Derby had touched on Church matters, the Queen expressed to him her sense of the importance of not having Puseyites or Romanizers recommended for appointments in the Church as bishops or clergymen. Lord Derby declared himself as decidedly hostile to the Puseyite tendency and ready to watch over the Protestant character of the Church. He said that he did not pretend to give a decided opinion on so difficult and delicate a point, but it had struck him that although nobody could think in earnest of reviving the old Convocation, yet the disputes in the Church could be perhaps most readily settled by some Assembly representing the laity as well as the clergy. Then follows the amazing example of the Prince Consort's foresight in this interesting matter. Albert expressed it as his opinion that some such plan would succeed, provided the Church constitution was built up from the bottom, giving the vestries a legislative character in the parishes leading up to Diocesan Assemblies, and finally to a general one. With this quite astonishing prevision of the details of the 1919 Enabling Act on the part of the Prince Consort we may perhaps leave this small consideration of the religious outlook of the Victorian Royal Family. Religion, of a sort, there was in plenty; plenty of reference to Providence, particularly in its dealings with Victoria and her family. There is firm adherence to the Protestant settlement which the Queen regarded herself as having been raised up by that same Providence to maintain. But there is nothing of a mystical nature in her religious experience, and no understanding of and sympathy with those startling new manifestations of Catholic sacramental devotion which to her seemed only a traitorous menace to the Protestant settlement of which she was the heaven-sent guardian. Yet our Victorian period piece owed much to Victoria and Albert. Their respectability, their conformity to the ceremonies of the Established Church, their exemplary home-life, provided that stable ethical background against which our church builders could build with confidence. Church of England Christianity would not stop at the limits which Victoria and her husband understood. There was new wine here, and the bottles of Erastianism were in danger of being broken. Yet the Tractarians and their friends could look up to the throne with respect even if they could expect scant sympathy from it. The Queen, as well as her Prime Minister, was on the side of the angels.

III

To our Tractarian, the Victorian religious background to his church building was largely an adventure in mediating the fullness of Catholic truth, with its newly discovered enrichments of sacramental practice and ceremonial stagecraft, to what he considered to be the arid deserts of unregenerate Anglicanism. To the Evangelical it was still the proclamation of the gospel of redemption as it had been derived from the fountain-head of Methodist inspiration, together with works of private and social charity and the eternal vigilance which was involved by being constantly on guard against the insidious advance of popish practices within the fold. Yet the Evangelical himself was by no means uninfluenced by the ideas of dignity and seemliness in worship which the Tractarians had introduced, and nowhere did he betray that influence more than in the architecture and ordering of the churches which he was building. To the Queen, the religious situation was an aspect of the political one; it required the loyal maintenance of the forms and ceremonies of the Established Church with herself as Supreme Governor, appointed by a Providence to whom she did not scruple often to refer, for the specific task of maintaining the Protestant succession; her immediate task was to restrain the encroachments of Puseyism by a careful watch over the appointment to the key positions in the Church. But how did the Victorian religious situation appear to the observant man of the world, and what did it mean to the rank and file of ordinary people in the new crowded industrial areas in which the new churches were being built?

We look in vain in Creevey's Papers for intelligent comment on Church affairs in the period covered by his literary life. This is disappointing, for his observations on the shifting political scene of the period of the Reform Bill and the accession of Queen Victoria are as illuminating as those of Greville and sometimes even more pungent. But the Church does not seem to have interested him greatly, and appears little in his pages as a target either for his appreciation or scorn. There is, however, one enclosed letter from Henry Brougham, M.P., to Creevey which deserves quotation as representing the view held about the Church of England by one of the most brilliant parliamentarians of the age. Here speaks the Erastian statesman, prepared to maintain the integrity of the Church as an instrument of public policy and ready to spring to its defence against the projected attack by Joseph Hume:

Don't let us deceive ourselves [he writes] There are millions—and among them very powerful and very respectable people—who will go a certain way with us, but will be quite staggered by our going *pell-mell* at it. The people of this country are not prepared to give up the Church. For one—I am certainly not; and my reason is this. There is a vast mass of religion in the country, shaped in various forms and burning with various degrees of heat—from regular lukewarmness to Methodism. Some Church establishment this feeling must have; and I am quite clear that a much-reformed Church of England is the safest form in which such an establishment can exist. It is a quiet and somewhat lazy Church; certainly not a persecuting one. Clip its wings of temporal power (which it unceasingly uses in behalf of a political slavery) and purify its more glaring abuses, and you are far better off than with a fanatical Church and a Dominion of *Saints*, like that of the 17th century; or no Church at all and a Dominion of Sects like that of America.

There was much talk on the part of politicians about reforming the Church in those days when the notion of reform was so much in the air. Even some of its best friends felt that drastic measures were called for. It is a surprising conclusion that it was the eminently reasonable plan of suppressing the redundant Irish bishoprics which provided the singular piece of enkindling in Keble's Assize Sermon of 1833. Reform and revivification were certainly on the way with the coming of the Oxford Movement, but reform was to be a process beginning from within. The Church of England was still rather too powerful and lively a society to suffer the drastic truncations which lay in the minds of Brougham and such-like of the reforming politicians. But there were other observant layment of the period more knowledgeable in Church affairs than Brougham and Creevey, and for their point of view we go to Greville.

Outside the confined circle of fervent idealists in every generation there always stands the fair-minded observer who has no particular ardour for theological causes but whose approval and support will always be thrown in on the side of what is decent and straightforward and honest and moral. There are always a vast number of intelligent Englishmen of this sort—the Church of England contains thousands of them—and Charles Greville, the diarist who has helped us considerably already, was a fair specimen of these. To his journals we may turn again for a picture of how the religious and Church of England situations appeared in the early and middle Victorian periods to a thoughtful and not altogether unsympathetic spectator.

It was the bigotry of English religious life that impressed Greville when he paused for reflection during his German tour in 1843. In the Rhineland he found two-thirds of the people Catholics and the reigning family in Baden Protestants. The clergy of both persuasions were paid by the State, education was in common, and the schools were open to teachers who gave separate religious instruction. Everywhere there seemed to be a more satisfactory and harmonious state of things with regard to religion than in England. There was more intolerance, bigotry, obstinacy, and *déraison* at home, he considered, than in all the world besides. Perhaps it was the conflicting theological loyalties in the Anglican Church which produced this bitterness. Even the royal ears were not spared the expression of it, for when Perceval and Hook, two of the leading High Churchmen of the time, were appointed to preach at the Chapel Royal, it was feared that they would take the opportunity of lecturing the Queen on their own particular tenets. The Bishop of London tried to keep Mr Perceval out of the pulpit by preaching himself on several Sundays, but when the Bishop fell off his horse and broke his collar-bone, Mr Perceval found his opportunity. The Queen, who had been warned to expect a strong sermon, heard the preacher make an attack upon Peel, reproaching him with sacrificing his conscience to political objects in consenting to Catholic Emancipation. Hook was even more forthright; he told the Queen that the Church would endure, let what would happen to the throne. Lord Normanby, who had been at the chapel, later said to her, "Did not your Majesty find it very hot?" "Yes", she said, "and the sermon was very hot too."

In 1841 Greville noted the increasing religiosity of society in a world "which often grows religious but never grows moral". Perhaps a symptom of it was the conversation at Holland House when Macaulay displayed his prodigious memory by discoursing with equal fluency on the subject of the Fathers of the Church, with special reference to a sermon of St Chrysostom in praise of the Bishop of Antioch, the use of children's dolls in ancient Rome, Milman's *History of Christianity under the Roman Empire*, and Strauss's book on myths. No wonder Greville could complain that his own farthing rush-light was instantly extinguished by the blaze of Macaulay's all-grasping and all-retaining memory. About the same time, he noted, in connection with a lecture by Mr Hullah on the teaching of vocal music in Poor Law Schools, that such plans which were founded in benevolence and a sincere desire for the diffusion of good among the people would gain every encouragement. In the midst of much indifference and prejudice there existed a growing disposition to ameliorate the condition of the masses, both morally and physically. The building of our Victorian churches is surely another evidence of this growing disposition. In March 1841, Sir Robert Peel made a striking speech rebutting charges of irreligion which had been levelled against him in a series of letters in *The Times* signed "Catholicus", and identifying himself with the side of social progress.

Greville appears to have made his first acquaintance with Puseyism in August 1841, when he met at dinner Dr Wiseman, the future English cardinal, then a bishop and head of Oscott, "a smooth, oily and agreeable Priest". Wiseman talked religion, Catholicism, Protestantism, and Puseyism almost the whole time. He spoke of the increase of Romanism in the manufacturing districts and attributed it to the violence and scurrility of the Protestant Association. He talked about Pusey and Newman, and Hurrell Froude whom Wiseman had known at Rome; he declared that the opinions of Pusey and himself were very nearly the same and that the great body of that persuasion, Pusey himself included, were very nearly ripe and ready for reunion with Rome. Wiseman assured his hearers that neither the Pope's supremacy nor Transubstantiation would be obstacles in their way. It is an interesting comment on the extent to which the official Roman view had misunderstood what was happening in the Church of England.

The Bishop of London's (Blomfield's) charge in October 1842 apparently attempted, like similar charges of the Bishops of Exeter and Oxford, to be conciliatory to the Puseyites by prescribing what Greville calls some formal observances half-way in advance towards their opinions. This desire to conciliate was put down by the diarist to the bishops' knowledge of and alarm at the Tractarians' remarkable superiority in everything which related to ecclesiastical learning. *The Times*, too, was reputed to be becoming decidedly Puseyite. It associated its Catholic tendencies with advanced notions in Poor Law reform, both subjects being, so Greville observes, of a highly democratic character. Thus early does it seem that in the public mind there was an association between High Church doctrine and enterprises of social reform, an association which came to fruition in the philosophy of Frederick Denison Maurice, and the activities of Bishop Gore and Stewart Headlam and their Christian Socialist confederates in the work of the Guild of St Matthew and afterwards of the Industrial Christian Fellowship.

Greville inquired of Blomfield about this time on the subject of pews and pew rents; the bishop replied that the whole thing was an anomaly, in some respects doubtful, but in many regulated by ancient usage or by local Acts of Parliament. Still, these weighty matters were interspersed with pleasing social graces, and episcopacy could even unbend on an occasion when there was no company to the extent of singing a duet with Lady Jane Grimston. Greville gives what for him is high praise to this Bishop of London; he describes Blomfield as an agreeable man in society, good humoured, lively, though a little brusque in his manner. He enlarges on the character sketch later by calling him intemperate and imperious but always distinguished for great liberality and a munificent disposition; he has a generous mind, is capable of forgiving an enemy and casting aside feelings of resentment and wounded pride. In his review of the year 1842 Greville notes that great and increasing interest was felt at that time in all the many grievances or pretensions of the various Christian denominations and that men's minds were much turned to religious subjects. One proof of that might be found in the avidity with which the most remarkable charges of several of the bishops had been read and the prodigious number of copies of them which had been sold. Of these, the principal were the charges of the Bishops of London (Blomfield), Exeter (Phillpotts), and St David's (Thirlwall). Phillpotts's charge was especially able and contained amongst other things an attack upon Newman for *Tract 90* and a very powerful argument in reply to a recent judgement by Brougham at the Privy Council on the subject of lay baptism.

In May 1843 Greville attended service at the Temple Church. It was, he said, most beautiful to see, though perhaps too elaborately decorated. The service was very well done, with a fine choir. Benson preached on justification by faith; it was not a good sermon, though he was a fine preacher. Greville listened attentively but found it all waste of attention. The preacher ended by a hit at the Puseyites (as he often rejoiced to do) and an extract from one of the Homilies which was the best part of the sermon. Brougham was there and had brought Peel with him. In June Greville reported that the whole country was full of distress, disquiet, and alarm and that religious feuds were rife. The Church and the Puseyites were at loggerheads in England, and the Church and the Seceders in Scotland. Everybody said it was all very alarming, and everybody went on just the same and nobody cared except those who could get no bread to eat. It did seem strange to him that after thirty years of peace, during which there had been so much reforming zeal and activity, England seemed to be in as bad a condition as ever. It was a great problem, said Greville, which he could not pretend to solve, and which it would task most men's philosophy satisfactorily to explain.

Through the pages of the journal there moves, appearing from time to time, that memorable figure which appears to have dominated the early Victorian ecclesiastical scene, Samuel Wilberforce, Bishop of Oxford. Son of the famous anti-slavery enthusiast, he inherited a good deal of the vigour and ability of his father. Greville characterizes him as a remarkable man, full of cleverness and vivacity, very unlike a Churchman in society and in Parliament, and yet, so Greville judges, deficient in that worldly tact which it might be thought he would most surely have acquired. Greville had some strong personal reason for passing this judgement. After a slight acquaintance, Wilberforce had called on him to discuss, so Greville thought, some detail of Eton College business. However, it turned out that he had heard that Greville had been dangerously ill and he had called to tender his spiritual advice and aid, and (in a rather commonplace style of writing) had urged him to listen to his religious exhortations. Greville was obviously at a loss to know what he had done to merit these attentions. In the whole course of his life, he says, he never was so astonished, for Wilberforce was about the last clergyman from whom he would have expected such an overture. His acquaintance with Greville had been so slight, that he could not conceive why he had selected him, the diarist, as the subject of a spiritual experiment. Greville determined, after some perplexity, to take his letter in good part, to give him credit for the best motive, to express much gratitude, but to decline to enter with him into any religious discussion. Moreover, he gave him to understand, though with great civility, that his proposal was extraordinary and uncalled for. These tactics succeeded well; the bishop took no notice of this answer, and Greville did not know what he felt about it as he did not see him again.

Other ecclesiastical butterflies flit across the early Victorian scene, and are pinned down by Greville in his delightful museum. Here, for example, is Whately, the Archbishop of Dublin, whom he meets at dinner at Raikes Currie's and thinks not at all agreeable. He has a "skimble-skamble" way of talking as if he was half tipsy, and the stories he tells are abominably long and greatly deficient in point. Here is the Hon. Edward Harcourt, Archbishop of York, who dies on 5 November 1847, in his ninety-first year, a man in no way remarkable except for the wonderful felicity of his whole life from first to last. It would perhaps be difficult, says Greville, to find a greater example of uninterrupted prosperity. The Church was a happy sphere in those days for men like Harcourt, nobly born and highly allied, full of professional dignities and emoluments and the inheritor of a large private fortune. When the Reverend Benjamin Armstrong paid his first visit to the home of Pelham, the new Bishop of Norwich, in 1860, he found that instead of the crazy old Palace of Bishop Hinde's time, it seemed as though an enchanter's wand had substituted a fairy medieval structure in its room. The entrance was very ecclesiastical, and the bishop's library and dining-room very spacious and elegant. Pelham had aristocratic connections and when, at his installation in June 1857, the words of the anthem were, "Thou spakest sometimes in visions unto Thy Saints and said'st 'I have exalted one chosen out of the people'", Armstrong could not resist commenting that the words were hardly appropriate for the scion of a noble family! Nevertheless, Pelham took his episcopal office very seriously, and, although not sympathetic to Armstrong's type of Churchmanship, the diarist speaks highly of his fairness and kindness, and praises his conscientiousness. He remarks in September 1859 that the Bishop of Norwich rose much higher than Sir James Graham's celebrated description of the office and work of a bishop, in which he said in Parliament that more bishops were not needed, their duties being merely an ordination twice a year and a Confirmation thrice. Pelham laid himself out for work. He ordained at all the Ember Seasons, revived ruridecanal chapters, preached in all the chief churches of the diocese, and instituted episcopal conferences to which all the clergy in their respective deaneries were invited. The leaven of Tractarianism was working in the high circles of aristocratic episcopacy; indeed, there were few departments of Church life which did not show something of its influence in spite of their declared lack of sympathy with its aims.

Greville displays considerable interest in the furious controversy which rages around the appointment in 1847 of Dr Hampden to the see of Hereford. Hampden had long been the object of the hatred of the Tractarian party on account of his supposedly heterodox theological opinions, and Lord John Russell's appointment of him was largely made as a gesture of defiance to that party. He was a dull, heavy man who, as Greville says, made more noise in the world than he deserved, but he did not turn out to be a bad bishop. Lord John Russell defended his protégé against the remonstrances of thirteen protesting bishops and a brilliant attack by Phillpotts of Exeter. The Archbishop of Canterbury also wrote a testimonial for Hampden when there seemed some likelihood of making him the first bishop of the diocese of Manchester, now about to be carved out of the Henrician see of Chester. The archbishop wrote that, during the ten years since Dr Hampden had been appointed Regius Professor of Divinity at Oxford, he had no reason to believe that Hampden had taught from the chair any doctrines at variance with the Articles of the Church of England. He had discovered nothing objectionable in the few publications by Hampden which he had seen and which were ably written, but of his discretion or talents for business he had no means of judging. Those qualifications, thought the archbishop, might be more than ordinarily required in the first bishop of such a place as Manchester. This favourable testimony Greville attributes to the archbishop's timidity, both natural to him, and due to his advancing years. Hampden was passed over for Manchester and the new diocese received as its first bishop Prince Lee.

Dean Merewether, one of Hampden's antagonists, is described as a very paltry fellow who had moved heaven and earth to get himself made a bishop. He had memorialized the Queen and written to Lord Lansdowne suggesting to him to put an end to the controversy by making him a bishop then and Hampden at the next vacancy. Greville regarded the whole proceeding as reflecting great discredit on the great mass of clergymen who had joined in the clamour against Hampden, and on the Oxonian majority who condemned him; it was pretty clear that very few, if any, of them had ever read his writings. "Sly Sam" of Oxford ("my would-be director and confessor") had covered himself with ridicule and disgrace. The disgrace was the greater because everybody saw through his motives; he had got into a scrape at Court and was trying to scramble out of it. But at Court, where the Queen and Prince Albert were following the controversy with hot zeal, he had been found out, and his favour seemed to be waning. Phillpotts of Exeter is characterized as an old fawning sinner for his part in the dispute. Indeed, the diarist works himself up into a perfect paroxysm of indignation at the scandalous motives of Churchmen which this case had revealed. Dispassionate men must be disgusted and provoked with the whole thing and at the ferocity with which these holy disputants assaulted and vituperated each other about that which none of them understood and which it was a mere mockery and delusion to say that any of them really believed. It was, he said, cant, hypocrisy, and fanaticism from beginning to end.

It is a relief after stirring these muddy waters to turn to two ecclesiastical appointments of which Greville sincerely approved. In February 1848 Dr Sumner, Bishop of Chester, was appointed Archbishop of Canterbury in succession to the timorous Howley. It was a great mortification to the Tractarians and a great joy to the Low Church; but he was so excellent a man and had done so well in his diocese, that the appointment would be generally approved. It is not without interest in this present study, for Archbishop Sumner was the great-uncle of Ella Sumner Gibson, who married Henry Robinson Heywood, the builder of Swinton Church. The appointment by Lord Aberdeen of Mr Jackson, rector of St James's, Piccadilly, as Bishop of Lincoln, gained the Prime Minister great credit in Greville's estimation. Mr Jackson was a man without political patronage or connection, and with no recommendation but his extraordinary merit both as a parish priest and a preacher. Such an appointment was creditable, wise, and popular, and would strengthen the Government by conciliating the moderate and sincere friends of the Church.

On such a favourable note we may end this short sketch of some aspects of the Victorian Church, drawn from the comments of a well-informed man of the world who would probably have described himself as a moderate and sincere friend of the Church. Whilst rejecting the overtures of the Bishop of Oxford to draw

8

him on such subjects, Greville in an entry on 2 April 1847, his fifty-second birthday, entrusts something of a private confession of faith to the security of his personal journal. "With regard to that great future, the object of all men's hopes, fears, and speculations", he writes, "I reject nothing and admit nothing.

> Divines can say but what themselves believe;
> Strong proof they have, but not demonstrative.

I believe in God, who has given us in the wonders of creation irresistible—to my mind irresistible—evidence of His existence. All other evidence offered by men claiming to have divine legations and authority are to me, imperfect and inconclusive. To the will of God I submit myself with implicit resignation. I try to find out the truth, and the best conclusions at which my mind can arrive are really *truth* to me."

The pages of ecclesiastical histories are too often written by the ardent protagonists of this side or the other; they would have us believe that all the truth lay with those who assailed or defended the orthodoxy of Hampden. They feel deeply on these questions and they would persuade us that men of the time ranged themselves as decisively on either side in the struggle. It is good to be reminded by such men as Greville that there were, even then, moderate and sincere friends of the Church who stood apart from the hot blood of battle, and, taking refuge in a reverent agnosticism, would say that on some points of doubt they rejected nothing and admitted nothing. Whilst, in the Victorian scene, Tractarians and Evangelicals belaboured one another soundly, whilst court chaplains fawned and clerical place-seekers crept up back stairs towards episcopal office, there were men like Jackson of Lincoln and Sumner of Canterbury who reached the highest rank on account of their ability and goodness alone.

The expansion of the Church went forward, the building of the Victorian period pieces increased, in spite of intrigue and self-seeking and theological acrimony. Church life prospered in spite of the suspicions of the Crown and the repressive hand of Prime Ministers and important people in high places in Church and State. It prospered, because no anachronisms of Erastian restraint could hold back the bounding zeal of vast new industrial wealth harnessed by men who were inflamed by religious enthusiasms. We have taken a glimpse of this renewed Church life as seen by a sympathetic observer from an aristocratic vantage point, with an unveiled contempt for the foibles and jealousies of aspiring Churchmen, but with a real sympathy with what was being done to ameliorate the social wretchedness of the time. We must now give some attention to that work actually in progress, to see how, in one or two parishes, the lower-placed clergy of the Church were trying to apply the healing doctrines of Christianity through the Anglican parish system to the densely populated areas of the industrial towns. The building of the period piece rose out of the spiritual, social, and educational zeal of these conscientious clergy. Let us examine some of their methods, see them actually at work, and note something of their success.

IV

There is a practically unexplored field of evidence for mid-Victorian parochial activities in the crop of parish magazines which were springing up all over the country at this time. Some time, perhaps, a full-scale book may be written which may do justice to this extremely important and influential type of popular journalism. For our purpose in illustrating the day-to-day parochial life of two typical Victorian parishes we shall touch briefly on the rich resources which lie within the pages of the handsomely bound volumes which stretch back in unbroken series to the 1860's. The local parish notes in each set are bound up with stock matter entitled "Parish Magazine. Edited by J. Erskine Clarke, M.A., Vicar of St Michael's, Derby." Canon Clarke had invented the parish magazine at St Michael's, Derby, in 1859. The London publishers were Bell and Daldy, 186 Fleet Street, E.C. The 1864 issue begins with an "Eastern Fable", entitled "The Bulbul and the Vulture", illustrated on the first page. Next comes a five-verse poem, "A Lyric of the New Year", by John Critchley Prince, a weaver, of Hyde, Cheshire, followed by six and a half pages of a serial story, "Ashford Feast", which runs into four no doubt eagerly awaited monthly episodes. Another eight-verse poem by J. B., entitled "The March of Time", is followed by an improving little illustrated article "Grandfather's Watch" (for the children). Then comes a short parable, "The other side of the Hill", another poem, "A New Year's Carol", by T., and then a forceful bit of Anglican propaganda based on the restoration of Newland Church and called "The Restored Window". "The Written Rocks" of Sinai are briefly described and illustrated, and the issue then ends with "A Short Sermon. The Abiding City: A New Year's Sermon, By W. Baird, M.A., Clare Market Mission Chapel, London." The text is Hebrews 13.14: "For here we have no continuing City; but we seek one to come." The inset covers twenty pages and measures 5 inches by 8½ inches. Its contents are worth quoting in full, for they illustrate the kind of literature which was being circulated very cheaply in thousands of homes in the country where the young people were learning to read in the new National Schools, which were being built in large numbers of parishes. The parish magazine must have been much prized in homes where the cheap literature of the age was beginning to be popular. Whether the serial story or the short sermon were the favourite feature we need not speculate, but the principles of the revived Anglicanism were being given the widest publicity in a more popular sort of *Tracts for the Times* which went into far more homes than their graver predecessors, and expounded sound Church teaching whilst combining business with pleasure in these catching little pennyworths. "And therefore, when one of those who differ from us says to me 'Your Church is a new Church, not much older than mine', I think of this window and answer, 'No: we cleared away the false doctrines and heresies which Rome had brought upon us; but we kept up our old line of descent from our original founding in the first century. If this is a new window, the Church of England is a new Church, not otherwise; for what was done to it, the same was done to us.'" Thus does Mr C. Witherby, B.A., drive home his moral in "The Restored Window", and thus does the new-born popular ecclesiastical journalism contribute to the substantial prosperity of the Victorian period piece.

It is when we look at the local matter bound up month by month with this sort of inset that we actually see the parishes at work, and for this purpose we propose to examine briefly the records of two typical Lancashire parishes, Prestwich and Swinton. Prestwich lies about four miles to the north of Manchester; it is one of the great pre-Reformation parishes of the Salford Hundred of Lancashire, and in medieval times stretched over ten miles to the north-east, to include the ground on which the small hamlet of Oldham stood with its daughter chapelry of St Mary. In the Industrial Revolution Oldham grew to be a large and densely populated cotton-manufacturing town; Prestwich remained a small village with its ancient church perched above a deep ravine or "clough" running towards the Irwell Valley, and in the middle of the nineteenth century it began to acquire popularity as a residential suburb of Manchester, and the villas of prosperous business men grew up within sight of the church. The living was financially well endowed and regarded as something of a "plum"; the local landowner was the Earl of Wilton, living in a large mansion rebuilt by Wyatt in Heaton Park about a mile from the church. The Earl of Wilton was patron of the living and a regular attender at the services of the church. The occupations of the inhabitants were mainly agricultural, with the exception of those who worked in a small cotton mill in the village and those employed in the large county asylum[1] which stood at no great distance from there.

The rector of this very delightful parish in the 1860's was the Reverend Henry Mildred Birch, a clergyman of some importance in the Victorian scene. When the time arrived for the young Prince of Wales to have a tutor the choice fell upon this Mr Birch, who took up his duties in 1849. He was the eldest son of the Reverend William Henry Rouse Birch of Bedfield Rectory, Suffolk, and had been a King's Scholar at Eton, where he became

---

[1] Opened in 1851; built on land purchased from Mr Oswald Milne in 1847 for £11,412 4s. 5d.

Captain of the School. He had a distinguished academic career at King's College, Cambridge, graduated B.A. in 1843, and was then elected a Fellow of his college. For four years he was under-master at Eton, and then in 1848 negotiations were opened with him which resulted in his being entrusted with the tutorship of the Prince. "The impression he has left upon me," wrote the Prince Consort to Lord Morpeth in August 1848, "after a preliminary interview, is a very favourable one, and I can imagine that children will easily attach themselves to him." The trouble seems to have been, according to Mr Hector Bolitho in his *Victoria and Albert*, that the young prince began to attach himself to the "young, good-looking, amiable man", as described by Prince Albert, to a degree of affection which the father may have considered a little too intense to be discreet. As Birch was to keep unrelenting watch on the young prince, so was Birch himself to be watched by Stockmar. The system laid down for the boy's education was so stern and arid and painful that no opportunity was given for the play of the natural childish affections and enthusiasms. It is suggested that the boy began to turn towards Birch with an affection and tenderness that he could not give to his father. He wrote affectionate notes to his tutor and crept into Birch's bedroom at night to put them on his pillow. Prince Albert considered this "unsuitable" and Birch was dismissed, to be succeeded by the prim and correct Frederick Waymouth Gibbs.[1]

The Royal Family seem to have retained a high opinion of Birch and to have kept in touch with him for the rest of his life. When the tutorship came to an end in 1851, Birch was ordained deacon in Lincoln Cathedral and, the following year, priest. He had not long to wait for a substantial preferment; in 1852, the same year as his priesting, he was presented to the wealthy living of Prestwich-cum-Oldham in Lancashire by the Earl of Wilton, and read himself in on 30 May. This was not the end of lucrative preferment, for in 1868 he was appointed Residentiary Canon of Ripon by the Crown, a benefice which he held in plurality with

---

[1] Disraeli, in his *Correspondence with His Sister, 1832–52* (1886), asserts that Birch was dismissed because he attached undue importance to the Church Catechism (quoted by Sir Sidney Lee, *King Edward VII*, p. 29).

his rectory of Prestwich. It is unlikely that these two pieces of preferment could have yielded the ex-tutor much less than £3,000 a year, and it may perhaps be set down to the good credit of the Crown that it was not unmindful of its erstwhile servant, who at one time stood in danger of being a menace to the emotional balance of the heir apparent. In Victoria's correspondence of 1861 there is a letter from Viscount Palmerston to Sir Charles Phipps which reviews the candidates for election to the office of Provost of Eton. Dr Goodford, the headmaster, was the successful candidate and reigned as provost till his death in 1884; the other three were Mr Coleridge ("a prejudice against him on account of his Puseyite tendencies"), Dr Chapman, late Bishop of Colombo, and Mr Birch, "formerly tutor to the Prince of Wales, scarcely of sufficient calibre for the office, and not qualified by a sufficient degree". The Ripon canonry no doubt came as adequate compensation seven years later for the loss of the Provostship of Eton.

In 1852 Mr Birch was appointed Chaplain-in-Ordinary to the Queen. In 1856 the Prince of Wales contributed gifts to the Prestwich Library and Reading-room, and in 1857 he and Prince Alfred, later Duke of Edinburgh, paid a visit to Prestwich, and lunched at the rectory on the occasion of the opening of the Manchester Art Treasures Exhibition. In 1868, the Prince of Wales stood sponsor to Albert Edward Henry, the only surviving son of Canon Birch, and presented him with a splendidly chased silver goblet. Birch died in 1884, and a west window made by Messrs Ward and Hughes of Soho Square, London, was erected in his memory. H.R.H. the Prince of Wales and H.R.H. the Duke of Edinburgh appear at the head of the subscription list as each subscribing £1 1s. od. towards the ex-tutor's memorial.

It might be suggested by the cynical observer that Birch, the pluralist, with his appointment to an unusually opulent benefice twelve months after his ordination, represented a type of aspiring clerical place-seeker who would have been more at home in the Anglican Church of the eighteenth than of the nineteenth century. There is certainly evidence that the Crown found it convenient to use pieces of Anglican preferment as a reward for services rendered as little as a hundred years ago. Duckworth, who had been governor to Prince Leopold, was pressed by Queen Victoria for the Westminster canonry vacated by the death of Kingsley, on the grounds that the Prince was at that time very ill and "the appointment would greatly gratify her poor sick boy". When the appointment was made, the Queen wrote to Disraeli to say that "He would have been gratified had he seen the pleasure which lighted up the emaciated face of the dear invalid." Yet the fact remains that many of these favoured gentlemen who had come to their benefices by special influence took their work extremely seriously and became, within the limitations of their own particular mental outlooks, first-rate and conscientious parish clergymen. Birch was probably a snob, in that he was justly proud of his intimate associations with families in the first rank of English life. At Prestwich he would dine occasionally with his wealthy Philips parishioners at the Park; but the young ladies at that establishment came from a dissenting and more radical tradition. They were not so impressed by the frequent references to the exalted circles in which the rector had moved before his banishment to the rural fastnesses of Lancashire. "Let's listen carefully," they used to giggle together before a dinner-party, "and count how many times he mentions the Prince of Wales." But, snob or no snob, Birch was determined to do his duty by the parish which was to be his home for over thirty years and he tackled jobs of church restoration, extension, and embellishment, and parochial organization amongst his poor parishioners, with all the zeal of a Camden Society Tractarian. In twenty years £6,500 was spent on the ancient church, for the rector regarded it as a matter of high principle to retain the ancient building as a symbol of continuity with the piety of the past in a neighbourhood where there was so much that was new. So the tale of embellishment and structural alteration went on with the years whilst other buildings for religious worship were erected in other parts of the parish, reading-rooms and libraries were opened, and National Schools were enlarged and rebuilt. A new care for the beauty of the sanctuary was displayed in fresh furnishings; two handsome carved oak chairs presented by James Prince Lee, first Bishop of

Manchester, kneeling stools, a new reading-desk, a new font, stained glass windows, the chancel enlarged and a new vestry built, brass book-stands for the altar, altar cloth and carpet presented, the Birch Chapel built by subscription at a cost of £500, the tower of the church repaired at a cost of £3,300, the west gallery re-moved, the nave and chancel re-roofed and other alterations made at a cost of over £2,000—here is a tiny local picture of that tremendous upsurge of Church life which was happening all over the country in the middle of the century. Finally, here is evidence of the advancing Churchmanship of the age, for the rector, though too much of a courtier to declare himself a Puseyite, was by no means unaffected by those encroachments upon the conduct of public worship which seemed to draw the Victorian Church a little closer to the customs of the Catholic past. In 1871, the sur-plice was worn by the rector in the pulpit for the first time on Easter Day. The chancel began to take on what the ecclesiologists would have called a truly Catholic appearance, with the gift of oak stalls with elaborately carved and tapering wooden canopies, and a sculptured reredos over the holy table. In 1877 the choir boys and men were put in surplices which had been given by Mrs Birch. Early celebration of the Holy Communion was held on every third Sunday in the month and Divine Service was commenced on Saints' days. The triumph of Tractarianism was in full flood.

As we glance through the pages of the local matter printed in the parish magazines month by month during the 1860's and the 1870's, we see clearly how the church was the focal point of the community life of the parish, and provided not only a scheme of services for public worship on Sundays but also opportunities of amusement and instruction on several nights of the week. Here, in the January number of 1864, for example, is a notice of a "Night School, open at St. Margaret's School Room, Rooden Lane, four nights a week, free of charge, on Tuesday and Thurs-day Evenings for Young Women, and on Wednesday and Friday Evenings for Young Men. The School opens each evening at half-past seven, and closes at nine." We are not told precisely the curriculum of the night school, but no doubt it was concerned principally with the teaching of the three Rs. The Prestwich

Library and Reading-room seems to have been a most important
feature of village life at this time. We are told in an advertisement
in the same issue of the magazine that it was established for the
recreation, instruction, and amusement of the working classes of
the parish. The National Schoolroom was opened every evening
from 6 p.m. to 9.30 as a reading-room, and the principal daily and
weekly papers were on the table. There was a good library containing about 2,000 volumes attached to the institution, and
occasional lectures and readings were given.

During that 1863–4 season it was reported that lectures had
been given by the Reverend Charles Glynn, Mr Leo Grindon,
and the Reverend St Vincent Beechey, incumbent of Worsley.
Readings had also been given from the English Poets, Lancashire
Sketches etc., by the Reverend S. E. Bartleet, Mr Bremner, and
Mr Wain. This type of entertainment developed into the penny
reading which was immensely popular and drew large crowds of
the illiterate villagers to hear the educated gentry reading poems
and passages from novels grave and gay. When Mr Beechey lectured on "Joseph in Egypt" the room was well filled, and all
present had very great pleasure in listening to the eloquent
descriptions and explanations of the reverend lecturer. The illustrations produced by Mr Beechey's trinoptic lantern were, we are
told, very beautiful, though a slight disarrangement of the
apparatus rendered them less perfect than they otherwise would
have been.

When Robinson Fowler, Esq., lectured on "Inside a Police
Court", the room was densely crowded. He spoke, as a magistrate, of the different kinds of cases that were principally brought
before him. He described the street quarrelling and street rows
and the various kinds of drunkenness he had to deal with. Then
there were the beggars, professional and otherwise, and those
who pursued fraudulent practices especially as regards weights
and measures. His comment on strikes is so symbolic of the
age that it is worth reproducing. He allowed that trades unions
were strictly lawful, yet he warned working men against per-
mitting themselves to be misled by delegates who were only
serving their selfish ends.

With the coming of summer there was the Whitsuntide school feast and the exhibitions connected with the floral and horticultural society. The Whitsuntide festivity was of a type similar to the scholars' processions which are a notable feature of Lancashire life and whose origins have so far baffled the investigations of the students of regional folk-lore. The procession of "not much under 1,000 children and teachers" proceeded to Heaton Park, the residence of the Earl of Wilton, where, after a good tea in the courtyard of the house, they amused themselves until evening. On the Friday in the same week, the teachers and adult scholars, to the number of 150, made an excursion to Alderley Edge, where tea was set out on a lawn in front of a farm-house. In the same week the floral and horticultural society held its first exhibition by kind permission of the Earl of Wilton in Heaton Park, in a large and commodious tent which the committee had hired for the occasion. The various classes for which prizes were offered were all well represented, particularly the fuchsias, geraniums, and calceolarias. Encouraged by their success, the committee proposed to hold an autumn show, but the funds in hand would not allow of the hire of a tent "unless some of the gentry of the neighbourhood will kindly help them with an additional subscription for the purpose".

Winter and summer saw a continuous round of activities, religious and social, organized by and centered upon the parish church. "Amateur choir practice", "singing class", "Bible class", "lecture", "reading", "drawing class", "night school", "French class", "old women's tea-party", "old men's dinner"; the monthly calendar is filled with such items as these, cheek-by-jowl with such interesting points of information as, "Sept. 9, People's Park opened at Dundee, 1864", and "Sept. 30, Dividend due on Indian Bonds". It would be a mistake to imagine that the parish church was merely the place of worship of the community; it was the educational, cultural, and recreational centre round which, apart from their working hours, the life of the population moved.

The impression to be derived from these faded parochial records of nearly a hundred years ago is of a suburban village community in which relationships were ordered in a nicely balanced pyramidal system which was apparently taken for granted and accepted by the large majority of the people. At the apex was the Earl, established in the dignity and opulence of spacious living in his Adam mansion at Heaton Park. Then came the gentry, a vague term embracing all those who were equipped with special privileges of wealth and education. The rector, from his peculiarly intimate relationship with the Royal Family, ranked rather higher than usual in the social scale, but performed his duties with exemplary devotion and conscientiousness. Then came the mass of ordinary people, farmers and farm workers, tradesfolk, factory employees, city clerks and warehousemen, railway workers and asylum attendants. The rigours of the system are softened by a definite sense of obligation which the privileged classes owe to those less fortunate. The Earl contributes with his wealth to the building of churches, schools, and reading-rooms; the large mansion and park are regularly thrown open for the recreation of the populace. The gentry teach in the schools and night classes, arrange concerts and lectures and "penny readings" for the education and amusement of the masses. The clergy and the wealthiest folk co-operate in relieving poverty by assiduous visiting and gifts of relief in food and money. The feudal structure of society is still firm; the trade unions and all the social uprising which they were to represent still remain a suspected menace against which the working man is warned for his own good. The society thus portrayed is not an unattractive one; if it contains less notion of equality before God than religion in these days is assumed to imply, it at least demonstrates a sense of greater obligation and stewardship. Victorian religion may have been deficient, according to modern standards, in much sense of obligation to promote social and economic equality, but it was not lacking in its sense of the duty which the privileged owed to the unprivileged. The suggestion that Christianity demanded an equalitarian ordering of society would have filled it with either amusement or horror. The Church may have been very far removed from its early experiments in apostolic communism; in its acceptance of feudalism it may have compromised with the world; but it certainly did much to hold the various classes of society together in a sense of the humanitarian obligation which the stronger owed to the weaker. We may condemn Victorian religion because it possessed no idea of the virtue of social equality which some, in a later age, insist is an integral part of true religion. Perhaps the task of such critics is less to vilify the Victorians on this count than to substantiate with any degree of finality that their own thesis, which they take for granted, partakes of the substance of ultimate truth.

When we cross the River Irwell to look at day-to-day life in the parish of Swinton, where our period piece is to be built, we find a less aristocratic community, one where the little hamlet of farmers and hand-loom weavers is rapidly growing up into a considerable industrial community. There is no earl actually in the village, though Ellesmere is not far away at Worsley and owns land in Swinton. Sometimes he helps by the gift of a piece of land for a new school or by a substantial subscription towards some building enterprise. But the leadership in the immediate neighbourhood falls to the local clergy and to a handful of factory owners and gentry who occupy the few big houses in Swinton Park. A writer of memoirs speaks of Swinton in the middle of the nineteenth century as a "mere hamlet, but rising in importance". He attends service in the church on 4 November 1849 and describes the "singing by a choir of probably 200 youths of both sexes, accompanied by the harmonious swelling notes of the lively organ" as "to my mind, next to enchanting". He believes that Swinton will thereafter be considered a place of importance, in consequence of the Manchester Union Schools of Industry erected there in 1842. They were, he says, a very handsome and commodious range of buildings in the Tudor style, and were calculated to receive nearly 2,000 children. They were taught useful trades or prepared for service. Their religious instruction was attended to by the chaplain, a clergyman of the Church of England, and a Catholic priest, each instructing those of his own denomination. The local villagers, however, regarded this architectural *tour de force* with rather less favour than it deserved; they saw something sinister in its rising walls, not clearly understanding the functions of this monumental pile in their midst, and thenceforward, for the remainder of its life of nearly a hundred years, it was known to the "locals" by the disrespectful title of "the bastille". The vast building outlived its usefulness, and in the 1930's, the local authority having bought the building and the site, the industrial schools were demolished and a new red-brick town hall in a rather more severely functional style of architecture rose in its place, to serve the needs of the community which had now grown into full adult stature by receiving the charter of incorporation which created the new borough of Swinton and Pendlebury.

This same writer of memoirs demonstrates how in its early days as an industrial community the life of the ordinary people of the village was interpenetrated by a religious sense. He refers to a visit "to the extensive steamloom establishment of Messrs Bowers and Yates in Swinton. In the month of November, 1849, Mr. Bowers very politely conducted me through his works, when I had the gratification of hearing the young female hands employed in one of the rooms to join in [sic] singing a very sweet hymn or psalm."

There is a passage of deep interest in Beatrice Webb's *My Apprenticeship* in which she describes visits paid in 1883, 1886, and 1889 to working-class relations in the Rossendale Valley in Lancashire; staying *incognito* amongst these humble mill folk, she begins that habit of social observation which was to lay down the main lines of her life's work. One of the chief things that impressed her was this same interpenetration of the lives of the mill workers by the religious interest, but, looking ahead, she was fearful as to what would take its place when the foundations of that interest had crumbled away.

In living amongst mill-hands of East Lancashire [she writes] I was impressed with the depth and realism of their religious faith. It seemed to absorb the entire nature, to claim as its own all the energy unused in the actual struggle for existence. Once the simple animal instincts were satisfied the surplus power, whether physical, intellectual or moral, was devoted to religion. Even the social intercourse was based on religious sympathy and common religious effort. . . . But one wonders what will happen when the religious feeling of the people is undermined by advancing scientific culture; for though the "Co-op" and the chapel at present work together, the secularism of the "Co-op" is half unconsciously recognised by earnest chapel-goers as a rival attraction to the prayer meeting and the Bible class. One wonders where all the *feeling* will go, and all the capacity for *moral* self government.

This visit to precisely the same sort of Lancashire environment which we are describing in connection with our period piece taught her, she says,

... the real part played by religion in making the English people, and of Dissent teaching them the art of self-government, or rather serving as a means to develop their capacity for it. It saddens one to think that the religious faith that has united them together with a strong bond of spiritual effort and sustained them individually, throwing its warmth of light into the more lonely and unloved lives, is destined to pass away.

It is this same intense preoccupation with religious issues and with a life centred in the activities of the parish church that we note in the industrial village that we are now considering. The records of its spiritual, educational, and cultural programme are patent in the pages of its early magazines. Perhaps in this particular parish the most important undertaking apart from the actual services of the church was the work of the Sunday-school. The numbers of people old and young who were touched by the life of the school were enormous. It provided a field of activity for well-disposed lay people with some education, and the "teachers' meeting" was probably the most extensive and important representative body of the laity in the parish before the days of the parochial church council. When the Reverend H. R. Heywood was ready to unfold his plans for the building of the new church, it was to the Sunday-school workers that he first broached the subject. In his diary on 4 March 1867 he notes: "At the School Committee meeting in the evening I brought forward —for the first time at all publicly—the subject of a New Church. No kind of opposition." In the field days, processions, parties, and excursions of the Sunday-school the mass of the people found their recreation and enjoyment.

Here again are the "monthly penny readings" which were noted as an important feature in the social life at Prestwich. The first of a series was held in the school-room on 14 November 1864. The readers were: Reverend H. R. Heywood, the Reverend J. P. Pitcairn, E. S. Heywood, Esq., Dr Morgan, and Mr Hillman. Between each reading, a glee was sung by a party of singers, who kindly gave their services for the occasion. £1 1s. od. was taken at the door, of which sum 7s. 3d. was afterwards spent in defraying the necessary expenses, leaving 13s. 9d. to be added to the funds of the infant school. Again the calendar contains notices of old people's dinner, congregational tea party, scholars' tea party, choir practice, night schools. In later years come the provident society, the sick and burial society, the temperance meetings (many of these to combat the evil of heavy drinking, undoubtedly prevalent in industrial areas at that time), the missionary meeting, and the communicants' meeting. The "choir practice and conversation meeting" sounds interesting, but what, we may wonder, was the "Druidesses club night" held on Saturday 2 September 1876? Then there is the general meeting of "church helpers" and the "children's guild meeting", the Sunday-school cricket club, and, for those who would venture a little out of the district, the "Eccles choral festival". So it goes on, every night of the week, the whole programme, interspersed between 1867 and 1871 with the thrilling adventure of collecting the money to build the great new church which we see slowly taking shape and rising under our eyes in these far-off pages.

In June 1870, the year after the consecration of the new church, the Reverend H. R. Heywood kept a diary in which he noted something of the daily activities of his parish and made comments on matters of topical interest. As far as we know, this is the only diary which has survived, apart from one which he kept to mark the progress of the new Church enterprise and which will be mentioned later. It is a pity that this energetic and nimble-minded clergyman did not persevere with his diary keeping. We might have had a record of mid-Victorian Church life worthy to rank with Kilvert and Armstrong in the nineteenth century, and Woodforde in the eighteenth century. However, this record of a busy fortnight's parochial labours has been preserved for us because it was printed in the July magazine. It is worth reproducing here to illustrate the work of a parish and a parish clergyman in a typical thriving mid-Victorian parish:

NOTES BY THE EDITOR, 1870

June 4. Received £1. 6. 3d. from Mrs. Redford, which she with others, had collected in order to buy a flag for "S. Stephen's", to be carried in the procession on Whit Friday. Very kind both of collectors and donors, but this Ragged School has called out a good deal of kindness.

June 5—Whit Sunday. A friend asked a friend how he liked the chant to the "Benedictus?" in the morning? Answer—"What is the Benedictus?" The Canticle which is sung directly after the Second Lesson. Answer—"Oh! I noticed you sang the wrong one of the two." No, we didn't, look to your Prayer Book, and you'll see we sang the right one of the two. However, about the chants? Answer—"Well, I didn't notice that one in particular, but I liked all of them, both in the morning and afternoon; they were all good to join in." No better reply could have been wished for.

Received an interesting letter from Mr. Harvey, who is in Bavaria. He gives a full and interesting account of what he saw the other day at Ober Ammergau. Cannot help wishing that the letter (which is chiefly about the miracle plays, which are being performed this year) was shorter, so that it might be printed here. A scrap of the "P.S." is as follows:—"One Sunday afternoon in Munich we came out of the English Church rather out of heart with the cold service, and went to Vespers at the Jesuits' Church; an enormous devout congregation, and beautiful music. We were much impressed; and what we felt we felt all the more coming straight from the preaching of our own prayers, but my wife said, 'Mind you, I could have gone from Swinton Church without feeling the same contrast in baldness and coldness.'" Again, "What has struck me in the Churches is the personal individual devotion of the people. Go into a Church wherever you please, and you will find somebody there praying. I have often counted a score or two."

June 7. Called on Mr. Atherton, who (without being asked) said, "You want £1000 I believe to complete the Church? I'll give you

9

£50, if the remainder is raised in six months, and if then you are £50 short, I'll give you a second £50." Coming home was waylaid and asked whether it was using vain repetitions to say, "Preserve me, body, soul, and spirit. Do we consist of three parts? or do soul and spirit mean the same thing?" Gave a reply, and noted the point as suitable to be explained in a sermon.

June 8. Read the Burial Service over the body of Miss Townsend at the cemetery. She is the first, I think, who is taken from the number of those parishioners confirmed here last October. To-day is Wednesday, and she was at the grave in which her body now rests last Thursday. Last Friday she was walking past our house here. "In the midst of life we are in death." Appointed Mr. Thomas Wrigley, of Holy Trinity, Bury, as organist, to succeed Mr. Whitley, whose departure is a cause of universal sorrow. If his successor in any way equals him, he will be a good fellow indeed, as indeed I hope he is. He brings an excellent character. I hear Mr. Hutchinson, of Pendlebury, is dead. We sat for years in adjoining pews at St. John's. The "S. Stephen's" flag came, but it is not what was intended, and the 26s alluded to above will buy another larger one, and altogether handsomer. It is too late to have it for Whit Friday, so for this week we must be content with what we have got.

June 9. Our trip ("our" being 450 people) to Blackpool and back successfully achieved. Fine day with a N.W. wind blowing, as those who went on the steamers for a sail can testify. We left Worsley at 5.40 a.m., and got back at 8.30 p.m. Blackpool was very full and very dusty. I went over to Poulton Vicarage, where I fell in with Mr. Green and a party of Miles Plattingers.

June 10—Walking Day. It was very threatening in the morning, but as it turned out fine the moment we were for starting, we had no use for our umbrellas at all. The Church School, Holy Rood School, and S. Stephen's School all proceeded together to Mr. Atherton's where the usual pleasant afternoon was spent. The schoolroom was not empty at tea time in the evening!

June 12. The newly-consecrated Bishop of Zululand preached in the afternoon. The Church was not as full as it might have been by a good deal, but the collection was probably better than any of us expected. Dr. Wilkinson (who is stopping with us two nights) promises to write a letter from Zululand by and bye for this magazine. One thing is certain, a good man and a self-forgetful man is going out on his Master's service to that far distant land.

June 14. Married Mr. G. H. Howarth, of Sindsley, to Miss Mary Campbell, of Bowness, at the old Parish Church of Bowness, or Windermere, whichever is its correct name. The Church is not exactly in a fit state for weddings; this wedding took place on a temporary platform in the vicinity of the Font, and close under a glassless window. The Church is being restored, meanwhile Sunday services are held in the Cemetery Chapel and in the Schoolroom. As it would be inappropriate to solemnize a wedding in either of those places, there was nothing for it but bravely to invade the Church, and there marry the couple somehow—glass or no glass, floor or no floor, roof or no roof!

June 15. The labels for the Alms Boxes (begged for in the last magazine) have been kindly undertaken. The second "want" for the choir vestry, it is still open to any "young ladies" who will, to supply. I see that the Holy Rood collections for the Curate's Fund in connection with that Chapel have only raised (in the first six months of this year) the sum of £8. 16. 7d. Might not the congregation do a little more than this? A shilling a day is something, but not a good deal. The Additional Curates' Society send word they cannot help this year.

June 17. Preachers are failing us for July 3rd. Archdeacon Anson, Canon Thicknesse, of Brackley, Mr. Body, of Wolverhampton, Mr. Russell Walker, of Ringley, and Canon Marsden, our Rural Dean, have all been asked, but none can come. The S. Stephen's Sunday School, I hear, is increasing, and I am told to look out for another teacher. The Girls' Night School also keeps up its numbers well. The Boys' Night School, spoken of in the May magazine, not being patronized, is non-existent for the present. The room therefore is at liberty on Wednesday, Thursday, and Saturday evenings. "Oh! for eyes to see ourselves as others see us." Somehow I did not look upon our services at Swinton as dead and heavy. Last Friday indeed was I not told of some one who rather hesitated about coming here, in consequence, "so it was said," of all the singing we have? To-day—this Friday—I was conversing with one who was for returning to the Church and Parish from whence that one came, and (so far as the Church and Church services were concerned) the grief would not be great, for our "service is so dull—Psalms only chanted once a day, Responses never sung, &c. &c.,"—indeed I came away feeling quite "last century" like. It only shows how much there is in custom.

June 18. In a letter which appears in this morning's Eccles Advertiser, it seems that, in the Patricroft Workhouse Chapel, on Whit Sunday, "flower pots were placed on the window sills, green leaves and crimson flowers waved and moved in the refreshing gentle breezes which entered through the open casements, a sight most pleasing and unusual to me in a place of worship. I thanked God that such a place had been provided for the spiritual welfare of the poor." This is capital. Guardians are looking up. Common sense is prominent. A Chapel may be made attractive as well as a sitting-room, and the flowers of the field may adorn the House of God as well as the house of man. When will the Manchester Guardians provide a Chapel (to say nothing of "green leaves and crimson flowers") for their Swinton children?

This brief record of parochial activity will suffice to round off our picture of Church life in an industrial neighbourhood in the second half of the nineteenth century. It is a picture which illustrates the various points which have been mentioned in this chapter on Victorian religion. It shows the Church of England at last overtaking the new situation which had been caused by the shifting social pattern of the developed Industrial Revolution. Tractarianism, with its emphasis on recovered Catholic beliefs and practices to a greater or lesser degree within the Church of England, is the inspiration and driving force behind the faithful priest and his ambitious project of church rebuilding. The project is successful because the new commercial middle classes provide money and leadership, both clerical and lay, for this busy Church life. The church is not only the worshipping centre but also the educational, cultural, and social centre of the community. She has no competitors in the field of social relationship, for, apart from politicians who solicit the votes of the ordinary people, nobody else has troubled to take an interest in them at any point in their lives. State interference is on a very small scale: the activities of local government are severely restricted. The Church accepts the presuppositions of a society based on class distinctions which are largely a matter of distinction of wealth and privilege: but she urges the duty which the better equipped owes to the under-privileged. The picture of Church life at this period is one that does credit to the virility of the religious impulse of the time. The fruits of that impulse remain with us in the shape of the impressive buildings which our grandparents built. But many distracting urges have appeared during the last eighty years to remove many human activities away from the Victorian period pieces which originally housed them all. One activity the trends of a commercialized and mechanized civilization can never remove, and to many souls in this vastly different age the Victorian church still remains the much-loved worshipping focus of the devout believers of the parish.

V

This chapter must conclude with a description of the local ecclesiastical situation, diocesan and parochial, which the Reverend H. R. Heywood found when he decided to rebuild Swinton Church. He was appointed in 1864 to the charge of a district chapelry in the ancient parish of Eccles. In early times the greater part of Lancashire had been included within the Midland diocese of Lichfield. There is evidence of a plan to create a diocese for Lancashire at the time of the suppression of the monasteries, and a Bishop of Fountains was to have ruled Lancashire and north-west Yorkshire with his seat at Fountains Abbey, assisted by a dean, six prebendaries, six minor canons and masters of grammar and song schools. The failure of this excellent plan to materialize was due to the threatening overseas situation which developed during Henry VIII's reign, compelling domestic reforms, both social and ecclesiastical, to give way to rearmament. A new see was erected at Chester with its headquarters based upon the monastic buildings there, and Lancashire had to wait another three hundred years until the Industrial Revolution and the pressure of a greatly increased population made the creation of the Manchester bishopric imperative. For three hundred years the Bishops of Chester ruled the great county palatine from Chester, and it is at least arguable that the distance of the remote parishes and their chapelries in this rugged countryside from the seat of adminstration and discipline was responsible in Elizabethan times for the failure of the Reformation to make substantial headway and for the strengthening of Roman Catholicism, particularly in the country parishes.

When the diocese of Manchester was created in 1847, the names of several prominent Churchmen of the day, including that of the so-called heresiarch, Dr Hampden, were canvassed for the responsibility of being the first diocesan. The appointment fell to James Prince Lee, the son of Stephen Lee, secretary and librarian to the Royal Society.[1] He was born in 1804, educated at St Paul's school and Trinity College, Cambridge, where he obtained a Craven Scholarship and graduated B.A., with high honours, in 1828. He subsequently became a Fellow of Trinity College, assistant-master at Rugby School under Dr Arnold, and head-master of King Edward's Grammar School, Birmingham, from 1838 to 1848. He was then consecrated first bishop of the new see created by Act of Parliament, and enjoyed an income of £4,200 a year. The episcopal residence was established at Mauldeth Hall in the parish of Heaton Mersey, in the churchyard of which he was eventually buried. He died on 24 December 1869, so that the consecration of the new Swinton Church must have been one of the last official acts of his life. His fine library of about seven thousand volumes, chiefly substantial folios and quartos, many annotated in his own hand-writing, is now part of the library of Manchester University. What precise use he himself made of an important section of it is not so easy to understand, for he is reported to have said, during the controversy which raged around the suppression of the choral services in Ringley Chapel, "that the Early Fathers contained the greatest trash that ever men read. . . . That between the last Canonical Writer and the Apostolical Fathers, there was a gulph as immense as that which separated Lazarus from Dives; that he had the profoundest contempt for these said Apostolical Fathers—their intellect as well as their writings—but he had not waded through all the endless rubbish contained in them, although he had, perhaps, one of the best collections of Patristic Theology in the country."

[1] Mr Roger Fulford in his *Prince Consort* asserts that the Prince was directly responsible for Dr Lee's appointment to Manchester, and that the appointment was so generally criticized that Dr Hook suggested that an ecclesiastical body should be set up to advise the Prime Minister about episcopal nominations (p. 189).

Bishop Prince Lee left the reputation of being a somewhat stern schoolmaster bishop who ruled his clergy with the discipline of a sixth-form master. The fact remains, however, that he did accomplish with conspicuous success the task that he had been sent to Lancashire to perform, namely to establish and extend the Church of England as a diocesan unit in an industrial area where the population had increased enormously over the previous hundred years, and where it was continuing to increase. There is no doubt that the Established Church had lost ground to organized Dissent by its failure to provide local organization which could press ahead with the work of erecting churches and schools to cater for the Anglican version of Christianity in the industrial districts. The work of the new bishop was to tap these vast sources of new industrial wealth, and to encourage the middle classes in providing spiritual and social amenities in the densely populated towns where their wealth was made. The record of the bishop's success is deeply impressive. Between 1848 and his death in 1869, Bishop Prince Lee consecrated 110 new churches, providing 77,177 sittings of which 39,948 were free. The cost of the new buildings alone was at least £450,000. Besides these new churches, twenty existing churches were rebuilt, of which Swinton was one, at a cost of £93,900. A total of 163 new district parishes and ecclesiastical districts were formed during this period. After Prince Lee's death the work went on, and during the reign of his successor, Bishop Fraser, from 1870 to 1885, 105 new churches were consecrated. Although late in the field, it is clear that once the convenient machinery was set up by the provision of a local bishopric, the Church of England in Lancashire was not slow in overtaking the arrears of enterprise. The loss of time, however, had resulted in the establishment of a strong Nonconformist organization throughout the area and the two systems went on side by side, for the most part working in sufficient amity, though occasionally with relationships somewhat exacerbated by such questions as the relative positions which each body was to hold in newly established public cemeteries.

In this vast industrialized sprawl which was south Lancashire, the ancient pre-Reformation churches were few and far between.

They had all governed large expanses of territory and all contained many or few chapelries which had been erected from the fifteenth century onwards to meet the needs of increasing populations. A great part of the enterprise of nineteenth-century church building in Lancashire was the rebuilding both of the medieval parish churches and of their chapelries. Many were too far decayed to permit of restoration and repair. The Salford Hundred contained ten pre-Reformation parishes which, together with the parish of Leigh in the West Derby Hundred and parts of the great parish of Whalley in the Blackburn Hundred, make up the present Manchester diocese. Of the ten pre-Reformation parishes in the Salford Hundred four have been completely rebuilt, whilst the remaining six have been so extensively restored and added to as substantially to alter their appearance from their original shape. Most of the chapelries have likewise been rebuilt, though a few eighteenth-century brick buildings like Astley and Tottington still remain. Without doubt the most conspicuously interesting of the lesser churches of the diocese is that of St Lawrence, Denton, a timber-framed building erected as a chapelry to the Collegiate Church of Manchester in 1533, and retained in its original condition ever since as a record of what many of the early post-Reformation chapels in large parishes must have looked like.

A scrutiny of the twelve parishes which contributed to the formation of the Manchester Diocese as they are recorded in Bishop Gastrell's *Notitia Cestriensis,* which was edited for the Chetham Society by the Reverend F. R. Raines of Milnrow in 1850, reveals that in those parishes there were thirty-three chapelries existing before A.D. 1700. Between A.D. 1700 and A.D. 1800 thirty-two new chapels were built, and between A.D. 1800 and A.D. 1850, ninety-two. During the one hundred and fifty years which saw the rise of the Industrial Revolution and ended with the creation of the Lancashire bishopric, Church enterprise furnished 124 new churches to cater for the expanding population. This is perhaps no bad prelude to the great torrent of church building which followed in the second half of the nineteenth century, when Manchester was the centre of its own diocese, ruled over by a series of exceptionally brilliant and energetic bishops. During that one hundred and fifty years it is not surprising to find that by far the greater amount of church building was done within the ancient parish of Manchester, which contained the greatest single aggregation of population. Before A.D. 1700 there existed nine chapels of ease to the Collegiate Church, some of them of pre-Reformation date. Between A.D. 1750 and A.D. 1800 twelve new churches were built and between A.D. 1800 and A.D. 1850, thirty-seven. The following table gives the picture of

Ancient Parish	Chapelries existing before 1700	Churches built A.D. 1700–1800	Churches built A.D. 1800–50
Ashton-under-Lyne	—	3	7
Bolton-le-Moors	5	3	9
Bury	3	2	6
Deane	2	1	2
Eccles	1	2	5
Manchester Collegiate Church	9	12	37
Middleton	2	—	3
Prestwich	3	4	11
Rochdale	4	4	6
Radcliffe	—	—	1
Leigh	2	—	3
(Whalley; Parish Church in Blackburn Diocese)	2	1	2
	33	32	92

church building in this period in the present diocese of Manchester at a glance. The figures would be even more impressive if we added those which are now proper to the diocese of Blackburn since the two dioceses formed one diocese of Manchester until its division in 1926.

Eccles is one of the ancient Lancashire parishes. There is evidence of Christianity having existed here in pre-Norman times, and a Saxon cross was found in the neighbourhood in 1889. A list of incumbents dates back to 1180 and the Coucher Book of

Whalley Abbey gives evidence of the advowson of the church
being purchased from the manorial lord Gilbert de Barton and
given, with its chapels, to the Abbey of Stanlaw, by John de
Lacy, Earl of Lincoln, in 1235. The influence of the monks of
Whalley, which succeeded Stanlaw, was strong throughout this
area until Reformation times, and they established a chapel at
Ellenbrook for their tenantry in that neighbourhood. In 1291 the
Church of Eccles was valued at £20 per annum, in 1834 at £500,
and the present value is given as £853. At the Dissolution of the
Monasteries the advowson passed from Whalley to the Crown,
and the Lord Chancellor still appoints the vicar in modern times.
Bishop Gastrell's survey gives fourteen halls as contained in the
parish and describes it as divided into three "quarters": Worsley,
Barton, and Pendleton. The Worsley quarter embraced four
hamlets, of which Swinton was one, Barton eight, and Pendleton
three. The first chapel to be erected in this parish was at Pendleton,
where a building for public worship was consecrated by Bishop
Markham of Chester in 1776.

At the end of the eighteenth century the population of the
hamlet of Swinton was about 1,000, and the only provision for
religious instruction apart from the services at Eccles Church was
in a school opened about 1786 in a farm-house at Broad Oak,
kept by a Mr Derbyshire. The school was transferred ten years
later to Dales Brow, but by that time progress had been made in
providing the hamlet, which was now increasing into an industrial village, with a place of worship of its own. In 1789 a petition
signed by a number of the inhabitants of Swinton, praying for
permission to erect a chapel, was presented to the ecclesiastical
authorities. On Sunday 10 April 1791 Swinton Chapel was
opened by licence granted by the Bishop of Chester. The sermon
on the occasion was preached by the Reverend J. Lemprière,
Headmaster of Bolton Grammar School; it was printed and
dedicated "To the subscribers of Swinton Chapel, with the fervent wish that religion may keep an equal pace with the increase
of the population and the improvement of manufactures in the
neighbourhood." The consecration by Bishop Cleaver of Chester
took place on Saturday 23 July 1791; the chapel was dedicated in

honour of St Peter, and the Reverend William Nuttall was appointed the first incumbent. The cost of the building was met by public subscription, the land being given by a Mr Watson, and formerly used as a bowling-green by the Bull's Head Hotel across the road, the first posting-house on the road from Manchester to Preston.

The building was of the usual type of late-Georgian chapel, of which some examples still remain; in Lancashire, similar buildings, heavily restored and grotesquely overcrowded with Victorian ecclesiastical furniture, may be seen at Tottington, Astley, and Edenfield. Recollections of elderly inhabitants and two existing photographs of the exterior recall a plain brick building, square and ivy-covered, with round-headed windows and a graceful cupola surmounted by a ball and cross. It was enlarged in 1828 and 1838 by the addition of transepts and galleries. Within were high-backed pews and a three-decker pulpit with its clerk's desk, prayer desk, and pulpit; a handsome many-branched chandelier hung from the ceiling, and candles fixed in brackets at the ends of the pews gave illumination in the winter months. The galleries were used by the general congregation, and the nave seats by the pew holders. In the west gallery were the choir, the musicians, and the Sunday-scholars. The schoolmaster's seat was in the west corner of the north gallery and there he would often stand so as to survey the scholars and keep order amongst them. Probably the seats under the galleries were free. The regular Sunday services were Morning Prayer at 10.30 a.m. and Evening Prayer at 3.0 p.m. Holy Communion was celebrated once a month, and the prayer book used on the prayer desk from 1791 onwards is still preserved in the church. Till 1828 there was no organ and the singing was led by a small orchestra. In 1805 the choir consisted of two treble singers, one alto, two tenors, and two basses, and the instruments of the orchestra were a violin, a clarinet, an oboe, a bassoon, and a violoncello. Musical enthusiasm was ever a mark of Lancashire people, and in 1805 when several local chorus singers were engaged to sing at a festival in Newcastle and found all the seats in the stage-coach were full, they set out to walk and completed the journey in three days.

There was a monthly club for the practice of vocal and instrumental music.

The services in the church can be easily visualized from contemporary accounts. The parish clerk stood in his stall which was the lowest of the three decks of the pulpit and announced the psalms as follows: "We will now sing to the praise and glory of God the 104th Psalm, common metre." The clergyman wore his surplice as he read the service from the "middle deck" but donned a black gown when he mounted to the top deck for the sermon. The Reverend R. Broadley, the second incumbent, had considerable musical ability, and copies of anthems composed by him still exist.

An account book exists which is almost filled with quarterly payments for pew rents in this old church. The accounts are kept by the Reverend W. Nuttall, the first incumbent, and are headed: "An account of what has been received from the Proprietors of Seats in the Swinton Chapel, also the sum each pays quarterly." The sums vary greatly, due perhaps to higher rents for better placed seats or to a combined payment for several seats in one pew—3s. and 3s. 9d. a quarter are common amounts in the book dealing with the years 1792–1833, but there are many larger payments, such as 15s. 7d., 19s. 4d., £1 14s. 3d., and (the largest) £2 12s. 2d. When the Reverend H. R. Heywood rebuilt the church he found that he had to carry over this system of pew rents into the new building: it was a system which he greatly disliked, and he strove for many years to abolish it. It was one of the greatest of his later achievements that he was able to do this and to set aside a sum of money which was invested to produce a revenue so that the stipend of the incumbent should not suffer by the freeing of all the seats.

Further endowment was secured for the living by the purchase in 1817 of a farm of fifty acres at Edgworth beyond Bolton. The property appears to have been bought from a Mr Wood, and although the purchase price is not recorded in contemporary records the bill of solicitors' charges amounted to £19 12s. 9d. A parsonage house and land were given by Mr James White. The first incumbent, the Reverend W. Nuttall, died in 1833 and was

succeeded by the Reverend R. Broadley, who for two years previously had been a curate at Eccles Church. He was remembered
as a good preacher and a competent musician who composed his
own anthems to be sung in the church.

He also possessed certain literary ability, and at least two small
printed books stand to his credit. One is entitled, "*Lectures on the
Services, Creeds and Offices of the Church of England*, by Robert
Broadley, Perpetual Curate of Swinton, Lancashire, author of
Christianity a Divine Revelation etc. etc." This book was published
by J. G. and F. Rivington of St Paul's Churchyard and R. H.
Moore, 162 Fleet Street, and bears the date 1836. The lectures lay
great stress on the Church of England as a scriptural Church, but
there is some evidence that the Tractarian leaven is working thus
early in the author's mind. Baptismal regeneration is emphatically
taught, and there is due regard given to the Church's sacramental
system. Such passages as the following betray the direction of
his sympathies and indicate that his outlook was not purely
Erastian:

Of the true Catholic and Apostolic Church of Christ, the Church
of England is one undoubted and essential branch. It was probably
first founded by one of the Apostles, or by preachers of the Gospel
who first came either in the time of the Apostles, if there be not
very strong reasons to believe that St. Paul himself first preached
and planted the Cross of Christ in this country. And ever since
those days there has never ceased to be a true branch of the
Apostolic Church amongst us; although it has seen its dark, as
well as its bright days, was for a long time corrupted by the errors
of Romanism, and was for a short period disturbed by fanaticism
and rebellion. Still, the Apostolic Church has ever remained in
this country with its Temples, its Altars, its Services, its Ministers,
and its blessed Sacraments—here it has been for nearly one
thousand eight hundred years—here it is at this day, bright,
blooming, flourishing as ever—"built upon the foundation of the
Apostles and Prophets, Jesus Christ Himself being the chief
corner stone".

During his incumbency the church was enlarged for the second
time in 1838 by the addition of transepts and a gallery to

accommodate the children.[1] Again the cost was met by voluntary
contributions and a grant of £500 from the Manchester and Eccles
Church Building Society which was procured by Hugh H. Birley,
Esq. Further gifts in this period included a stone font, a new east
window, and churchwarden's staves. The vast range of buildings
in the Tudor style of architecture called the Schools of Industry
which were to occupy an important place in the future development of Swinton were erected by the Manchester Board of
Guardians in 1842. Broadley died in 1864, and the stage was set
for the coming of the Heywoods and the Victorian period piece.

On 8 March 1864 the vicar of Eccles in a note to Henry
Robinson Heywood, then assistant-curate of Pendlebury, offered
him the incumbency of Swinton which he accepted. The population then was said to be six thousand, and the stipend of the living
£200 a year. It was clearly his intention before accepting to make
the rebuilding of the church his first enterprise; his father warned
his elder brother Percival that Henry would need his financial
help in the matter and Henry made his intention to build quite
plain to the gentlemen who waited upon him so cordially to welcome him to the living. But before building could begin it was
necessary to establish the separate parochial status of Swinton.
The district attached for ecclesiastical purposes to the Swinton
Chapel was technically a district chapelry. There had, hitherto,
been no *legal* district but only a conventional district. In the summer of 1864 the new incumbent raised the matter with the Bishop

---

[1] A small notebook in Broadley's handwriting records communicant
numbers and collections at Holy Communion from 1840 onwards. Communicants at Christmas, 1840, numbered sixty-seven; at Easter, 1844, eighty-
one. There appears to have been a regular monthly communion and also a
celebration on Good Friday. On Good Friday, 1842, there were thirty-nine
communicants who contributed 19s. 9½d.

Heywood continues Broadley's notes in the same book until the new
church is opened. There were, e.g., on Easter Day, 1867, nine communicants
at the "Early Communion" who contributed 12s. 4½d.; at "Mid day" there
were 141 and the collection was £8 os. 2d. The vicar notes "Both for poor."
With the opening of the new church there are printed vestry books which
continue in unbroken succession to the present day. Other collections were
for the sexton, the organist, the Cotton Famine Relief Fund (on 25 January
1863) amounting to £22 18s. 2½d., and on "Fast Day", 7 October 1857,
£20 8s. 3¼d.

of Manchester and the vicar of Eccles, with the result that a map and description of a proposed district were forwarded to the Ecclesiastical Commissioners for approval. In the autumn, the Commissioners replied that they approved of the district and would forthwith submit a representation of the case to Her Majesty, praying that an Order in Council might be passed which would legalize and complete the business. At a Court held at Osborne on 7 January 1865 the requisite Order was made, and a print of the *London Gazette* of 10 January, which contained a copy of the Order, was received by the incumbent and deposited in the church chest. A portion of the fees for churchings and burials had still to be paid to the vicar of Eccles, so Swinton was not yet a separate and independent parish. The new incumbent reported to his people in February 1865 that by virtue of the Act of Parliament under which the district had been formed, it would become a parish at the next voidance of the vicarage of Eccles. But in the following month he was able to tell the people that an arrangement had been made with the vicar and clerk of Eccles by which all the Swinton fees due to them during the incumbency of the vicarage of Eccles by the Reverend J. P. Pitcairn would be compensated for. The necessary papers were signed on Monday 13 February 1865, and from that date Swinton existed as a separate parish.

3

THE ARCHITECTURAL APPROACH

I

THE eighteenth century attempted to bury its romantic impulses beneath the solid masses and horizontal lines of a strict and unemotional classicism. The well-regulated proportions of a Palladian façade reflected the love of settled order and suspicion of aspiring enthusiasm which John Wesley found to be his implacable enemy in other manifestations of the human spirit. Yet that solidly conventional classicism was not imposed without some restless stirrings in quarters entirely different from popular Methodist evangelism. Even Viscount Torrington, assiduous traveller and shrewd observer of the later Georgian scene, sound constitutionalist though he was, can almost weary us by his ceaseless plaint for the vanished Gothic past and by his lugubrious nostalgia amid monastic ruins in his pursuit of the "cult of the antick". "I feel a pleasure", he remarks at St Asaph, in 1784, "in seeing any of our churches resume their papistical grandeur; and emerge from the devastation of fanatics and sectaries". Had he lived sixty years later he would undoubtedly have been found in the ranks of the Camden Society; the following entry in his 1785 diary seems to be uncannily before its time: "In every place in this country are the bases of the old crosses, as well as the holy water basins in the churches; which I am Roman Catholick enough to regret the demolition and disuse of, as they recall'd the mind to acts, and memory of devotion, without and within the church: now both are neglected: and those who forget greater duties are not likely to attend to lesser offices of obedience."

But the romantic spirit in the eighteenth century was not

confined merely to an effortless sighing over the departed glories of a Gothic past. Enthusiastic amateurs were beginning to dabble in the prospect of recreating the Gothic idiom in the contemporary building programme. Horace Walpole with his Strawberry Hill Gothic is generally regarded as the pioneer in this field; perhaps Sanderson Miller of Radway is only a little less well known in the same sort of enterprise. If Miller is the architect of the four-square classical bulk of Hagley, there is no doubt that his versatility displayed itself in another direction in the important work which he did for John Ivory Talbot in the Great Hall of Lacock Abbey. It is the Gothic revival stirring early when we can read Talbot's letter to Miller in 1755 and know what tremendous satisfaction the new look had given to admiring visitors. "My Ceiling is the delight of all eyes, yet I fancy will lose some of its abundance of Praise when the Chimney Piece makes its appearance. . . . The Niches are carved and are Beauties. . . . The Grand Opening will be deferred till about May, when all my friends who are in this Country and whose Arms are emblazoned on my Ceiling will do me the Honour of their Company: and a Grand Sacrifice to Bacchus will be the Consequence." We are glad that Miller's reputation as a builder in the Gothic style was not involved in the ruin of the tower of Wroxton Church which he built in the spring of 1747 and which fell down in the following winter. Horace Walpole permitted himself an unkindly sneer at this misfortune, but Lord Deerhurst wrote consoling words in a letter to his friend which also assured him of a further commission in the shape of a Gothic stable front: "The downfall of Wroxton Tower, my dear Miller, would have drawn an earlier Condolence from me had I come to the knowledge of it sooner than I did. I am glad, indeed, that it was delayed so long as I can now assure you that your fame for Architecture is not at all diminished by it. A Friend of mine, apprized of this accident came to me yesterday and told me that he was going to build a Gothic Front to a stable, and, that as no one was so great a Master of that style as yourself, desired I would procure a draught of one from you."

We may regret that hardly anything survives of Miller's exercises in ecclesiastical Gothic. It appears that Hagley Church

10

was perhaps his most ambitious enterprise in this field, with its
chancel entirely new, the windows "adorned on the sides and
every part with Gothick ornaments in hewn stone, and all the
other parts of it in stucco". On the ceiling and at each end were
the arms of the paternal ancestors of the Lytteltons, and the east
window was of rich painted glass dated 1569, together with
shields, scripture pieces, some Flemish glass, and a border of blue,
purple, and green glass made at Stourbridge. Three windows on
each side were in the Gothic style with a bordering of coloured
glass thrown in pretty Gothic forms. The gallery was adorned
with carved wooden roses. The Communion rails were Gothic
and there were numerous funerary monuments. Alas, all this
courageous pioneering in the Gothic spirit was swept away in
1858 to make room for one of Street's Victorian period pieces.

But we are not without many remarkable examples of
eighteenth-century churches which demonstrate the early stirrings of the Gothic renaissance. Shobdon, in Herefordshire, built
in 1753, is a priceless relic of adventurings in architectural antiquarianism which succeeded in evolving a style which could only
satisfactorily be called "rococo Gothic". Croome d'Abitot, the
vast Adam seat of the Coventrys in south Worcestershire, has a
church which plasters Gothic trimmings on to a classical base
with charming effect, and St Paul's, Bristol, which combined
pointed windows and geometrical tracery with classic pillars and
architrave in the nave and delicate plaster scrollwork in the Adam
style over a painted chancel arch, displays a considerable inventive
genius on the part of Daniel Hague, the builder, in making the
best of both worlds. Tetbury in Gloucestershire by Francis Hiorn
in 1777–81 is a magnificent *tour de force* in a revived Perpendicular
style, with its bold use of window space and its slender clustered
columns of wood over iron from which springs the impressive
vaulting of the nave and false aisles. This church, which was
highly regarded by its contemporaries, seems to lead us forward
naturally to the architecture of the period which immediately
followed the Napoleonic Wars, when the Commissioners' architects had travelled far enough to realize that to build in the
Gothic style was not the sportive whim of some rich antiquarian

dilettante but the intelligent revival of the genuine tradition of English religious architecture. It is with a few of these Commissioners' churches in and around Manchester that we are now concerned in studying our architectural approach to the building of a Lancashire Victorian church. Eighteenth-century Gothic building is a fascinating background to the genuine Gothic revival of the nineteenth century, but as far as we are aware there are no examples of this architectural harbinger in the country around Manchester.

The Parliamentary Act of 1818 which is generally known as the Million Act made possible the enterprise of church building on a larger scale than had ever been possible before. Apart from providing a large sum of money to ease the burden of providing new churches, it removed certain legal obstacles which had previously proved formidable. It had, for example, been necessary to procure a private Act of Parliament for the building of a new parish church, and the consents of bishop, patron, and incumbent of the parent parish had sometimes been the cause of a delaying action rather than an expression of good will and expedition. The Reverend Hammond Roberson in issuing his prospectus for the building of Liversedge Church, Yorkshire, in 1811 gives a useful background summary of the conditions against which a new church had to be built, and refers to the delays and hindrances with evident resentment:

The difficulties which present themselves to an individual, or to a number of private persons who might wish to unite to build a church, will be strongly felt by every person acquainted with business of this nature. The sum of Money requisite is very considerable; and the necessary arrangements are attended with trouble and inconveniences, which discourage the well-disposed from making those attempts, which, under different circumstances, they would be glad to venture upon. . . .

The 1818 Act removed certain difficulties and facilitated the building programme, though some churches were still built under private acts. A parish had to contain not less than four thousand persons and its church accommodation to be less than a thousand before it could qualify for benefits provided under the Act. The whole of the cost of the new church could be provided from the Commissioners' funds or they could make grants or loans towards it. The liberality of the Act produced a crop of new churches, especially in the rapidly increasing industrial districts, and most of our cities contain one or more of these great smoke-blackened edifices, too often now stranded as a "down-town church" near the centre of the city from which the tide of population has ebbed away into the suburbs.

It is a pity that we do not know a good deal more about the architects who built these Commissioners' churches. Some, like Smirke and Barry, have attained fame by reason of their other great architectural exploits, but the architects of the lesser-known churches are lucky if they have escaped a complete and quite undeserved oblivion. Local architectural enthusiasts might do a useful piece of work in rescuing them from such oblivion. Thomas Taylor, Regency architect of Leeds, has recently been presented to us afresh by the admirable researches of Mr Frank Beckwith, which have been published in the transactions of the Thoresby Society. Here we are given an illuminating picture of a little-known and painstaking architect who worked both with the assistance of the Million Act and private Acts to produce a number of Yorkshire churches between 1812 and 1826, which are important milestones along the road of the Gothic revival. We must give due credit to the Million Act which facilitated church building, and thereby provided extended scope for architects to experiment in Gothic styles which were slowly being recovered by arduous and sometimes not completely intelligent antiquarian research. Britton, the elder Pugin, Rickman, and others were producing drawings of ancient buildings which provided excellent copy-book material for the new builders. Yet so often their results were only a stiff and formal repetition of certain medieval *motifs* applied in a formal and unintelligent way. Why was Gothic favoured by some of the Commissioners' architects? Three arguments at least were used: first, medieval ecclesiastical models, capable of a wider variety of detail and expression than the classical rules afforded, were regarded as more appropriate to the religious character of the intended building. We shall see how this argument was taken up and elaborated by the ecclesiologists later in the century. Second, it was believed that Gothic was cheap; and third, that it was more pleasingly ornamental. Scott, in 1857, gave as his reasons for advocating the use of Gothic that it was nearest to the facts of construction, closest to nature in decorative detail, and belonged to the native tradition of building. Later critics have doubted whether any one of these arguments in favour of Gothic could be sustained. A church could be equally dear in either style, and whether the builders have succeeded in achieving something beautiful with their pleasing ornamentation has been gravely doubted by some writers. Perhaps the pendulum of taste may now be swinging away from that extremity of condemnation which moved Canon Overton to write in 1894 that "unmitigated ugliness and hopeless inconvenience are their chief characteristics. . . . They have not even the merit of originality in their ugliness; they are either absolutely nondescript or sham Gothic. Still less have they the merit of cheapness; they were very expensive indeed."

Henry Heywood, the builder of Swinton Church, was a Manchester man, and may be presumed to have studied the architecture of some of the better-known Manchester churches before he decided upon the sort of church he wished to build. Very early he had made up his mind that his architect was not to be Medland Taylor, the local diocesan architect, or any other local man, but an architect of outstanding national reputation. His choice eventually fell, as we shall see, upon George Street. It is interesting to speculate whether his acquaintance with Manchester churches of earlier in the century had nourished some artistic appreciation in his mind and had determined him to enlist only the services of the very best man that English architecture had to offer. A consideration by Heywood of some of the existing Manchester churches, is, hypothetically, at any rate, part of the architectural approach to the building of Swinton Church.

We may imagine him as having visited the family bank in St Ann's Square and making his way to his old home at Claremont, Pendleton, or to his own house in Swinton Park during the years of his curacy at St John's, Pendlebury. The first church he would pass would be the rebuilt Trinity Chapel over the river in Salford, now known as the parish church of Sacred Trinity. Here he would find one of the seventeenth-century chapelries of the Collegiate Church, rebuilt in 1752. It is a small rectangular building with round-headed windows and heavy galleries in the authentic style of Georgian building of the time. At the west end stands a gallant attempt to formulate a Gothic tower with pointed windows and pinnacles. Sir Stephen Glynne described it in 1865 as rebuilt "in the most uninteresting and unecclesiastical quasi-Italian style". He has a word of praise, however, for the tower, which, he says, seems to be original, and remarkable as a specimen of Gothic of that period, yet not thoroughly debased. Perhaps this interesting survival in the Gothic vernacular with its buttresses, embattled parapet, and rather crowded pinnacles may be the expression of the debt owed by some local seventeenth-century Lancashire craftsman to the striking Perpendicular example in the tower of the Collegiate Church of Manchester which he could see across the river, not many hundred yards away, as he worked.

Proceeding in a homeward direction along the Salford Chapel Street, Heywood would next pass the large Commissioners' church of St Philip, and here we may pause with him for a moment to examine this early nineteenth-century building in which the architect has not adopted the Gothic style. It is an essay by Sir Robert Smirke in the prevailing Greek taste of the third decade of the century. The plan is cleverly adapted to the lay-out of the surrounding buildings, and since it was the south side which presented itself most conspicuously to passers-by in Chapel Street, from which it is set back a little at the end of a small square, the architect throws his main decoration against this south side. It carries a semi-circular porch with six columns in the Ionic order, above which soars a high steeple with a cylindrical belfry, peristyle, and cupola. The interior has a wide nave and galleries supported on square pillars surmounted by Doric columns which carry the flat ceiling. The main entrance nowadays, in spite of the elaborate porch on the south side, is at the west end, which presents a perfectly plain and unadventurous front towards the Salford Royal Hospital. Mr Whiffen considers that the architect gave the

Mancunians and the Commissioners their money's worth by providing accommodation for 1,828 worshippers for the moderate sum of £14,000. Contemporary estimates of this essay in classical antiquarianism were not apparently as favourable as might be ours to-day when we view it as an interesting though highly transitory phase in the development of nineteenth-century archaeology enlisted in the service of the English architectural tradition. Dr Hibbert-Ware, the historian of the Manchester Ecclesiastical Foundations, tells us that it was erected at the sole expense of His Majesty's Commissioners for building additional churches. He describes it as a plain Grecian structure, consecrated by Dr Blomfield, Bishop of Chester, on 25 September 1825 and containing 2,000 sittings, 1,200 of which were free. Then comes the devastating comment in a footnote: "Its peculiar design ought to be studied by every architect—*to be avoided.*"

Dr Hibbert-Ware's sympathies were undoubtedly in the Gothic direction, and we may perhaps at this point allow Henry Heywood to turn back in his tracks to visit the other two Commissioners' churches in Manchester which were built before 1830, "agreeably to the Act passed in Parliament for the erection of new churches". The first, St Matthew's, Campfield, off Deansgate, consecrated on 24 September 1825 by Dr Blomfield, bears the impress of a name sufficiently well known in the story of nineteenth-century architecture. It is the work of Charles Barry, later designer of the new Houses of Parliament, who is also represented in the Manchester diocese by the suburban village church of Stand in the parish of Prestwich built in 1826. In each of these churches we see Commissioners' Gothic asserting itself with full strength and confidence. St Matthew's, now unhappily derelict,[1] is described by the contemporary Hibbert-Ware as "perhaps, with the exception of the Collegiate Church, one of the most beautiful structures in Manchester, built in the vilest of situations". Stand, more fortunately circumstanced, has been the recipient of constant care and further embellishment during the last hundred years and now remains as a most perfectly preserved specimen of the zeal for extended church accommodation combined with

1 It was demolished in 1952 whilst this book was preparing for the press.

architectural experimentation which characterizes the Commissioners' Million Fund churches. There is stiffness and rigidity which comes from the slavish imitation of such piecemeal medieval examples as their builders knew. There is enslavement to symmetry in the balance of the design and in the details of window tracery, as is typical of the period. Spacious effect has been lost by the necessity for the heavy-fronted galleries, and the slender columns of the naves appear to be carrying a weight to which at first glance they would seem unequal. But there is ingenuity in the plaster vaulting, and the details of the decoration, whilst not over-subtle, are by no means contemptible. Whilst we realize that the Gothic revival has a long way to travel before it reaches the perfection of the best of Scott's or Street's or Bodley's or Austin's work, we must allow merit and a certain measure of power and impressiveness to these earlier pioneers.

The second Commissioners' Church in the Gothic style built in the 1820's is Francis Goodwin's St George's, Hulme. Mr Whiffen describes Goodwin, who was born at King's Lynn in 1784, as one of the typical architects of the age. He was already represented in Manchester by the steeple he had added to St Peter's Church and by the old Town Hall, a classical building. Most of his churches are Gothic and Whiffen epitomizes his particular hall-mark as a liking for fat pinnacles and lean towers. He apparently devised a type of church which pleased him sufficiently and then repeated it with minor modifications of detail until either he or his clients grew tired of it. Whiffen describes St George's as "a very large and showy church with a western tower, burgeoning in an even more extravagant crop of pinnacles than is usual in Goodwin's designs". He compares it unfavourably with Barry's St Matthew's, Campfield, and whilst admitting that Goodwin's Gothic is skilful and efficient credits Barry with a quality which he considers lacking in Goodwin, namely, "sensibility".

Whether Miss Jane Austen would have approved of Goodwin's St George's, Hulme, or not, it is clear that others of his contemporaries did, for Dr Hibbert-Ware describes it as the most attractive object at the entrance to the town from Chester. It might be worth while to reproduce in a little more detail this writer's account of the origins of this church. The population of the township of Hulme, the western suburb of Manchester, having, he says, increased in very rapid proportion within a few years, a grant of £14,000 was obtained from His Majesty's Commissioners for the erection of a new church in that neighbourhood. A plot of land was provided for the purpose by the munificence of Wilbraham Egerton, Esq., of Tatton Park, and the foundation-stone of the intended structure, dedicated by the name of St George, was laid with great solemnity by the Right Reverend C. J. Blomfield, Lord Bishop of Chester, on Thursday, 7 September, A.D. 1826. The building was carried on with great diligence, and although the edifice was of a size sufficient for the accommodation of more than 2,000 persons, it was nearly completed on 9 June 1828, when the Reverend Joshua Lingard, B.A., of St Mary Hall, Oxford, was appointed to the curacy, on the nomination of The Very Reverend the Warden and the Reverend the Fellows of Christ's College, Manchester. After some unexpected delays, which took place in consequence of the translation of Bishop Blomfield to the see of London, the church was eventually consecrated, the 9 December following, by his successor Dr Sumner, who preached an excellent sermon on the occasion.

Hibbert-Ware's next paragraph reveals how the medieval Gothic models were interpreted by the early nineteenth-century builders. He says that the church is of a pure and uniform style of architecture, prevalent in England for a period of more than 160 years, from the reign of Richard II to that of Henry VIII, and known by the names of the florid Gothic, and Perpendicular English style. It is clear that these early Gothic revivalists were already arriving at a fairly firm classification of period styles.

The incumbent of the church, who was prepared to dilate, as most incumbents are, upon the unique beauty of his own church, supplied Dr Hibbert-Ware with a detailed description of the new building which is an interesting piece of contemporary architectural description. He describes the body of the church as remarkable for its simplicity and the beauty of its proportions :

The tower [he says] is of a most ornamental character and displays the talent of the architect to the greatest advantage, and may perhaps be reckoned the most beautiful of his many beautiful works. It is of four stages; and such is the singular felicity of its construction, that it bears the appearance of much greater elevation than in reality it possesses. The bold projecting buttresses, which are set square at each corner of the tower, are carried up the three lower stages, and terminated at each set-off by a canopy and finial; from the upper part of the third stage there springs, at each angle of the tower, an octangular turret, which rises to the summit of the tower, and shooting above the battlement to a very unusual height, is surmounted by a crocketed pinnacle and finial. Between each of these turrets, on the four sides of the tower, there are three lower pinnacles:—the two extreme ones surmounting a flat buttress, brought up from a battlement carried along each side of the tower at the second stage; the one between, which is rather higher than the others, rises from a buttress which springs from the top of the bell-chamber window. The whole of this arrangement, which is very novel and striking, adds much to the richness and effect of the structure.

The interior of this church, which is neat and handsome, corresponds rather with the simplicity and elegance of the body of the building, than with the rich and highly ornamented architecture of the tower.

The burial ground surrounding the church, which is very extensive, is enclosed by a handsome Gothic palisade, executed, together with the gate pillars, which are extremely rich and beautiful, after the designs of the architect of the church.

The incumbent's eulogy, with its emphasis on the tower and pinnacles as the central feature of the design, is firm evidence for Mr Whiffen's note as to the architect's preferences which is quoted above. It is worth observing that these earlier pioneers of the Gothic revival were not so enslaved to the notion of the decorated or geometrical period of Gothic architecture as being the highest and most perfect of the styles, and the only one that should be imitated in true Christian architecture.

Having viewed these two Commissioners' churches in the Gothic style in Manchester, we will now allow the Reverend Henry Heywood to proceed homewards towards Swinton Park.

A short distance beyond Sir Robert Smirke's Greek temple of St
Philip, Chapel Street, he will pass the church of St Thomas,
Pendleton. This will probably interest him a little, as Pendleton
was the first chapelry to be carved out of the ancient parish of
Eccles in 1776, as St Peter's, Swinton, was the second in 1791.
Bishop Markham of Chester had consecrated the first building in
1776, but the Commissioners had come to the aid of the people
of Pendleton who desired a larger church fifty years later; the
work had begun in 1829, and the new church was consecrated on
7 October 1831. It is another typical example of Commissioners'
Gothic which, of course, is Perpendicular Gothic, heavily battle-
mented, sternly symmetrical, and clumsily pinnacled. It is not so
imposing and adventurous as either St Matthew's, Campfield, or
St George's, Hulme, but it indicates that the Gothic idea has now
become firmly established in architects' minds as common currency for the smaller type of parish church. Roman and Greek
have been abandoned in the search for suitable *motifs* for the
parish church, and Gothic is respectably established. Its style is
copyist and dull; it is not inspired copying such as Gilbert Scott
produced, and it is certainly not possessed of any natural beauty.
But it is a harbinger of the real Gothic-revival spring, and its
architect, whoever he was, reminds us that Scott and Street are
on the way. Inquiry has so far failed to elicit the architect's name
and it does not seem to have been retained in any of the church
documents. At a guess we may hazard the name of Thomas
Taylor, the Regency architect of Leeds. Pendleton Church has
many points of resemblance to Taylor's churches of Liversedge,
Christ Church, Bradford, Holy Trinity, Huddersfield, and Dews-
bury Moor. Mr Beckwith, whose monograph in the Thoresby
Society publications has rescued Taylor from obscurity, tells us
that he died as a result of an illness which began by sleeping in
damp sheets during a visit to Manchester, and the *Leeds Intelli-
gencer* in its obituary notice describes him as having been appointed "architect to the new churches at Manchester, Ripon and
Almondbury". This new church at Manchester has not been
identified, and Mr Beckwith suggests that it is possible that another architect brought the churches to completion and took the

credit. The great objection to attributing Pendleton to Taylor is that Taylor died in 1826, and the Pendleton Church was not consecrated till 1831. Nevertheless it was begun in 1829; and as St Andrew's, Travis Street, which Mr Beckwith thinks may be the Taylor church, was also not consecrated till 1831, it is at least as likely a guess that Pendleton Church may be attributed to Taylor. Possibly further evidence may subsequently emerge which will clear up these doubtful points and allot these churches to their rightful authors.

There is one more church to be mentioned before the Reverend Henry Heywood reaches his home in Swinton Park, and it is a church with which he is closely familiar, for his present appointment is as curate to this church of St John, Pendlebury. It is a small building consecrated in 1842, and not without a certain architectural interest as being one of the few in Lancashire built at that time in the Norman style. Not, of course, that it incorporates any massive round columns in the nave arcading, for the fact is that it possesses no arcading whatsoever. Its plan is almost square, its chancel is a shallow protrusion at the east end, it possesses no nave; but its seats stretch right across the church, and additional accommodation is provided by a heavy gallery at the west end. Yet its windows are round headed, the chancel arch is rounded, there are varieties of mouldings which suggest that the architect has studied his subject in the original; that, having been a little tired of the clumsy imitations of Perpendicular Gothic which he had seen in churches of ten years earlier, he had resolved to strike out on a fresh line of his own and had indulged in a private experimentation according to models suggested by Durham or perhaps Kilpeck. The interior furnishings suggest a presentation of religion still untouched by the notions of the Oxford Movement; ceremonial would not only be abhorrent in such a church, it would be a physical impossibility. It is, *par excellence*, a neat and comfortable little preaching house built to accommodate a company of attentive hearers, and the neat little parsonage in the same pseudo-Norman style which nestles close beneath its wing proclaims irresistibly that it was built with what was left over from the church. Very curiously, a later hand has added to the chancel an amazing rococo altar and reredos, which brings a splash of colour into this sober exercise in Anglo-Norman, and rather suggests some exotic Italian cousin executing a *pas seul* on the platform of a Mothers' Union concert.[1]

This flight into the Norman style was by no means unknown to contemporary builders. It was tried in a few places, and James Barr in his *Anglican Church Architecture*, which was published in 1842 (the year in which St John's was built), wrote that "the Anglo-Norman style possesses many peculiarities and elements of beauty, that ought to recommend its occasional adoption; and although it may not be altogether applicable for a place of worship whose dimensions are so large as to require aisles, since the bold and massive character of the piers or pillars must always necessarily interfere with the convenient arrangement of the interior of the building, yet from its great simplicity it is peculiarly adapted for small rural churches; which ought not in this style to be designed of very lofty proportions". It might be thought that St John's had been built by someone who followed pretty closely James Barr's instructions. It is essentially a small rural church, certainly of no lofty proportions, and containing no bold and massive pillars. What the architect has in fact succeeded in doing is building again the eighteenth-century galleried preaching house overlaid with a few trimmings which he learned from Norman originals. But the mind of the best architects of the time was moving beyond this sort of thing.

Between the centre of Manchester and Pendlebury, Henry Heywood was able to view a symposium of contemporary architecture. As an intelligent man with some acquaintance with ecclesiology, he was well aware that twenty years after St John's, Pendlebury, better things had been done than that rather jejune imitation of the Norman style. Worsley Church was good in its way, probably as good a copy of earlier perfections as could be

[1] It is only fair to say that while this book was being written certain adaptations have been made to this singular piece of furniture, which, though conforming it a little more closely to sober Anglican taste, have certainly deprived the church of its most astonishing *trompe-l'œil*.

managed, but adaptations of the Gothic theme had gone ahead rapidly since the time when Worsley Church was built, and Scott's pupils had outstripped their master. The idea of a new church for Swinton, the best that the 1860's could produce, was in his head for a long while before it became a practical policy. Its completed design bears testimony to the enlightenment which came to English architecture between the time of the Commissioners' churches and the date of its building. The pace at which that enlightenment proceeded was amazingly rapid; we seem to be standing in two different worlds of achievement when we contrast the Commissioners' Perpendicular of 1831 with Bodley's adaptations of the Gothic theme in the 1870's or even Street's in the 1860's. If Heywood was able to build something fine and satisfying at Swinton in 1869 he had much for which to thank one man who imparted an entirely new spirit to the Gothic revival and led it away from the unimaginative stiffness of its earliest models. That man was a genius of French extraction, A. W. N. Pugin.

II

It is to Augustus Welby Northmore Pugin that we owe the spiritualizing change which came over the English attitude to Gothic architecture in the middle of the century. The Commissioners' architecture took up the style for utilitarian reasons: it was, so they said, cheap, and it was pleasingly ornamental, and there was some dim notion that in some way it was more appropriate to a building dedicated to the uses of religion. But the younger Pugin brought to the dissemination of Gothic ideals all the burning ardour of a Catholic crusader. Auguste Charles Pugin, the father, was a French refugee: whether he was a Catholic or not, the son was brought up as far as religion was concerned by his mother and was constrained to attend upon the interminable ministrations of Edward Irving in Hatton Garden.

Foreign tours enthused him with the grandeur of continental churches, and in 1834 he became a Roman Catholic. It was, he decided, from the Catholic religion only that valid architecture could spring, and valid architecture was the flowering of the developed Gothic style in the later Middle Ages. It was an evangel as logical as it was thrilling, but like most evangelists he found what should have been a ready audience singularly slow and stupid in adopting it. The fact was that the Roman priest said his Mass in a little over-ornate chapel in the Italianate style, and in the latter years of his life Pugin's ideas received far more sympathy from Anglicans whose thin trickle of Catholicism afforded doubtful evidence of their possession of the fullness of true faith which was the *sine qua non* of true architecture.

So, to sustain his thesis, we have the creation of that amazing roseate view of the later Middle Ages which has had considerable currency amongst the incurable romantics and which, in the realm of architecture, at any rate, we may attribute largely to the younger Pugin. His conception of the medieval city effulgent with faith, symbolized by a veritable hedgehog of bristling spires, deserves careful study in the print which reproduces his picture in Sir Kenneth Clark's *Gothic Revival*. There are multitudinous spires, but naturally no slums, and Pugin was apparently unaware of the hideous filth which characterized the medieval city. The same romantic *urbs beata* theme is pursued in the remarkable series of sketches called the *Contrasts*, where a glamorous version of the supposedly best of medieval building is set side by side with the most dreary and commonplace of early nineteenth-century achievements. The effect is ruthless as propaganda and may easily be successful in convincing the unwary; the student of Pugin's *Contrasts* should dose himself with a stiff dose of Coulton before allowing his judgement to be completely swept away.

It is apparent that good Anglicans lapped up this make-believe medieval world which Pugin created for them, and in 1839 came the Cambridge Camden Society. The story of the flowering of the Gothic revival has been told to perfection so often, and nowhere better than by Sir Kenneth Clark in the classical book of that name, that it seems otiose to do more than make the briefest reference to what was going on in the minds of these eager and devout Anglicans who were faced with the task of building and restoring their churches. But the Camden Society is at least worth mentioning; for Henry Heywood was a member of Trinity College, Cambridge, in 1852, and although the headquarters of the Society had, by that time, been transferred to London, it cannot be supposed that its traditions would be unknown to the devout and impressionable youth who was preparing for a life of service in the Church of England.

The Camden Society was founded in 1839 by J. M. Neale and Benjamin Webb, to "promote the study of Ecclesiastical Architecture and the restoration of mutilated architectural remains". It published many pamphlets in furtherance of these aims and in 1841 founded a magazine called the *Ecclesiologist* to stimulate intelligent interest and criticism. So we may say that the Camden Society begat ecclesiology, never perhaps an exact science, but one which set a vast number of earnest Churchmen in the way of brass-rubbing, sketching, plaster chipping, and kindred works of virtue. Amateur architectural studies became such a favourite feature of mid-Victorian culture that there were even *Aunt Elinor's Lectures on Architecture* to initiate the young ladies of England in a hobby which they might pursue with the utmost propriety.

But the devout practice of Tractarian Churchmanship must be the basis of every ecclesiological field-day. It needed a pious acceptance of the neo-Catholicism of the Oxford fathers to produce a right appreciation of Gothic architecture, and the spate of imitation Gothic building and church restoration of the second half of the nineteenth century is surely a symbolic manifestation of the new spirit which was astir in the minds of sincere Anglicans. That manifestation was reckoned to have reached its highest expression in an attempt to reproduce the architecture of the fourteenth century or Middle Pointed Gothic. The "Norman", "Early English", and "Perpendicular" styles had been known to the Commissioners' architects: the first quarter of the century had seen many attempts to build thus, but this was before the blessed light of Tractarianism had dawned upon the Church, and these buildings were suspect as the habitation of Evangelicals and other kinds of theological Liberals. No, the fullness of faith had come with the Oxford Movement and Decorated Gothic was the outward and visible sign of a militant Tractarianism. The blossoming of intricate ornament, flowing tracery, ball-flower decoration, all these were symptomatic of the perfection of the Late Middle Pointed period, and in the pages of the *Ecclesiologist* contemporary building was judged accordingly. Besides, what boundless opportunities for Christian symbolism did this style afford! Neale and Webb's translation in 1843 of the first book of the *Rationale Divinorum Officiorum* of Willielmus Durandus, Bishop of Mende, in the thirteenth century, opened the floodgates to a torrent of symbolic enthusiasm which reaches almost unbelievable limits of extravagance.

It was really symbolism run riot. Every tiny detail of the building must be pressed for some symbolic significance; even the music and the flowers are symbolical. The triune Deity can be traced in the threefold division of nave, chancel, and sanctuary, of arcade, triforium, and clerestory, and in the three towers of large churches. Christ said, "I am the door", therefore doors symbolize Christ; he also said, "I am the Light of the World", therefore windows symbolize him, the true light, that lighteneth every man that cometh into the world. There is no stemming this flood; even the four walls of the church must be held to represent the Four Evangelists, the pillars in the nave are bishops and doctors, the capitals are the opinions of the bishops and doctors, and the ornaments of the capitals are the words of Sacred Scripture. Even the tiles on the roof of the church symbolize the soldiers who defend the church from its enemies; they bear witness to that in the course of their homelier duties of keeping out the rain. It is a strange frolic of medieval imagination: but the ecclesiologists solemnly took it all in and when, in 1850, Neale lectured on "Symbolism", he produced a long and vastly impressive list of writers of the Western Church who had written on this subject. It is no wonder that the mid-Victorian architect devoted himself so willingly to Decorated as the queen of the styles when, besides its quite exceptional facility for allowing him

11

scope for prettiness in his building, it supplied a whole series of elaborate details, each of which was capable of a transcendent significance.

But the ecclesiologists did not have it all their own way: they were involved in the general assault which was made upon Tractarianism when the reaction set in after Newman's secession to Rome, and the whole movement became deeply suspect. Leading Evangelical preachers thundered against elaborate schemes of building and restoration as an evidence of the recrudescence of popery. The Camden Society itself came under fire and in 1845 severed its connection with the *Ecclesiologist*; it had even been accused by one Protestant enthusiast as likely "in all probability to lead to great and violent political commotions, and it may be to distress and bloodshed". This was a lurid accusation to level against an innocent covey of Saturday-afternoon brass-rubbers, but it was a reflection of the heated tempers of the time. There is a curious story about the excellent Bishop Prince Lee, first Bishop of Manchester, whom we have already met as the energetic sponsor of much church revival and extension in Lancashire. It is recorded in the *Ecclesiologist* of February 1851 that a chancel had been added in the Decorated Gothic style to the church of St John, Higher Broughton. When the bishop saw it he gave an exhibition of what the writer calls maniacal fury, throwing cushions and altar cloths about. He screwed off carved ornaments and threw them on the pavement, saying, in reference to Mr Bayne, the builder of the chancel: "Mr. Bayne? *Saint* Bayne, I suppose you mean. . . . The man must either have been a knave or a fool." He also said that he wished "the boys might break the stained-glass windows of the church". It is an incredible incident and can perhaps be understood only in the light of the extraordinary tempers which were engendered by the Tractarian controversy in the early days of its parochial adventures. Prince Lee was an ardent advocate of church extension, but there is other evidence to suggest that he had scant sympathy with Tractarianism. He seems to have acted in a thoroughly arbitrary and unreasonable fashion in his suppression of choral services in the Ringley Chapel in Prestwich parish during 1850. His Lordship is said to have remarked that the people of Ringley were an "ignorant set" and could not understand singing, and he ridiculed the idea of colliers and labourers taking a prominent part in the church service. He considered intoning stuff and trash . . . and it was absolutely wrong to have choristers in ordinary parish churches, as the people did not and could not join in the service, and it was, in short, Romish, because it admitted of vicarious worship. It is only fair, however, to say that in regard to some complaint about a clergyman who had introduced a credence table, he replied, "Pooh! Pooh! what do I care about a credence table? it is a matter of perfect indifference."

It was perhaps the Protestantism of Ruskin which finally reconciled the suspicious to the respectability of Gothic architecture. That one who was such a bitter antagonist of Romanism could exhibit such enthusiasm for this sort of architecture robbed it of its sting and made it a "safe line" for every type of builder in the Church of England.

One of the earliest entries in Henry Heywood's diary of the building of Swinton Church is a note dating from the latter part of 1866 in which he says that suggestions had been put into his head that whenever a new church was built *Street* had better be the architect. He thereupon wrote to Street, determined that no Manchester man should have the work, and invited Street to visit him at his home at Moorfield, Swinton, when he next came into the neighbourhood. Street replied to say that he would do so. By March 1867 the question of the architect was receiving very careful consideration; Heywood determined that there was to be no competition, but an attempt must be made to secure Street, Scott, Butterfield, "or else Mr. Taylor or Paley". Medland Taylor was the diocesan architect and is responsible for many churches in the Manchester area; a letter of application for the work was read from him at the first meeting of the building committee on 1 April, but at that committee it was proposed and seconded and carried unanimously that Mr Street should be the architect. Setting Taylor aside, we have here in this note the names of four of the greatest architects of the second half of the nineteenth century, and some account of their work may conclude this brief sketch of the architectural trends which led up to the building of Swinton Church.

Sir Gilbert Scott is the most extensive popularizer of the ideals of the Camden Society in the story of nineteenth-century architecture, and he has left the imprint of ecclesiology upon a very large number of Victorian period pieces. The Middle Pointed Gothic style with its flowing tracery and intricate ornament reaches its dizziest heights in his work, but the most serious criticism that can be levelled against him is that whilst he was an intelligent copyist, his work lacks the sense of initiative and adventure which led later architects like Bodley and Paley to a technique of adaptation which, whilst retaining the genuine Gothic spirit, produced buildings which succeeded because of the freshness of their originality. The brilliance of Scott is the brilliance of a highly intelligent copyist; the genius of the later architects is in the spontaneity of their designs and in their grasp of the truth that Gothic architecture was not only a matter of joyful resurrection but also a progressing adventure in newness of life.

Scott may be regarded as the mediator of Puginism to the Anglican Communion; after surrendering himself with the rapture of a convert to Pugin's gospel he could write that every aspiration of his heart had become medieval. The *Ecclesiologist* tended to regard him with some disfavour when it found him submitting designs for the rebuilding of the Lutheran Church of St Nicholas, Hamburg. It was a condonation of theological heresy which would have infuriated Pugin as a betrayal of the true genius of Gothic, and the *Ecclesiologist* stigmatized it with the reproof that the temporal gains of such a contract were a miserable substitute for its unreality, "and—we must say it—its sin". Still, we have no evidence that he ever departed essentially from his conversion standpoint that English Catholicism was the genius of Gothic architecture, and that since Catholicism had been part of the texture of the common life of Englishmen in the greatest periods of building it was logical that civic architecture as well as religious should follow that style. He fought that battle to its last stages with Lord Palmerston in the matter of the Government Offices. Perhaps we may regard the Albert Memorial as being as much a monument to Scott's cherished convictions about the paramount position of Gothic in everyday life as a tribute of respect to the Prince Consort. Certainly that is much more how it would be regarded by lovers of everyday things in England to-day; it earned him his knighthood and he himself said that it was the result of his highest and most enthusiastic efforts.

Henry Heywood had ample opportunity of studying Scott's work at first hand, for, in the next parish to Swinton, Scott had had the unlimited resources of Bridgewater wealth to build the parish church of Worsley for the Earl of Ellesmere in 1846. It is a fine piece of building and shows what ecclesiology could do when not even the tiniest detail was stinted for lack of means. Worsley Church is magnificently situated on a hill nearby the great mansion which Edward Blore had built for Francis Egerton, when he and his wife decided to live in the place from whence their wealth was derived. It has a soaring spire rising from an elaborately pinnacled tower, and it follows with richly embellished detail every canon of the Middle Pointed style. Its arcades of clustered columns, richly decorated mouldings, gargoyles, carved heads, flowing tracery, show how meticulously Scott had mastered the minutiae of the Decorated style. Its fittings are chosen with equal care and executed regardless of expense. The rather heavy stained glass of the east window is not characteristic of the period but an importation of original medieval glass from Flanders. Likewise some of the elaborately carved woodwork, particularly in the pulpit and the organ case, is a collection of old panels brought from elsewhere; but the ironwork separating the Ellesmere Chapel from the chancel is surely as impressive an example of Victorian craftsmanship of that character as could be found anywhere.

It is an opulent church; it bespeaks a pious aristocracy lavishing its new-found wealth in the worship of God and enlisting the services of a skilled medievalist to work with unlimited resources to that end. But when all is said and done, it is not a piece of great and inspired building. It is Decorated Gothic resurrected in the middle of the nineteenth century by an archaeologist who was very sure of himself. But it is precisely at that point that it illustrates so admirably both Scott's cleverness

and his weakness. Set Worsley Church alongside Bodley's St
Augustine's, Pendlebury, or Temple Moore's St Anne's, Royton,
or Paley and Austin's St George's, Stockport, and of these last
three churches one is compelled to say: "Here is true genius; the
unfettered spirit of man creating something that arises from a real
generative power within him. He is the heir of the ages; he
acknowledges his debt to the traditions of master craftsmen who
have gone before him, but he is in no sense their slave. Out of
the treasury of architecture he is bringing forth things new and
old, but he is not merely copying them for our delectation. He is
assimilating the best they have to teach him, and from their
lessons he is storing up knowledge. His own God-given spark of
genius is bringing to the birth a creation which is unique, the offspring of a divinely inspired master spirit." A man might sit in
Worsley Church and say, "This is really very pretty; this reproduces the atmosphere of the Decorated Period very cleverly."
But in St Augustine's, he must be almost overpowered with a
feeling of awe. Bodley succeeds where Scott fails in raising up the
sense of the numinous. Such a man will be singularly unimpres-
sionable if Bodley, by his work, does not bring him to his knees.

The second name suggested by Heywood was that of
William Butterfield, and one wonders whether, if he had been
given the commission, Swinton might have been blessed with a
church in what has been called the "streaky bacon" style of
decoration and made of red brick. Butterfield's interpretation of
the revived Gothic is not to be despised; he was not a mere
imitator and he introduced certain original features into his
buildings which were used to great effect again by the great
masters who followed him. He may be thanked for reconciling
the ecclesiologists to the use of red brick, and, above all, he gave
us All Saints', Margaret Street, and St Alban's, Holborn, which
have long been the nerve centres of parochial Anglo-Catholicism
in England. Butterfield was an intensely religious man, and his pursuit of architecture was Puginesque in its religious significance. He
was born in 1814 and died in 1900, and his inspiration again derived
from the Camden Society. Three features of Butterfield's work
seem to stand out conspicuously: his use of brick construction

for churches, his lavish employment of colour for interior decoration, and his rediscovery of the unbroken roof line as a medieval idea worth recovering.

It is difficult to understand why the early ecclesiologists dis-liked brick as a material for church building, but Butterfield apparently converted them, and their model church, All Saints', Margaret Street, was built of brick. But even more characteristic of Butterfield is his lavish use of different coloured bricks, marbles, and garish coloured glass to enliven his interiors. "Polychromatic architecture" had a certain vogue after All Saints' had set the fashion; red Peterhead granite, Cornish serpen-tine, Devonshire marble, alabaster combined with mosaic, frescoes, and gilding to dazzle the eye. This was in large measure the influence of Italian *motifs* which the mid-Victorians had learnt in their foreign travel. Street passed through a phase of enthu-siasm for this sort of thing and introduced marble patterns in several places in Swinton Church. But it was criticized on two valid grounds, first that what was suitable beneath the sunny skies of Italy was not necessarily congruous in the grey and sometimes dismal atmosphere of England, and second, that over-elaborate coloration might be liable to distract the mind of the worshippers from the contemplation of heavenly thoughts. The original "whirling maze of variegated colouring", as one con-temporary critic called it, must have reached its zenith when St Alban's, Holborn, was first seen. We are not in a position to judge of the first startling impression which this "constructive coloration" must have made upon the first worshippers, for in all cases time has subdued the garishness, and St Alban's, Holborn, has been lost to us by the swift judgement of Hitler's bombs. Keble College Chapel succeeds by reason of its magnificent pro-portions, but the over decoration is at any rate not in accord with modern taste. But St Alban's and Keble Chapel illustrate Butter-field's reintroduction of the unbroken roof line; it was a useful discovery of a medieval feature which most architects of the Gothic revival had overlooked and it was used to great effect by Bodley and other later nineteenth-century architects.

We may be sure that if Butterfield had rebuilt Swinton Church we should have had a finely conceived building. But we may be relieved that he was not chosen. It would have been all too easy in a neighbourhood where stone was not too close of access to have had ready recourse to his favourite brick. Brick and polychromatic decorations in the Lancashire atmosphere would quickly have assumed a dingy and neglected appearance. We are not without considerable evidence as to how brick buildings of that period look after standing up to the Lancashire industrial atmosphere for eighty years.

It is a little surprising that Edward Graham Paley was not the favoured candidate, for he had more popularity in Lancashire than perhaps any other single Victorian architect of national reputation. Lancashire abounds with Paley and Paley and Austin churches. Paley was a grandson of the author of the *Evidences*, and was a pupil of Edmund Sharpe of Lancaster, who himself had been a pupil of Rickman. Sharpe had a flair for the Romanesque style, but Paley's principal work is Gothic with a strong bias to the Perpendicular period. Sharpe and Paley were partners from 1845 and many well-known Lancashire churches, including Wigan parish church, derive from this partnership. The two churches of Lever Bridge, near Bolton, and Holy Trinity, Platt, Rushholme, represent an interesting but disastrous exploit in building construction. An Industrialist of Bolton, Fletcher by name, claimed to have discovered a cheap method of building elaborately decorated churches by the use of terra-cotta as a medium. Lever Bridge and Platt were designed by Sharpe and Paley and were actually built in this medium; but from the time of their completion the terra-cotta began to disintegrate, and the care of the structure of these two buildings has proved a heavy anxiety and expense ever since.

Paley worked independently from 1851 to 1868, and himself was responsible for several Lancashire churches during that period. In 1868 began the partnership with H. J. Austin, and together they built over forty new churches, mostly in the north. Many of them were within easy reach of Swinton, and the large parish church of Leigh was completed in 1873. Henry Heywood attended some of the earliest services held in the building and wrote interesting notes about the manner of conducting public worship there in his own parish magazine. The crown of this partnership is surely the superlative church of St George, Stockport, though there is reason to suppose that Austin had the greater part in this achievement, for it was consecrated in 1895, the year that Paley died. Here is the revived Perpendicular style developed to perfection; it excels exactly as Bodley excelled and as Scott never could have done, for though it derives its inspiration from such a late medieval model as Holy Trinity, Stratford-on-Avon, it is an adaptation and not a copy, and succeeds precisely because it is a spontaneous product of the architect's own genius. It is curious that the Camden Society should have so disliked the Perpendicular style; it regarded it as a declension from the purest peaks of Gothic architecture in the Decorated period. The *Ecclesiologist* even advised the removal of Perpendicular clerestories and the insertion of circular windows in their place. We may be grateful that such architects as Paley and Austin emancipated themselves from this arbitrary tyranny, and we may be fairly sure that if they had been entrusted with the rebuilding of Swinton Church we should have had a building in the adapted Perpendicular style.

III

The chosen candidate for the rebuilding of Swinton Church was George Edmund Street. A memoir by his son, Arthur Edmund Street, was published by John Murray in 1888; it is a scarce book, which the author in his preface describes as crude and incomplete, setting forth rather his father's opinions and some description of his more important works than his home-life and the more intimate side of his character. He says that it suffers from a want of continuity and cohesion, and there is justice in this self-criticism; nevertheless, the book contains a large amount of interesting information about Street and his work, and the two

lists of his original works and of his restorations and additions
are extremely long and impressive. There is also printed, as an
appendix, the course of five lectures which Street delivered on
architectural subjects before the students of the Royal Academy
as Professor of Architecture in the spring of 1881, the year he
died.

George Edmund Street was born at Woodford in Essex in
1824, but when he was a boy of six his family moved to the Grove,
Camberwell, which was where he grew up and went to school.
His education was at Mitcham and afterwards at the collegiate
school at Camberwell; this was brought to an end when the
family moved again, on the retirement of the father who was a
solicitor, to Crediton in Devon. Sketching became the boy's
earliest hobby and whilst in Devon it became his practice to sketch
the old churches and houses in the neighbourhood of his home.
After his father's death in 1840 there were periods of residence in
Exeter and Taunton with further opportunities of drawing and
sketching, but in 1841 he began work in the architect's office of
Mr Owen Carter in Winchester. It is Winchester Cathedral which
appears to have been the operative influence in this part of his life,
and for three years he served an assiduous apprenticeship making
himself intimate both with the great building and with everything
of architectural interest within a wide radius round the town. In
1844 he transferred himself to the office of Messrs Scott and
Moffatt in Spring Gardens, and he was taken on there provision-
ally to help with the work on the cathedral at Hamburg which
Scott had just undertaken. He acquitted himself so satisfactorily
that his temporary place became permanent and he remained in
Scott's office until he began in an entirely independent sphere of
his own.

The 1840's were the great years of ecclesiology, and Street
could not have found a better place than Scott's office for im-
bibing its principles at the fountain-head. Year after year, he and
his brother spent their holidays touring and sketching amongst
the great churches and abbeys of the country. Visits to Sussex,
Lincolnshire, the Lake District, Durham, and the Yorkshire
Dales are recorded, and his letters reveal the youthful enthusiasm

with which he was beginning to discover that intimate connection between religion and great architecture which Pugin had passed on to Scott and which Street was now learning both from his master and his own experience. "I daresay you have smiled", he writes in a letter in 1845, "at the way in which I connect architecture and religion; it may perhaps be the bias of a profession which makes me do so, but I cannot but think that architecture as well as, not more than, the other fine arts is a great and most important assistant to religion."

Street's first commission was Biscovey Church, Cornwall, for the clergyman, Mr Prynne, who, moving to St Peter's, Plymouth, whilst the work was in progress, afterwards gave him the work of restoration of this latter church. Street now felt justified in opening an office on his own account: in 1849 he severed his connection with Scott and Moffat, and independent commissions began to flow in rapidly, especially in the west country. Through the Ecclesiological Society and his friendship with the Reverend Benjamin Webb, Street became acquainted with Butler of Wantage and soon there were commissions for a new vicarage and new schools there. In 1850 he settled in Wantage and his introduction to the Bishop of Oxford, Dr Samuel Wilberforce, led to his appointment as diocesan architect. Street was now assured of success; 1853 saw the building of Cuddesdon Theological College and the work for the East Grinstead Sisterhood, and a year or two later a start was made upon the notable church of St Peter, Bournemouth.

Succeeding years brought tours on the Continent which both furnished the material for Street's standard works on architecture and showed their influence upon the churches which he built. Thus, in 1855 was published his *Brick and Marble Architecture of North Italy*, and the church of St James the Less, Westminster, bears the impress of certain Italian ideas which have become assimilated into the architect's own specific genius. Three tours in 1861, 1862, and 1863 enabled him to publish in 1865 *Gothic Architecture in Spain*, which is probably his most important piece of writing, and which was highly praised both in this country and in Spain. At the height of his powers and reputation it seems reasonable to select the Protestant cathedral of Christ Church, Dublin, the nave of Bristol Cathedral, and the new Law Courts in the Strand as his three most important commissions. Indeed, the work on the last named was not complete when he died in 1881, and it was his friend Sir Arthur Blomfield who carried the work through to its conclusion and the ceremonial opening by the Queen in December 1882.

Out of the abundance of information which the son's biography gives us it may be most suitable to consider only the quality of Street as a man and the place which his work holds in the progress of the Gothic revival. First, then, it is essential to understand that his work as an architect was conceived as a vocation and that his Christianity, interpreted through the channels of mid-Victorian High Churchmanship, was the mainspring of all his work. Street's character is another of the astonishing triumphs of ecclesiology, of which perhaps the most notable feature was its extraordinary success in influencing the outlook of a very large number of Victorian Churchmen. "This great truth must be grasped," he said, "that Christian Art is never properly developed except by an essentially Christian intention on the part of the artist, as well as on the part of those who employ his talents." Again he says, and this is perhaps the most explicit of statements in regard to the matter, "The Church architect must thoroughly believe the doctrines of the Church for which he builds, and must lead a life of—to say the least—fair conformity to her rules and discipline. He must also be fairly acquainted with her ritual and usages." It is an intriguing doctrine, this notion of good art and good men being inextricably mingled; for Street we have suggested that it derives from Pugin and is mediated by Scott. The lives of some of the most eminent of the religious artists of the Renaissance are perhaps a little difficult to square with the universal application of ecclesiology as part of the ultimate moral law. But the Victorians may not have been as well informed of the private lives of their predecessors as Lytton Strachey has now made it possible for us in this enlightened age to be informed about the lives of the eminent Victorians. At any rate, we may be quite sure that the ecclesiologists took themselves very seriously and went to some pains to practise in their private lives the religious principles which they held to be fundamental to their artistic canons.

It was the qualities of truthfulness, abnegation of self, and consistency which, in Street's view, ought to animate every church architect. Such moral qualities he tried to develop by his association with the well-known Tractarian church of All Saints', Margaret Street. There, during the incumbency of Mr Upton Richards, he served as a church officer and, in fact, held the churchwardenship for many years. He insisted on every single seat being kept free and also saw that men and women were segregated in separate blocks of seats. He was a member of the Council of the Free and Open Church Association and also of the English Church Union, of which he was one of the most active lay members. In 1866 he was one of a committee formed to present the first vestments to All Saints' Church and himself designed them.

In later life Street was able to achieve what had been always a great ambition, namely to build a country church near his country home at Holmdale, which he completed in 1876. An ecclesiastical district was formed out of six contiguous Surrey parishes under the name of Holmbury St Mary, and the church which was Street's personal gift was consecrated in 1879. On Sundays and weekdays he was assiduous in his attendance at the services of the Church, and, although born a townsman, took with zest to all the typical pursuits of the country. When he died in middle age it is said that he had about sixty buildings on hand. The enormous output of men like Scott and Street is in itself a matter of wonder; we may admire their skill in being able to make the best of both worlds, to be immensely successful professional men, running true to type in establishing themselves as country gentlemen with their well-earned wealth, and yet at the same time sincerely religious men, the highest product of all that ecclesiology strove to commend.

There is a curious note amongst the papers relating to the rebuilding of Milnrow Church near Rochdale, written by Canon Raines, the vicar, to a Mr Blackburn. The exact context of the letter is not clear, but it appears to deal with some extra item of

expense to Captain Schofield the donor of the church; Raines
writes: ". . . I have received what I consider a very curt and ill-
mannered letter from Mr. Street which I enclose with my reply.
I have not heard from him since. . . . I find him to be more overbearing than I like and I am not sorry that my intercourse . . .
should have ended. But great men have great power, and resistance is not always a wise measure." This is the sort of private
comment which does not always reach the official biographies,
and we can only judge it for what we think it to be worth. On the
other hand, amongst the many papers connected with the building
of Swinton Church there are many both in Street's private hand
and of that of Mr Wood his clerk. Nothing in this correspondence
suggests anything of the harsh overbearing character that we
might deduce from Canon Raines's letter. There is, in fact, one
letter which contains an extremely generous offer of a kind which
bears out the suggestion in his son's biography that Street showed
no alacrity in charging for work in what he considered was a
deserving religious cause; he obtained his position as Oxford
diocesan architect because he was prepared to do for nothing the
work for which Benjamin Ferrey wanted £100 per annum.

On 14 November 1867 Mr Wood, writing from Street's office
at 51 Russell Square, sends the following message: "Mr. Street
desires me to say that he has prepared a drawing shewing the side
elevation of the church in 5 bays—instead of 4—as in the drawings already submitted, which he thinks will be a great improvement, and as soon as I can get the drawings out of the surveyor's
hands, I will forward same to you. Mr. Street will (in the event o
your committee agreeing with him that the alternative above
refer'd to is an improvement) be glad to pay the cost of it
himself." A second note in Street's own handwriting confirms
this alteration in the elevation and renews the generous offer:

On looking at my design again I am not quite pleased with the
side elevations of the aisles, and I have made an alternative design
with five bays and windows on each side instead of four. The effect
is to make the Church look altogether higher, the spans being
narrower and the arches more pointed, and I have made the side
windows of 3 lights instead of four. I feel sure that you will like

the elevation better. I have got Horsman to go into the additional cost which he makes come to £50 and if you will allow me I should be very glad to make this contribution to the work. You and your Committee are taxing yourselves so much for the sake of making the work good that I should be sorry to let the aisles go unaltered. The columns and arches will remain unaltered. But they and the windows have no necessary connection.

At the foot of the letter Street appends two pen-and-ink sketches of the proportions of the windows according to the four-window and five-window designs.

Whether Street was in the habit of being over generous or not, it is curious to find the great and successful architect pleading shortage of ready cash and pressing his clerical client for prompt payment in order to buy a larger office building. On 27 November 1869 he writes:

I should be very much obliged if you could let *me* have a payment. . . . It so happens just now that I have a rather urgent call for all the money I have owing to me, as I am obliged to provide myself with larger offices than I have here and my only good chance of doing so seems to be by a considerable outlay in the purchase of a house, so if you can accommodate me, I shall be very grateful.

It looks as though the Swinton building committee and other outstanding debtors were able to accommodate Mr Street to his satisfaction, for subsequent letters are addressed from the more commodious premises at 14 Cavendish Place, Cavendish Square, W. But relationships between architects and building committees were never easy when it came to matters of payment, and whilst we do not hear of the Reverend Henry Heywood passing such sharp judgements upon Mr Street's character as did the Reverend Canon Raines, there is at least one letter from Street to Heywood showing that the even surface of the transaction had been somewhat ruffled by what the architect considered the committee's cheese-paring tendencies:

I am very sorry [he writes on 3 August 1870] the Committee express themselves so strongly. The truth is that if anything should be deducted from Horsman it could only be the value of the cement filleting. . . . [then follow certain details of a technical nature] . . . All this is nothing to you save by way of showing that an architect in attempting to adjust such questions equitably may not succeed in pleasing either side. Also as regards the charge I have made, I may mention that besides my donation to the work, I charged you £8 less than my book showed me . . . for travelling expenses. I should not have mentioned this but I think your committee seem to me to be a little inclined to deal too rigorously with me.

However, this little irritation did not upset the friendly relationship between the architect and the vicar. This letter concludes:

The drawing at the R.A. was not for sale, but if you care to have it you are quite welcome to it and I will send it to you when it comes back.

When Street died in 1881, Henry Heywood caused a memorial inscription to the great architect who was buried in Westminster Abbey to be incised on one of the tower arches in Swinton Church.

We have written sufficient about the personal character of Street, and it now remains to give some description of the kind of work he did and the place he occupies in the story of the Gothic revival. Street was an ecclesiologist and regarded the English Gothic church of the Decorated style as being the highest achievement of religiously inspired building. Yet he was not merely an exact copyist in the way that Scott his master was. He may be said to hold a half-way position between the precise enslavement to medieval models for which Scott has been rightly criticized and the free adaptation of the Gothic tradition blossoming into buildings of fresh genius and character which is associated with such names as Bodley and Temple Moore. Street is a Gothic enthusiast, but it is Decorated Gothic with a difference. Perhaps the difference crept in because Street himself was a practising Churchman, and his buildings shaped themselves into the ideal shape for rendering the liturgy of the Church of England according to the best Victorian tradition which Street, who had sung in a Church choir, understood so well. Tractarian liturgical formulae had led public worship into the custom of an elaborate Mattins or Sung Eucharist, sung by a surpliced choir in full view of the congregation at the east end of the church. Addleshaw and Etchells describe this as a dignified but not very congregational act of worship and consider that for such a service the great Victorian architects designed a church very successfully.

It was part of Street's originality to break away from the strict medieval plan and to design a broad nave to bring a large congregation in sight of the altar and to make the aisles little more than processional avenues. Street has not adopted this plan at Swinton, where there are two substantial aisles under their own separate gabled roofs, but at the neighbouring church of St Augustine's, Pendlebury, Bodley has carried the idea to its extreme form and the aisles are merely passages four feet wide pierced through the internal buttresses. At Swinton, however, Street has devised an extremely wide chancel with the choir set well back on each side so that it does not seem unnecessarily over-weighted and obtrusive and stealing the interest from the altar, as in some Victorian churches. Here again Street has broken away from a strict medieval plan whose imitators often made their chancels far too long and narrow. It has been said that his original plan, which had to be reduced because of shortage of funds, provided for a chancel which extended two bays farther eastward than the present chancel. There is no concrete evidence of this, as diligent search has failed to recover these lost original plans. But the chancel as we have it now seems quite in accord with Street's notion of wide and shallow chancels. It projects very little farther eastward than the Lady Chapel and the organ chamber, and escapes the mistake of placing the altar at the end of a long vista which, whilst no doubt effectively picturesque, destroys its significance as the accessible focus of congregational Eucharistic worship.

Street was also to some extent an innovator in his use of constructive coloration, which he learnt from his explorations amongst the Italian and Spanish churches. It shows itself in small details in Swinton Church in the use of geometrical patterns of marble mosaic in the panels of the pulpit and the low chancel wall, and in

12

the ornamental arcading against the east wall on either side of the altar. The church of St James the Less, Westminster, is one of the least restrained of his efforts at this sort of coloration; it is frankly Italian in its sympathy, and Eastlake in his *Gothic Revival* criticizes the "restless notching of edges, the dazzling distribution of stripes, the multiplicity of pattern forms, and exuberance of sculptured detail". Street's son defends his father in the *Memoir* against the criticisms which were levelled against similar work which he did on a large scale in the Wellington Barracks Chapel. The mosaics were disparaged as looking cold and poor in colour, but Street contended that they would be improved by time and exposure, and his son asserted that this forecast had been completely verified. Constructive coloration was to be effected in English building not so much by decorative materials which were part and parcel of the building construction but by a system of veneering which he regarded as an opportunity for a rich treatment of wall spaces in a permanent way. This is the kind of use which we see made of the method in the arcades filled in with marble mosaic at the east end of Swinton Church.

Street was a great believer in the architect being responsible for every detail of decoration and furnishing in the church which he built. Hangings, frontals, brass ornaments should assert the supreme control of the master mind producing one complete achievement. At Swinton it seems as though Henry Heywood conceded this principle. We find that Street designed the church wall and gate piers, and on 15 June 1869 he was given instructions to design an "altar cloth". The altar cross, the lectern, the credence table, the reredos, and the sedilia were all part of the original plan. It would be well if present-day improvers and restorers were to bear in mind the homogeneity of these Victorian churches. It is a mistaken idea that future generations are entitled to pull about and rearrange and add to the building and furniture so as to tune in to every prevailing wind of topical fashion. These buildings and their contents were the master plan of great minds, and the whole scheme of building and furnishing hangs together. Too often a new incumbent approaches a Victorian church with some preconceived prejudice about the so-called ugliness of the pseudo-Gothic and at once begins to ask himself: "How can I improve this?" So, with the aid of a few enthusiastic amateurs in the cult of architecture and ecclesiology, *this* is pulled out and *that* is put in, with an exuberance which even the grandmotherly supervision of the diocesan advisory committee finds it impossible to curb. The result is something which perhaps induces self-satisfaction in the incumbent and his friends, at any rate for the duration of one incumbency, if not for one whole generation. The result may be satisfying, but it is not just what the Victorian architect who was a master mind intended his church should be. He has long departed this life and is therefore defenceless, but it may be that history may work its strange retributions and posterity may execrate the name of our twentieth-century "improver" for daring to trifle with the achievements of the great Victorians, in the same way that it is the fashion at present to vilify the ecclesiologists and the Camden Society for doing what they ventured to do by way of restoration to the ruinous and crumbling churches which they found in their day.

Street was a genius; we are allowed to say as much as that, even in these days when the habit of disparaging the Victorians has not quite reached the end which is certainly in store for it. His son in his *Memoir* hit upon "an excess of boldness or bluntness, a tinge of eccentricity, a truthfulness in displaying construction" as his father's distinguishing traits. He explained them as a form of protest against the dull and meaningless symmetry which had been the leading character of church architecture before the Gothic revival. We may say that Street took the Decorated Gothic of the English Middle Ages, which the ecclesiologists had admired so greatly, and which Sir Gilbert Scott had copied and reproduced with such pedestrian and uninspired faithfulness, and used it and adapted it by the impress of his own genius. It is unlikely that men will build churches like St Peter's, Bournemouth, and St John's, Torquay, again, but how much poorer would be the achievement of the English architectural tradition without them. If we end the matter by saying that Street's churches possess "character", we are perhaps pitching our climax on an indefinable note. Yet "character" has its specific meaning and we may fix Street's churches in their proper place in the march of English architecture by regarding them as symbolic expressions, the very highest outward and visible signs, of the genuine Catholic spirit which earnest and sincere Tractarianism had implanted in the minds of their builders.

The Reverend H. R. Heywood in his parish magazine took some care to keep his parishioners well informed as to Street's qualifications as an architect and also noted the honours which subsequently fell to him. In May 1867 he introduced him as the author of *Brick and Marble Architecture of Italy* and *Gothic Architecture in Spain*, etc., etc. In August 1868 he quoted in full a description of Street which had appeared in the *Illustrated London News* about two years previously. This sets out the main facts about his life which have been already outlined, and instances several of his most important buildings; it mentions that he obtained second place in the European competition for the cathedral at Lille and one of the prizes in the competition for the Foreign Office. He had been selected as one of the first six architects appointed to compete for re-building the National Gallery, and for designing the new Palace of Justice. As early as 1851 Mr Street had been appointed architect to the diocese of Oxford and at a later period became also diocesan architect for York. He was a Fellow of the Institute of British Architects, a Fellow of the Society of Antiquaries, an Honorary Member of the American Institute of Architects, and of other societies. This article described him as enthusiastically devoted to Gothic art and as never having executed a design in any but his one favourite style. His churches were specially remarkable for purity of style, for evidences of foreign study, always harmoniously assimilated, nor less for honesty and solidity of construction. In May 1869, whilst the Swinton Church was being built, the magazine reported that Mr Street had received his diploma as Foreign Member of the Imperial and Royal Academy of Fine Arts at Vienna. Quoting the *Architect* the note continued: "This recognition of the claims and merits of English architecture in the person of one of our most representative architects, if we may be allowed the term, is a matter for congratulation. Mr. Street is one of the men who have helped to form the character of the art of the present day, and his work, though much of it is no doubt open to criticism, is yet always conscientious, and marked by science, learning and taste. Its peculiarities must be, we should fancy, very strange in the eyes of a Viennese artistic body, and we are the more glad that its undoubted merits are thus recognised."

In the August 1871 magazine, the editor reported that at a meeting of the Royal Academy, held on 29 June, Mr G. E. Street was elected a Royal Academician in the place of Mr Westmacott who had retired. This time the London *Guardian* was quoted to the effect that "Mr. Street's election to the full honours of the Royal Academy will give great satisfaction as a deserved, if tardy, acknowledgement of his abilities." The editor appears to have missed the final honour which was conferred on Street when in May 1881 he was elected President of the Institute of British Architects; it was an honour which, however, he lived only a few months to enjoy. Nor does the Swinton Parish Magazine record the death of the architect of Swinton Church, which occurred on 18 December 1881. But on the west side of the northeast pillar of the tower arch, the vicar caused the following inscription to be incised:

✠ IN : MEMORY : OF
GEORGE : EDMUND : STREET : R.A.
ARCHITECT : OF : THIS : CHURCH
BORN : JUNE : XX : MDCCCXXIV
DIED : DECEMBER : XVIII : MDCCCLXXXI
HIS : BODY : WAS : BURIED : IN
WESTMINSTER : ABBEY
ON : DECEMBER : XXIX : FOLLOWING.
✠

4

THE FAMILY APPROACH

ONE of the most moving pictures of the Reformation in Lancashire is that of the imprisonment of George Marsh in Lancaster Castle from Easter to the autumn of 1554. George Marsh, native of the parish of Deane, near Bolton, was one of the principal evangelists of Protestantism in Lancashire. The circuit of his apostolical preaching was wide, the depth of his influence profound. During the Catholic reaction in the reign of Queen Mary he was arrested and finally condemned in the Bishop's Court in Chester Cathedral on a charge of having "most blasphemously and heretically within the parish of Dean, Eccles, Bolton, Bury, and other parishes within the diocese", preached "directly against the pope's authority, the Catholic Church, the blessed mass, the sacrament of the altar, and many other articles". Marsh was burnt at Spittal Boughton near Chester on 24 April 1555; to him and his martyred colleague, John Bradford, is principally due the firm establishment of Reformation doctrines in the Lancashire towns.

During his imprisonment in Lancaster Castle in the previous summer he used every opportunity both for spreading his teachings in the neighbourhood of the prison and of strengthening the faith of his own converts who lived at a distance by writing them letters. One letter describes how he and his fellow prisoner, Warburton, "every day, kneeling on our knees, read morning and evening prayer with the English Litany, twice, before noon and after, with other prayers, and also read every day certain chapters in the Bible, commonly towards night, with so high and loud a voice that the people without might hear us read, and sit under our windows". The letters written to his convert families in the neighbourhood of his native village were treasured in those families

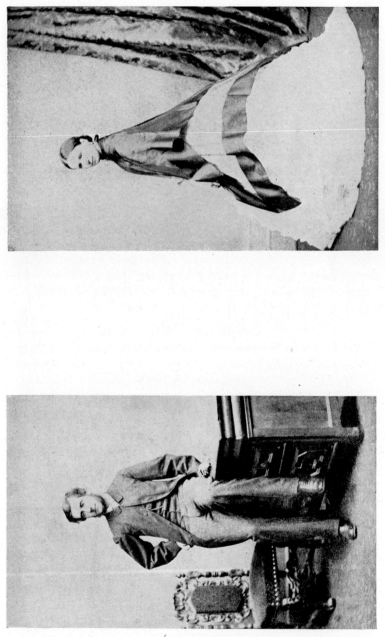

THE YOUNG INCUMBENT AND HIS BRIDE

The Reverend and Mrs H. R. Heywood in the 1860's

THE COMMERCIAL ARISTOCRACY IN THE SERVICE OF THE CHURCH

The Vicarage Family, Moorfield, in the 1880's

(*Back row*) : Jane Davies, Isabella Sherratt, Pollie Beighton, Gertrude (?), Mary Henley
(*Front row*) : Arthur Heywood, Geoffrey Heywood, Mrs Heywood, Miss Dorothy Heywood,
Canon H. R. Heywood, Bernard Heywood, Miss Molly Heywood, Christopher Heywood

ARCHITECTURAL APPROACH

Swinton Chapel, 1792

[*Facing page 171*

for many generations. To the teachings of George Marsh we owe the stalwart Puritanism of the Bolton families of Crompton, Lever, Langley, Bradshaw, Assheton, and Heywood. There is a ravine on the side of Rivington Pike where seats were roughly cut in the rock, and here, it is supposed, the followers of Marsh met in the years of persecution to read the letters of encouragement addressed to them from his prison. After his death the letters continued to be read, and the circumstances of his death rehearsed over again, until George Marsh began to acquire the status of a venerable martyr in their estimation. Nor was miracle lacking to enforce that claim in a manner that savoured rather of medieval superstition than of Protestant enlightenment, for on the pavement of one of the passages in Smithills Hall, where Marsh underwent one of his preliminary examinations before Mr Justice Barton, his followers professed to discover the outline of a man's foot at the place where their master had stamped to emphasize his innocence. It has been stated that Marsh's letters were long preserved in the Puritan homes of the Bolton district, that they were copied by school-boys and handed round the farm-houses and cottages of that moorland country, so as to impress the kind of religion that Marsh taught upon the people of the countryside. It is from such a mould and in such circumstances that the religion of the Heywood family takes its earliest shape.

There is some evidence, and it has always been believed in the family, that the branch of the Heywoods which concerns this story was a cadet branch of the family of Heywood of Heywood Hall, an ancient mansion in the town between Rochdale and Bury. But the Reverend Oliver Heywood, the dissenting divine who alludes to this connection, dismisses it with the pious observation that it is "not as much material what family we are of so that we be of the household of faith", a sentiment which, whilst satisfactory to the dissenting minister, scarcely seems to ring as true of his aspiring baronet descendants in the nineteenth century. The first member of the family to emerge with any clarity from the mists of history is John Heywood, who is described as living at Little Lever, a hamlet in the close vicinity of Bolton, in the reign of Edward VI. His grandson was Richard Heywood, whose house at Little Lever was pillaged by the troops of Prince Rupert during the Civil War in the course of a march from Bolton to York. In the next generation we have Oliver and Nathaniel Heywood, sons of Richard, who took Holy orders and were found amongst the ejected because of the Act of Uniformity at the Restoration.

It is not hard to form a picture of these sturdy Puritan families of Bolton and district in the seventeenth century. We see them tightly knit together by marriage ties, the Levers, the Pilkingtons, the Critchlaws, the Bradshaws, the Cromptons, the Brightmets, the Heywoods, heirs of the Protestant traditions of George Marsh, Commonwealth men, strong to resist oppression when it attempted to coerce their consciences or to silence their favourite preachers. Their rank in society was not so elevated as that of the more prominent Puritan families in and around Manchester. They were men of the moorlands, farming their own lands and weaving their own cloth. Perhaps they might most easily be classed as yeomen, but they were men of considerable wealth, employing all the labour of the district, and, when acting unitedly, as powerful as any one great territorial family. They were united by their veneration for the memory of George Marsh and by their practice of the interminable Puritan devotions which derived from his teaching. "Many days of prayer have I known my father keep among God's people", writes Oliver Heywood, "yea, I remember a whole night. . . ." These were the praying yeomen of Commonwealth Lancashire who cultivated their lands and wove their cloth, and succeeded in imposing an extreme brand of Genevan Protestantism upon large portions of the towns of Rochdale, Bury, and Ashton, and upon the dwellers in the miles of rolling moorland between.

The women were as zealous and influential as the men. Here, for example, is the mother of Oliver Heywood, the wife of Richard, who had been Alice Critchlaw of Longworth near Walmersley. Not only was it her practice to "keep private days and fasts" and to "procure pious preaching ministers for the chapels"; she was also active in demolishing relics of superstition in the countryside. She did her work, we are told, in a "warrantable and peaceable manner" by obtaining leave of the officers to break the windows of the churches near Bolton. This is one of the most astonishing and perhaps delightful pictures in the long Heywood history, the picture of the vigorous Alice Heywood of Commonwealth times, diligently traversing the moorland villages of east Lancashire with a strong stick and delivering shattering blows at each stained glass window she met. It ought perhaps to be noted that her descendants of the nineteenth and twentieth centuries did much to redress the balance, and the celebrated stained-glass-window makers of the later time, Clayton and Bell and the rest, must have been considerably enriched by the orders for their brightly coloured wares which came from the Heywood family. The "painted puppets" destroyed by Alice crept back into their own again in the windows of Swinton, Denstone, and St Augustine's, Pendlebury.

Or here again is the grandmother of Oliver Heywood, born of the family of Hulton. She attended upon the faithful preaching of Mr Hibbert, Puritan minister of the chapelry of Ainsworth, in the parish of Middleton, but like many devout wives she found her husband's piety inadequate. He "being carnal" exercised himself on Sunday afternoons in shooting at the butts on Lomas Moor. The advice and remonstrances of the stricter brethren were tendered in vain, but when Mrs Heywood sought the counsel and prayers of the Reverend Mr Hibbert, the result was much more satisfactory. It happened that old Mr Heywood was attending Bury fair and, the parish church being open for lecturing, he went in and heard the lecture of the eminent preacher, Mr Paget. This time the earnest appeal reached his conscience and his heart; "from that time he set his face heavenward" to the great comfort of his wife and the spiritual welfare of his children. Presumably Sunday afternoons at the butts saw him no more.

Oliver and Nathaniel Heywood, the two sons of Richard Heywood of Little Lever, whose house was pillaged by Prince Rupert's soldiery, are eminent figures in the story of Nonconformity. After taking Holy orders, Oliver became vicar of Coley near Halifax in Yorkshire, and Nathaniel became vicar of Ormskirk in Lancashire on the presentation of the Countess of Derby.

Both were ejected at the Act of Uniformity and adopted the Presbyterian polity in Nonconformity. It is a little difficult to assess the amount of actual privation which these ejected clergymen actually suffered whilst deprived of their livings, for they had many friends both amongst the laity and the conforming clergy, and they did not lack opportunities of preaching both in licensed meeting-houses and sometimes in churches. Oliver Heywood, for example, was ejected from his chapelry of Coley in the parish of Halifax and his excommunication was published in Halifax Church on 2 November 1662. Crossing the border into his native Lancashire he was able to preach for another month until excommunicated by the Bishop of Chester on 7 December. But even after that he was able to exercise an itinerant ministry and to preach in churches and chapels with the approval of the clergyman or wardens; he was even found in his old pulpit of Coley Chapel. Nathaniel Heywood, the vicar of Ormskirk, had also been one of the King's preachers for Lancashire. These men were appointed in Elizabethan times to preach Protestantism in the most Catholic parts of the county for a stipend of £40 or £50 a year. Mr Ernest Axon, who has written about these King's preachers and traces their survival until their abolition in 1845, quotes Calamy's estimate of Nathaniel Heywood as a pious Puritan who was "very useful in saving many persons and families in these parts, from being perverted by the Papists". He was ejected as a Nonconformist in 1662 but continued preaching, privately in houses and publicly in licensed meeting-houses, until his death in 1677. He was buried in the chancel of Ormskirk Church. To his itinerant preaching may be traced in part the Nonconformist congregations of Wigan, Warrington, Liverpool, and Preston.

The next figure of importance in the Heywood family is Arthur Heywood, grandson of the ejected Nathaniel, who commenced business as a banker in Liverpool under the name of A. Heywood and Co. We have now reached the period of the Industrial Revolution, and with the new upsurge of commerce and trade the fortunes of the family enter upon a new chapter. Whilst the earlier recorded names are pre-eminent in the sphere of religion, we now pass to a time when Heywood is a household name in Manchester banking. But it is well to remember that the banking members of the family were shaped by a religious tradition which took its rise from the earliest teachings of the Protestant martyrs of Lancashire, was nourished by the stern Puritanism of the succeeding century, and was sealed by the indignities of the Ejection of 1662.

The banking firm of Arthur Heywood and Co. was founded in Liverpool in 1773. About 1784, on the suggestion of several eminent Manchester merchants, the firm was persuaded to open a branch or agency in Manchester for which premises were obtained in King Street. This first enterprise was not a success; it appears that the chief clerk from Liverpool who was put in charge of the new branch proved inadequate for the work, and although Mr Arthur Heywood himself came over to superintend the business he decided to close down the branch in 1786. In 1788 a fresh attempt was made to establish the Heywood bank in Manchester, this time by two nephews of Arthur, namely Benjamin Arthur and Nathaniel, who were sons of Arthur's brother, Benjamin Heywood. Benjamin Arthur was thirty-three and Nathaniel twenty-eight when this second venture was made. Offices were established in Exchange Street, and business commenced on 26 May. In 1788 the bank of William Allen failed, and the Heywoods bought its premises and removed to Bank Street, adopting as their title, the "Manchester Bank"; here they remained until 1796, when they bought from T. B. Bayley his mansion in St Ann's Square. Offices were built behind the mansion and the building became the permanent home of the Heywood's bank. To-day it stands rebuilt and bearing the name of Williams Deacons' Bank, but the traditional association is still recorded by the additional superscription "Late Heywood Bros. and Co."

Arthur Heywood and his brother Benjamin died in 1795, and Benjamin's two sons, Benjamin Arthur and Nathaniel, now became the proprietors of the Manchester Bank, conducting it under the name of Heywood Brothers and Co. They lived on the premises, worshipped at the near-by Independent Chapel in Cross Street, and became leaders as well of the cultural life of the town as of the business community. The Literary and Philosophical Society provided intellectual society for Manchester residents, and the Billiard Club was the most exclusive social organization. Nathaniel was treasurer of the former and an active member of the latter.

Benjamin Arthur Heywood never married; in 1812 he went to live at Clifton Hall in the Irwell Valley, and in 1825 removed to the country estate of Claremont at Pendleton, a place which now enters our story for the first time and which will be frequently referred to as the headquarters of the Heywood clan. His brother Nathaniel married, in June 1791, the daughter of the eminent Manchester physician, Dr Percival, and continued to live at the bank until his death in 1815; he was buried in Cross Street Chapel. His family consisted of five sons and a daughter, the eldest son, Benjamin, becoming a partner in the bank shortly before his father died. Benjamin is a figure of the greatest importance in this part of our story, for he was the father of Henry Robinson Heywood, the builder of Swinton Church. In 1816 he married Sophia Ann, the daughter of Mr Thomas Robinson of the Woodlands, Cheetham Hill, and the first home of the young married couple was at 41 George Street. In 1820 they removed to Acres Field, near the father's house at Claremont, separated from it only by gardens and pleasure grounds. It is perhaps difficult in these days when rows of box-like houses of red brick have covered these estates, to realize that this neighbourhood between Bolton Road and Eccles Old Road at Pendleton was a stretch of rolling country and park-land of great beauty and charm.[1] Acres Field stood at the crown of the hill, 240 feet higher than Manchester Town Hall, surrounded by lawns and luxurious trees. Farther towards Pendleton on the same side of the road stood the great square bulk of Chaseley, later to become the residence of one of Benjamin Heywood's sons. On both sides of Eccles Old Road, stretching

---

[1] "The high and elevated situation of the old road to Eccles, leading from Pendleton renders it a most interesting neighbourhood. From places contiguous to it, beautiful and extensive prospects may be gained, not only of the towns of Manchester and Salford, which appear to be on a plain, but also of more distant towns. The view is bounded by the Cheshire and Derbyshire chain of hills." (Love and Barton, *Manchester as it is*, 1839.)

from Pendleton to Eccles, were the mansions of wealthy Manchester merchants and manufacturers, the Potters at Buile Hill, in a house designed by Sir Charles Barry, the Armitages at Hope Hall, and others. Small wonder that in its heyday this stretch of road earned the title of the "millionaires' mile", for even in the dereliction of these later democratic days it has not entirely lost the spaciousness and elegance of its early-nineteenth-century prosperity. This right-hand side of Eccles Old Road as one travels towards Eccles was, *par excellence*, the Heywood domain, and though only one of the family houses, Chaseley, now remains, adapted to industrial uses, the names of the former mansions are recalled in the Claremont housing estate and Acresfield Road.

In 1828 Mr Benjamin Arthur Heywood died at the age of seventy-three and his nephew Benjamin came into possession of the Claremont estate, moving thence from Acres Field. His two younger brothers, Thomas and Richard, who had been associated with him in the business, now retired from the bank, leaving Benjamin in sole possession, under the title of Benjamin Heywood and Co. Mrs Nathaniel Heywood, his mother, lived at Acres Field until her death in 1847 at the age of eighty. Of the two younger brothers, Thomas[1] purchased in 1833 from the Moulton-Barrett family the estate of Hope End near Malvern and died there in 1866; Richard bought Banners House near Bath and lived there until he died in 1867. Out of this tangle of complicated family relationships we need only concentrate upon the family of Benjamin Heywood living now at Claremont and rearing a numerous family of whom one is the future builder of Swinton Church.

The later development of Benjamin Heywood's religious outlook was no doubt influenced by his early education. His first school was conducted by the Reverend Edward Lloyd at Fairfield,

---

[1] He had two daughters and a son born at Swinton. The elder daughter, Margaret, married, in 1846, her cousin, Sir T. Percival Heywood, the second baronet, and lived principally at Doveleys. She became a Roman Catholic in later life. The younger, Mary Elizabeth, married, in 1848, the Reverend George Sumner, youngest son of Bishop Charles Sumner of Winchester. He was appointed Bishop of Guildford in 1888. Mary Sumner is justly famous as the founder of the Mothers' Union.

Warrington, and here the heir to the great dissenting traditions of the family appears to have come under the influence of the teaching of the Established Church. At his second school, that of the Reverend John Corrie, in Birmingham, he was under the influence of Dissenters. It is evident that from boyhood he was exposed to these conflicting theological opinions, and even within the family there was by no means unanimity of outlook, for his grandfather, Dr Percival, though he never joined the Church of England, was always a warm supporter of it. In November 1809, debarred by the disabilities from which Dissenters still suffered at Oxford and Cambridge, Benjamin entered Glasgow University, and studied there for two years till in 1811 he returned to take his place in the family business and settled at the Bank House. Changes were taking place at this time in the theological outlook of Cross Street Chapel, the family place of worship.[1] The Arianism of Dr Barnes was giving place to the Unitarianism of Mr Grundy, and when Benjamin married Sophia Robinson in 1816 the wedding took place at the Collegiate Church and the service was conducted by the Reverend Dr Smith, the High Master of the Grammar School.

The *Memoir of Sir Benjamin Heywood* compiled by his brother, Thomas Heywood, F.S.A., and printed for private circulation by Thomas Fargie of Manchester, gives extensive extracts from his private devotional meditations. These reveal him to have been a man of deep religious faith, and in the 1830's it is plain that his beliefs were in complete accord with Christological orthodoxy. At this time he lost three children, all of whom had been baptized at Cross Street, and it may be inferred that the speculations as to time and eternity which these private sorrows evoked failed to derive satisfaction from the Unitarian creed. We are not surprised therefore when we find that, between 1841 and 1842, Sir Benjamin conformed and became a member of the Established Church. His biographer simply states that he exchanged the Unitarian Chapel for the Church of England "in whose services

---

[1] An interesting note on the intellectual climate of Cross St Chapel at this time will be found in a description by Susanna Winkworth quoted in *Elizabeth Gaskell*, by A. B. Hopkins, on p. 47

he found the greatest assistance". Whilst questions of ecclesiastical partisanship scarcely arise in his time, it is safe to assume that his theological conviction became rooted in the High Church tradition which was then renewing its life through the discoveries of the Tractarian fathers. The classical Catholic apologists of ancient and modern times became the constant subjects of his reading. St François de Sales, Thomas à Kempis, the Anglican Caroline divines, Vaughan, Arnold, Pusey, Keble, Newman, Manning, and many others were the guides to his thought, and with some of the Tractarian leaders he was personally acquainted. It was left to his son, Sir Percival, the second baronet, to become one of the foremost leaders of the Anglo-Catholic party in the next generation. A personal friend of Lord Halifax, enthusiastic member of the E.C.U., protagonist of Woodard Schools and particularly of Denstone College near his country home, Sir Percival occupied a position of great influence in the councils of Anglo-Catholicism; his championship of Sidney Faithorn Green, of whose church he became the patron on his father's death, is a valiant though a sorry episode in the story of the Manchester diocese. This championship of the imprisoned former curate of his brother Henry dragged itself out to a dreary conclusion in litigation with Bishop Fraser on the question of patronage. The unfortunate business saddened the lives of all who were concerned with it. It was in this home atmosphere of deepening Tractarian devotion and developing Anglo-Catholic partisanship that Henry Heywood was reared.

It seems a far cry from the iconoclasm of Mrs Heywood, amongst the chapelries of the Bolton moors, and the privations of the ejected Oliver and Nathaniel to the exuberances of Anglo-Catholicism in the first flushes of its adolescent enthusiasm. It was a transformation of sentiment in the Heywood tradition upon which newspaper critics did not sometimes fail wryly to animadvert. Yet it was a transformation by no means uncommon in the Victorian scene. If the Oxford Movement produced a fairly substantial trickle of recruits to swell the renaissance of the Roman Church in England, it is equally true that the Established Church was immeasurably strengthened by the accession of wealthy and able Nonconformists who joined its ranks. We shall not suppose that it was because they could not bear the strictures of their critics such as Arnold and Bagehot. *Insulae in insula* they may have been from the broad view of English cultural life, but many of them were nevertheless exceedingly proud little islands. We have noted how proud the Philips family remained of their independence of the aristocratic tradition, and the insularity which had been forced upon them was the result of many generations of the cramping restrictions of exclusive and intolerant legislation. There were probably some Dissenters who conformed for the sake of public advantage, but there were many others who, like the Philips family, remained Dissenters and others, like the Heywoods, who conformed with as much show of principle as that of their seventeenth-century ancestors whose conscience led them out with the "ejected" of 1662.

This phenomenon is well discussed by Katherine Chorley in her *Manchester Made Them.* She believes that the Nonconformity of the *haute bourgeoisie* of the later nineteenth century of which she writes would have withstood any number of penal laws, yet deriving from such a tradition she noted that the uncles and aunts of her childhood mostly went to church, and with complete sincerity. The reason for their conformity, so she believes, was the alluring beauty and majesty of the liturgy; the Church of England had been cemented by Cranmer's prose. A further consideration is that Unitarians, perhaps alone amongst historic Dissenters, suffered no loss of caste in attending the Unitarian Chapel, because, as she supposes, some of the leading—and, we may say, richest—Manchester families happened, like our Philipses and Heywoods, to be Unitarians. So, she concludes, when a Unitarian went over to the Church of England, it was presumably from conviction, though she suspects that the lure of Cranmer's prose may occasionally have had something to do with the conviction. No one who reads Sir Benjamin Heywood's private meditations could doubt that it was the most earnest conviction, and conviction alone, which led to his conforming: and no one would be surprised that in that family, with its habits of regular family devotion, and with the deeply impressive pattern set by the father, one of the sons would naturally turn his thoughts to the ministry of the Anglican Church as his life's vocation.

We have seen that sympathy and enlightenment were the main answers of the rich and privileged middle class to the problem of working-class wretchedness in the nineteenth century. Enlightenment was to be disseminated through education, and education was not to stop short at what the National and British Schools could do for children. Educational opportunities were to be offered to adults, and one of the favourite modes of conveyance was the Mechanics' Institute. The Mechanics' Institute began in Manchester in 1824 at a meeting presided over by Benjamin Heywood. Some of the most eminent men of the town joined the original committee of twenty-two, and the Institute held its first meeting on 30 March 1825, when Heywood delivered his first presidential address. The address sets forward the objects of the Institute:

That the instruction of mechanics and artisans in those branches of science and art, which are of practical application in the exercise of their several trades, is of the utmost importance, making them more thoroughly to understand their business, giving them greater degree of skill in the practice of it, and leading them to improvement with a greater security of success.

The Institute was supported by the subscriptions of wealthy friends and by the contributions of the students themselves. The former class supplied the directors, and this oligarchical form of government at first caused some controversy in which the great Brougham himself shared by contributing a pamphlet on the popular side entitled *The Education of the People.* Eventually, however, the basis of government was broadened by the inclusion of representatives of the second class of subscriber on the governing body. The sum of £4,000 was subscribed at the start for the purchase of land and the erection of a building. In 1830 it appears that modifications were made in the original ambitious scheme of instruction. Heywood in his address of that year had to confess to some disappointment that the first ideals of the founders were slow of realization. He had thought that the study of physical

13

science would essentially contribute to moral advancement by its tendency to impress the mind with the infinite wisdom and goodness which the Creator had displayed in all his works. He had to confess that he had been disappointed. It had been necessary to modify the original plan by adapting the instruction more to the taste and capacity of the working classes, to make it more elementary and more entertaining, and yet to point to the wisdom and benevolence of the Creator as the end of all physical research. He wanted popular lectures on a series of subjects which he suggested in some detail and which embraced the security of property, the improved condition of the working classes, the advantage of machinery, the regulation of the wages of labour, the advantage of friendly societies and banks, and the operation of the Poor Laws. It is not impossible to see, in this programme of sociological study which the wealthy banker insisted upon setting before the emerging working classes, the raw material for the socialist philosophy of life which the working classes were soon to embrace so avidly. It is interesting to note that when the wealthy middle classes were most philanthropically inclined, they were in fact sowing the seeds of their own ultimate destruction. But Benjamin himself could visualize a time, as he wrote to his son Oliver in 1854, "when the working people will get the upper hand". It was, to some extent, these Mechanics' Institutes which had opened their eyes to the possibility that the "upper hand" might some day be theirs.

But it was not only by way of sociological study that Heywood desired to widen the horizons of the working classes. He wanted to see a new and more active spirit infused into the institution to promote the amusements of the working classes out of doors. He wanted to see, in the neighbourhood of the town, public walks, where rich and poor, high and low, might enjoy a summer evening. He wanted plots of ground enclosed where "some of the manly games of our ancestors" might be revived. He wanted swimming baths, and holiday excursions organized by the Institute. When he built his own little philanthropic colony centring on the church of St John's, Miles Platting, complete with baths, he was disappointed to find that the baths were not received by the population with the enthusiasm which they merited. "The improvement of the working classes", he concluded, in his presidential address in 1832, "is an object of paramount and urgent importance; and as it is the duty of every man to mark out for himself some sphere of active usefulness to his fellow-men, I would select the furtherance of this object for mine."

The Hammonds in *The Bleak Age* suggest that these Mechanics' Institutes, useful though they were, failed to accomplish all that was expected of them. Perhaps, as the Manchester records suggest, they flew too high and attempted advanced instruction for artisans who had not the bare rudiments of reading and writing. Perhaps the intellectual fare which they offered was too strong a meat for workpeople whose bodies were jaded after long days of physical toil. Perhaps, too, in certain quarters, there was resentment at a suggestion that the institutes were "supported by patronage and conducted by patronage".

In 1851, by which time Sir Benjamin had transferred his active interest in the Manchester Institute to his son Oliver, we find a comment in one of his letters that "the character of the thing is changed". He was glad "for old sake's sake" that Oliver was present at some social function, but it was somewhat humiliating that the sober speeches should be the stopgaps between the acts. It suggested a crack in the age of seriousness. But if their influence was not as widespread as their founders had hoped, there can be no doubt that many artisans must have taken advantage of what was offered and have improved their knowledge, and perhaps their position in life, by attendance at this early form of night-school.

Henry Heywood came to manhood a good deal later than the period of his father's interest in Mechanics' Institutes. Yet we may be quite certain that he grew up against a background in which education, both juvenile and adult, was synonymous with enlightenment. As a clergyman, in later life, he advanced children's education by his assiduous attention to the work of the Church day-schools which were maintained and added to during his incumbency. But by one parish organization he may be regarded as continuing the sort of adult education which his father had initiated in the Mechanics' Institute. The Mutual Improvement Society, which was founded in 1881 originally for young men, was typical of an association which grew up in many parts of the country during the century for the spreading of useful knowledge. The Hammonds refer to these societies, some of them ephemeral, but others maintaining an organized life for many years. Working men banded themselves together to meet regularly "to improve themselves by mutual intercourse". The Leeds Mutual Improvement Society was started by four young men in 1844, and progressed from elementary lessons in reading, writing, grammar, and arithmetic, to lectures on chemistry and French. It is a matter of some pride to Swintonians that their Mutual Improvement Society has continued, without a break, to this present day; its members may trace their lineage back through Henry Heywood, its founder, to Benjamin his father, with his social idealism and his conviction that the enlightenment of the working classes could be accomplished by popular education and, for adults, by the Mechanics' Institute.

Benjamin Heywood's parliamentary career has already been referred to in a previous chapter. It was short and by no standards exciting, though he showed considerable dexterity in avoiding the attempts of Mr "Orator" Hunt to push him further in a Radical direction than he was prepared to go. The County of Lancaster at this time returned two members, Lord Stanley and Mr Wilson Patten of Bank Hall, Warrington. In 1830 the agitation for parliamentary reform was reaching its peak, and on 22 March of the following year the Government of Earl Grey managed to carry a Reform Bill by a majority of one vote. But in April an amendment that the total number of members for England should not be changed was carried by 299 votes to 291, and Mr Wilson Patten voted with the majority against the Government. He having thus disgraced himself, it is not to be wondered at that Mr Patten was rejected by the freeholders of the county, who now cast around for a candidate who could be thoroughly trusted in this matter of reform. Manchester, Salford, Oldham, Rochdale, Bolton, Bury, Blackburn, and Warrington were expecting enfranchisement and two reliable members were needed to make sure that their aspirations were implemented. The Manchester committee of freeholders approached Benjamin Heywood on 28 April, and on the following day resolved that "from his known principles and integrity" he was admirably qualified to represent the county on that momentous occasion. Heywood accepted the honour thus thrust upon him, in a speech of becoming modesty. The next day, at Liverpool, he pledged himself to support reform, and promised to work for the abolition of all commercial monopolies. During the following month electioneering was carried on in the principal Lancashire towns, and the popular reform candidate was greeted everywhere with triumphal arches, flags, bands, processions, and enthusiastic crowds. On 9 May the candidate and his supporters moved in procession from Leaf Square, Salford, to Lancaster, where he and Lord Stanley were returned as members for the county. On 11 May the cavalcade returned through the countryside amidst the usual scenes of unbounded enthusiasm, though the popular new member does not seem to have taken particular care to notice the somewhat subversive sentiments which were apparently emblazoned on some of the banners of his supporters. For the last lap of this triumphal procession, the horses were removed from his carriage, and it was drawn by the people to his home in St Ann's Square.

There were speeches *en route* and speeches at the beginning and end of these progresses, the details of which may be studied in contemporary issues of the *Manchester Guardian*. It is pathetic to note the high hopes of the people which accompanied the passage of the Reform Act; so much was expected from it, and the slowness with which the wheels of social reform began to move in the new parliaments encouraged the development of Chartism, whose supporters had been amongst Heywood's keenest advocates. On 17 June 1831 he took his seat in the House, and was an assiduous attender at all the debates which resulted, after many curious vicissitudes, in the Bill's passage and the receiving of the Royal Assent on 7 June 1832. Parliament was prorogued on 16 August and dissolved on 3 December 1832. It had been a time of particular strain for all members, and Heywood soon realized that he was overtaxing his strength. He left a memorandum amongst his papers to show that on eighty-five occasions the House sat until hours extending between 1 a.m. and 5.15 a.m. In declining health he struggled through the session, busying himself on important matters including the new division of his county into two county parliamentary divisions and eight new boroughs. His correspondence increased to alarming proportions, and he served on two Select Committees, on "the State of the Silk Trade" and "the Factory Bill". His brushes in the House of Commons with Henry Hunt have already been noted, and it is likely that such debating fracas were little to the taste of such a peace-loving character. At all events it soon became evident to him that he was in no way suited to a continued parliamentary life and, in June 1832, he notified the chairman of his Manchester election committee that on grounds of health he did not propose to present himself again as a candidate for county representation.

His interest in parliamentary affairs remained unabated until the end of his life. He presided at the dinner given on 27 December 1832 in honour of the return of Messrs Philips and Thomson as the first members for Manchester. He entertained Lord Brougham, Lord John Russell, Lord Palmerston, and Lord Morpeth at Claremont and took the greatest interest in James's (his youngest brother's) parliamentary career. On 16 June 1838 a letter which we may regard as not altogether unexpected was penned by Lord Melbourne at Downing Street: "My dear Sir—Your station in society and the recollection of the political services which you rendered during Lord Grey's administration, entitle you, in my opinion, to some public acknowledgment and some mark of distinction. This disposition is strengthened by my own personal esteem, and if it should agree with your feelings, I should be happy to ask Her Majesty to confer upon you the dignity of baronet." Very sensibly, Benjamin Heywood did not feel the scruples of the Philips family; Lord Melbourne's sentiments were agreeable to his feelings, and on 28 June 1838, he was gazetted, with many others, on the occasion of Her Majesty's coronation. Middle-class commerce had "arrived". With a suburban home at Claremont, a seaside house at West Hey, Blackpool, a country estate at Doveleys in Staffordshire, and a town house in Hyde Park Gardens, where their carriages mingled with those of the Philipses—still dissenting and untitled—the Mildmays, the Dorchesters, the Roseberys, and the Tecks, the middle-class bankers had achieved that sublime apotheosis amongst the county families upon which John Morley commented in 1868. It was an astonishing consummation for the descendants of the ejected divine who regarded it as little material what family he was of. But it was typical of the march of English society, and an achievement of which far more men than Sir Benjamin Heywood were less worthy.

We must now turn from the public life of the first baronet to his private and home life which is portrayed in his brother's memoir, and there we are permitted some intimate glimpses of the environment of a typical wealthy, middle-class Victorian home and of the influences which played upon the childhood and upbringing of the future church builder. Sir Benjamin and his wife had fourteen children, of whom six died in early life. Seven of them, namely Elizabeth, Sarah, Thomas Percival, Samuel, Oliver, Mary Isabella, and Arthur Henry, were born at their parents' first married home in George Street. The three following, who all died in 1836, Sophia Caroline, Annie, and Benjamin, were born at Acres Field, and the four last, Edward Stanley, William, Henry Robinson in 1833, and Charles James at Claremont. It was an idyllic home life for these children whose father's devoted care and interest is most clearly marked in his letters. The family headquarters was at Claremont, Pendleton, of easy access to the bank and to Manchester interests; in 1831 Doveleys was bought, a simple farm-house on a little estate near Ellastone in Staffordshire. This property became the home of Thomas Percival, the eldest son, after his marriage to his cousin, Margaret Heywood, daughter of Thomas Heywood of Hope End, in 1846. The simple farm-house received many additions, and, after a serious fire, was rebuilt and enlarged to an ungainly size which proved unmanageable after the Second World War, and compelled the family to dispose of it to the less dignified though more edifying uses of an approved school. There was a London house at 9 Hyde Park

Gardens, which succeeded a previous house in Dover Street, and in 1838 Sir Benjamin built West Hey at a newly discovered fishing village called Blackpool on the Lancashire coast where the air was good, thus contributing an early mite to the growth of the future grand Babylon of Lancashire pleasure-seeking. The year was passed between periodic visits to these family houses, and the delights which they afforded to the growing young folk are plain in the letters.

The varied interests of the father and his family become increasingly vivid as the letters come thicker in the *Memoir* in the late 1840's and the years following, until Sir Benjamin's death in 1865. Business and active parliamentary life have long been left behind; it is with the concerns of his growing family that the father finds the greatest pleasure. His sons become his confidants, and every plan of social reform, every political and economic idea is discussed with them. In 1843 he is made a Fellow of the Royal Society in recognition of his services to political economy, science, and social progress, and in the year 1847 a letter to his eldest son reveals some of the practical manifestations of his interest in social progress. He went, he says, with his brother-in-law, to inspect the Miles Platting property, an estate in a dreary neighbourhood a little way out of Manchester along the Oldham Road which had come into the family's possession in discharge of a bank debt. The improvement is very great; paving, flagging, and draining have made such a difference that it has half reconciled him to the expense. A school is in process of building, which it is proposed to fit out after the Dukinfield model, with a gallery, desks, and an assistant-teacher. Winstanley, the agent for the property in the district, is in high favour. Five years later came the request from the diocesan authorities for the site for a new church, and the beginning of the St John's, Miles Platting, enterprise, to which reference is constantly made.

By 1848, Harry and Charlie are at school at Harrow—their elder brother, Percival, had been educated privately—and the return of the boys for the holidays is an eagerly awaited delight. His letters regale these two youngest lads with sound religious advice; he is delighted with the good reports he has received on their accounts, but warns them that they are not to think of themselves more highly than they ought to think, but to go on striving in their good course.

Here is a delightful family holiday on the North Wales coast in April 1850. They examine the engineering details of the tubular bridge on an expedition to the Menai Straits, and at Carnarvon the boys climb to the top of the Eagle Tower. The day concludes with father reading aloud scenes from Pickwick, including the story of Mrs Leo Hunter's fancy breakfast: it had begun with Scripture reading and family prayers. The next day they went to service in Bangor Cathedral— it was two hours before the sermon was reached—and in the afternoon there was a drive to Beaumaris. In the following year they are holiday-making at Bowness in the Lake District, and on 15 August 1851, "Henry and Gibson are gone on ponies to Helvellyn."

By this period the older end of the family are grown up and mature, and are taking on the responsibilities which were formerly associated with the father. Sir Benjamin declined the shrievalty of Lancashire in 1849, but he was delighted when his eldest son became sheriff in 1851. It was a conspicuous year, the occasion of Queen Victoria's visit to Manchester, and Percival occupied one of the open carriages which attended the Queen in procession from her lodging at Worsley Hall to the ceremonial receptions at Salford and Manchester. "All must be done handsomely," writes the father to the son, "and I am sure you will be a pattern sheriff."

Social problems are gravely occupying the father and the elder sons as the century draws towards its mid-point. Sir Benjamin was in London and shared the anxiety of all thoughtful folk as the Chartist movement worked towards its climax in 1848. He saw and reported to his sons the special preparations which were made by the middle classes to meet the threat to law and order. But he approached the social problem with a greater degree of sympathy than many who regarded Chartism as a mere revolutionary threat to be subdued with the severest measures of force. His Miles Platting experiences had shown him that behind the grumbling discontent there were legitimate grievances for which the middle classes had to help to find remedies if there was to be any hope of social peace. "Sympathy and Enlightenment" were, to his mind, the larger part of the answer. Oliver, his second son, has to deliver a speech in Miles Platting in October 1849, and Sir Benjamin offers him advice about its contents. Let him point to the improved condition of the working classes and the hopeful prospect in front of them. Let him appeal to their good sense and intelligence, and dwell a little upon his confidence in them. He may refer to the cholera and show how needful it is that the people should be better cared for, in and about their dwellings, and that they themselves should be mindful of temperance and cleanliness. He had been reading, he said, Richson's education bill; he had read it carefully and with frequent interruption of objections. He criticized it because it virtually extinguished voluntary effort; free education, which was its fundamental principle, he was not yet prepared to think desirable.

Turn now again to the younger end of the family and particularly to Henry, the future church builder. He is eighteen in 1851 and in his last few months at Harrow. It is evident from his father's letters that the boy's ideas are turning towards the ministry of the Church as his life's work. His father is pleased to hear that he is a member of the school debating society. It is capital practice for him, and he must not mind "trips" at first. Henry must be careful early against the great hindrance, namely of thinking how he will appear to others or what success he will have. Sir Benjamin referred in the same letter to the fact that Mr Greenwood, the classical professor at Owens College, was dining at Acres Field that night and sleeping at Claremont. A few days previously he had given the introductory lecture at the opening of the college. It was on the value of Latin and Greek as a mental training, and he had combated energetically the idea that the classics had no sort of connection with the pursuits of a great commercial community; on the other hand, they were most important, to those absorbed in the *material* and the *present*, as a counteracting influence. This letter concludes with a reference to a life of a young Scotch minister, McCheyne, which had been lent to Sir Benjamin by a tenant, Mr Robertson, a missionary. This book described a pattern clergyman as "a Boanerges and a

Barnabas in one". "So", adds the father, "you see what you must aim at." The "pattern clergyman" had already begun to take shape in young Henry's mind as his life's ideal.

In 1852 Henry is at Trinity College, Cambridge. His father writes soon after his arrival there that everything seems to have begun very happily and that Henry will be quite at his ease with the examination over. His elder brother, Percival, had sent them a sketch of his room, and many little details of what was and would be around him, which presented a very pleasant picture. Most happy and appropriate, as Percival said, was the Collect for the eighteenth Sunday after Trinity for the event of his entrance on his college career, and it would often, he was sure, mingle with his prayers. His father wished he could have seen him at chapel in his surplice. In the spring he hoped to do so. He wanted to hear how his son liked the tutor who had been recommended; he felt that his congeniality was a great point and one not often attained in a college tutor.

How unmistakably are religion and domestic life intermingled here, when the boy's departure for Cambridge is linked up with the relevance of a prayer book collect! Yet this Anglican devotion interpenetrating the family life at every point is continually cropping up in the letters. Even a stone seat, we may note, at the country home at Doveleys, is inscribed with the last verse of Keble's hymn for Septuagesima Sunday. Contemporary religious topics occupy much space in the father's letters to his son at college. In October 1853 he describes how interested he has been in the newspaper abstract of the Bishop of Oxford's sermons at Denton. The bishop had said: "The slumbering energies of the Church must be roused in Manchester, the masses must be got at, the rigidity of external forms must be relaxed, short services, moving addresses must be employed." Sir Benjamin quite agrees with him, but he had not expected such prescriptions from him; he thinks the sermon will be published by and by. "To rouse the slumbering energies of the Church in Manchester, to get at the masses"—that was what the Manchester bishopric had been created for, that was the whole object of the work of Prince Lee and his successors in the episcopate. It is significant that no parish

priest more energetically than Henry Heywood assisted his bishop
in this great work of evangelizing the industrial masses. Sixteen
years only after he had received this letter from his father, a great
new parish church had been built at Swinton, district churches
and schools were on the way, the whole life of a growing suburban
area was being shaped by the mounting enthusiasm of energetic
Churchmanship. How much of that enthusiasm had been infused
into the mind of an impressionable youth, we may wonder, by
the letters and words, and above all, the affectionate example of a
completely sincere and devoted father?

At this same time, in 1853, Sir Benjamin writes to his eldest
son that he and his daughter Sarah are reading together the first
volume of Dr Arnold's published sermons with great interest.
The sermons contain from time to time words of guidance to
parents in the early religious training of their children, which he
thinks that Percival and his wife would value. He has also received
from his daughter-in-law one of Dr Pusey's sermons which he
describes as "an old friend". To Henry, in November, he writes
that he was much interested in Professor Maurice's pamphlet to
Dr Jelf on the author's removal from the chair of theology in
King's College because of some heretical exposition of the word
eternal in Scripture. The pamphlet was more on the injustice
done to him than on the interpretation of the word, for which it
referred to other writings. The eternity of suffering, commented
Sir Benjamin, had ever been a difficulty with him, and it would
be a relief to him to be able to believe that the word might be
otherwise construed. The temper of the pamphlet was not gentle,
but the question would of course now become a public one. On
the following day, writing again to Henry, he speaks of the influence which Bishop Selwyn had exercised over his son. There is
evidence here that it was the powerful personality of the great
New Zealand bishop which was impelling Henry in the direction
of ordination. There is an inference that Henry had expressed the
desire to work in the mission field, but his father indicates his
disapproval of his seeking his usefulness abroad; the masses at
home were far more urgent. Sir Benjamin visualized for his son a
sphere like Mr Richardson's at Miles Platting, or Mr Dewes's at

Pendlebury, which stood foremost in his mind as a field for
earnest labourers. Even for such a field as this, however, his father
did not think that Henry was physically adapted for any length
of time. It would be a wholesome training, but his mother had
always felt that Henry had a constitution which needed strengthening, and his father thought that his work must be tempered
to his fitness for it. He had a happy recollection of Bishop Stanley,
who had occupied a pleasant family living at Alderley in Cheshire
and afterwards became Bishop of Norwich; Stanley's object had
been to serve his people, ever amongst them, loving and beloved.
Sir Benjamin believed that his thoughts for his son had been in a
station like that, but he would be guided aright when the time
came. In the event, Henry's destiny was not to serve the Church
overseas, in spite of his admiration for Bishop Selwyn, but something much more like that which his father had visualized for him,
though the pastures were not to be the preserves of the Cheshire
aristocracy but the somewhat drab streets of a Lancashire
industrial suburb.

In February 1854 Sir Benjamin wrote to Henry from his
daughter's home at Caldy Manor; they were staying there "over
Monday, perhaps till Thursday, for we shall not move on Ash
Wednesday". Even the travelling arrangements of a devout
Church of England family in mid-Victorian times were con-
ditioned by the ecclesiastical calendar. In July of the same year he
takes up social topics again with Oliver, one of the older sons.
During a holiday at Grasmere he had been reading an article in
the *Edinburgh Review* entitled, "The Great Social Problem",
dealing with the relations between labour and capital. It was a subject never far removed from Sir Benjamin's cogitations. He thought
it a great subject for his beloved Mechanics' Institutes to take, for
he felt all the importance of instructing the working classes in that
matter. But no teaching would prevent strikes at certain seasons,
any more than it prevented drunkenness. The natural man acted
against conviction when temptation came, and in that case circumstances shook conviction, and intimidation often overpowered it.
The time might come when the working people would get the
upper hand; but he hoped it would not be yet. He thought the

reviewer was hardly just to the working classes in some points and certainly he kept out of view their employers' errors.

The principal interest in 1855 was the building of St John's Church, Miles Platting. In February 1852 he had been approached by the Diocesan Church Building Society for land to build a church. They wanted his only frontage to the main Oldham Road and he gladly gave it them, for the enlightenment of this dreary congested area was a project he had long had in mind. He felt that with a church, bath, and washhouses, schools, and mechanics' institution, some impression would be made on the place. It seems as though he also provided the money for the church building, for in February 1855 he reported to his eldest son that the four estimates for the church had come in, all being reliable contractors, and the lowest estimate had secured the job. Mr Gregan was preparing the contract, the ground was to be broken that month, and the first stone was to be laid the next month. In the May of that year he was reading the Bishop of New Zealand's Cambridge sermons; he had a great admiration for this man who had nearly allured his son overseas, but he did not always quite agree with him. His zeal, he thought, was somewhat too exclusive, but he always quickened his readers both to shame and better purpose. He was thinking of his son Henry that morning as he was reading, he said, and hoping that his labour would be among the heathen at home. He wished there was a Bishop Selwyn to take their cause in hand. Perhaps, father-like, he hoped that his son, Henry, might occupy that role.

In 1854 Thomas Percival Heywood records in his private journal how he paid a visit to Cambridge in November to hear Bishop Selwyn preach. On the Sunday Henry and Charlie had secured seats in St Mary's to hear the Bishop of New Zealand's sermon. St Mary's was crowded in every part, and so was the Town Hall on the following day when the bishop spoke again at great length at a meeting of the S.P.G. He called on Selwyn afterwards and had ten minutes' talk with him, finding him grateful for the promise he had made him of £100 a year for five years. When Selwyn died in 1878, Sir Thomas Percival Heywood, as he was then, was one of the pall-bearers with Lord Powys, Lord

Hatherton, W. E. Gladstone, Sir William Martin, the Provost of
Eton, and Archdeacon Allen, and always spoke of this as one of
the greatest honours he ever had.

By October 1855 the new church was practically finished. The
chosen clergyman, Mr Richardson, was regarded as a fortunate
find and bells were mentioned as "rather a vision". On 12 December Sir Benjamin wrote to Henry acknowledging a birthday
greeting—sixty-two years since he first opened his eyes in the
old original bank in St Ann's Square. The first lesson on Sunday
morning came home very much to him, "What could have been
done more to my vineyard?" Who can doubt that the influence
of George Marsh is still there and the blood of his Puritan ancestors still runs strong in the veins of the elderly banker? Each
day is still filled with devotion, and his whole life regarded as a
piece of carefully entrusted stewardship. The conclusion of the
Miles Platting enterprise marks one of the spiritual ambitions of
his life safely accomplished. The church, he writes, is intended to
be consecrated on 27 December, and they are busy completing.
The bell, to come from London, is note B, and it is reported as
"solemn and animated".

At the Lent ordination in February 1856 Henry Robinson
Heywood was ordained deacon in Worcester Cathedral on a title
to the parish of Southam, the Reverend Temple Hillyard, M.A.,
being rector, in the diocese of Worcester and county of Warwick.
The family approach to the building of the Victorian period piece
is rapidly converging with its three other avenues upon Street's
achievement of 1869.

His father wrote to him on the eve of his ordination; Henry had
been very much in his thoughts, and he was longing to know that
he was more at ease. Now all would be happy with him. They
would be together in spirit at his ordination on the morrow and
would remember him in their prayers. Another chapter of his life
was closed and a new one begun, bright and hopeful. It was a
great pleasure to him to give the new direction to his letter, and
he hoped that it might be the first his son received. He prayed
that God's guidance and blessing might be ever with him and
their guardian angel ever about his path. During that summer Sir

Benjamin paid a visit to the pleasant Warwickshire town of Southam where Henry was serving his first curacy. He found everything most happy, and wrote that he felt as if Henry could hardly have entered upon his new career more advantageously or more agreeably. Mr Hillyard, the rector, was particularly congenial. Henry always retained a hearty respect for his first rector, and Hillyard was one of the special preachers whom he brought to Swinton during the celebrations which marked the consecration of the new church in October 1869. Sir Benjamin considered that the opportunity of regular and quiet reading to strengthen his son for an advancing position was very valuable. They were also much pleased with the house. It could not have been in a better situation, for Henry's duty and the taste and comfort within had quite impressed his father. Lissey, his sister, and Henry together had certainly been very successful. Henry had had everything beautifully arranged for his visitors and had quite a knack in the disposition of the things in his rooms; visitors would say how comfortable and suitable and tasteful everything was. On the following day, Sir Benjamin was to hear Henry for the first time when the young curate was to read prayers in the morning and to do the whole duty in the afternoon. On the previous day they had driven to Leamington. He intended to call with Henry on Dr Jephson, who was now blind but well; they had seen the statue of the celebrated physician in the Jephson Gardens.

It is a pleasant picture of the life of a mid-Victorian curate whose lot had fallen in a fair ground. One thing more was required to complete his happiness, and that was his marriage, which took place in 1858, to Ella Sophia, eldest daughter of the Reverend William Gibson, rector of Fawley, Hants, and granddaughter of Bishop Sumner of Winchester. It was an idyllic union which was broken by Henry's death in 1895: his widow survived into a different age, continuing to live at the old home at Moorfield, Swinton, until her death in 1928 at the age of ninety. Shortly afterwards, the new East Lancashire trunk road swept through the grounds. Moorfield was demolished, and no single trace now remains of the house from which the Reverend Henry Heywood and his wife exercised their beneficent influence over the lives of their parishioners for so many years. From the very start it was a partnership not only in exceptional domestic bliss but also in public service. At the announcement of the engagement the union had been blessed by the old baronet's approval. "Henry's happiness is engrossing to-day," he wrote in November 1857, "and we are writing to Fawley with a cordial response. It comes to my mind with full satisfaction." After their first year of married life he could write that "Harry and Ella are so happy at Caldy that they remain there and give up their Lake journey."

Henry proceeded M.A. in 1860, and his father wrote to him expressing his great satisfaction that this final event of his college career had been accomplished. He hoped that he would go on his way rejoicing and that Ella would be happy. He gathered that Henry had found various old friends when he had stayed at his college to take his degree, and that he had graced the dons' table. He reported to his son that their good pastor, presumably the vicar of St John's, Pendlebury, had visited Claremont with his daughter on the previous night. After discussing, with suitable propriety, biblical prophecies on the eve of fulfilment, they had placed him in the armchair and read a chapter of the *Minister's Wooing*, which unfortunately called forth his disapprobation. Sir Benjamin feared that he would think them doubtful friends for his daughters. Even the Heywoods found it hard to support the stiffness which was associated with clerical behaviour in some circles at this period of the Victorian Church revival.

We are allowed one or two last glimpses at the bank before this delightful collection of letters comes to an end. To his brother Thomas, Sir Benjamin wrote in January 1860 that he did not think that the business was ever in greater prosperity than at that time, or the people so well employed and paid; nor did he see anything to hinder its continuance. They were in no excess. Their own business went on increasing. They had an excellent working staff, and his four sons were pattern bankers. He was very thankful to have been permitted to see their well-doing. In October 1860 arrangements were in train for the substitution of Heywood Brothers and Co., for Benjamin Heywood and Co., a reversal which, as Sir Benjamin said, was very happy to him and which, until lately, he little thought he would live to see. In August 1862 he inspected the premises of the Manchester and Salford Bank in Mosley Street. He was much struck with the magnitude and convenience and luxury of all the arrangements and could not but smile as he compared them, in his mind, with his own early memories of St Ann's Street. He went down to the safe and to the lavatories, etc., and up to the board room. When Sir Benjamin retired from active participation in the bank in 1860, his sons Oliver, Arthur Henry, Edward Stanley, and Charles James were the partners, but in 1874 the business was transferred to the Manchester and Salford Bank whose luxurious premises had so impressed their father. At this time private banking was certainly reaching its zenith. The Heywood family had established a considerable fortune by careful and conservative business in the banking world, but they had not attained to the dizzy heights of Samuel Jones Loyd, whose family wealth had originated in the successful bank which his father Lewis Loyd had founded in Manchester. Lewis himself, long before his death, was accounted one of the richest commoners in England, with a property estimated in the aggregate at three millions. His son, who was created Lord Overstone in 1850, amassed a fortune which far exceeded that figure. In the *Great Governing Families of England, 1865*, the author states that "the chief of the new commercial aristocracy is supposed to be Lord Overstone, one of the wealthiest subjects in the world, his fortune being estimated at five millions". This is the *ne plus ultra* of Manchester banking; it was not achieved by the Heywood family, but they laboured in the same tradition and were not very far behind it.

In 1859 Henry Heywood resigned the curacy of Southam and returned to be curate of his home parish of St John, Pendlebury. Perhaps it was felt that he owed the duty of being near to his ageing father; perhaps as a Lancashire man he believed that his duty was to work in his native Lancashire. He and his wife established themselves in a house in Swinton Park, and, in spite of one offer which at first seemed tempting, never left the neighbourhood for the rest of his life. By 1861 Henry had been in orders for five years, and it was obvious that a clergyman with such substantial advantages of family connection, education, and ample means would not be long in being offered a parish of his own. There appears to have been some suggestion in 1861 that he should have taken charge of a new district in Patricroft which was about to be carved out of the parish of Eccles. His father did not feel, however, that he had a call to Patricroft, but professed to a trust that a fitting charge would present itself in due time. Henry, he said, could not be in better waiting condition than he was, and he would like to talk with him of his many thoughts on the matter. The summer of 1861 passed happily for the young people at Pendlebury. In June, Sir Benjamin reported that he had had some pleasant talk with the Bishop of Winchester, Henry's grandfather-in-law; he had come to call—perhaps at an awkward moment—"after the half-hour gong had sounded". In this letter, which was to his son Oliver, he mentioned that Henry, with Richard Barton who had married his daughter Lissey, had heard Mr Boyd in the morning of the previous Sunday and Dr Goulburn in the afternoon: Dr Goulburn stood first in their estimation. On the Saturday Blondin, the famous tight-rope walker, had been their attraction. On 18 August he was congratulating his clerical son on his twenty-eighth birthday, and reminding him that it was on a Sunday that he first saw the light, the eleventh after Trinity. In October he was writing to Henry about his sermon reading; Dr Vaughan's sermons had interested him much, and he was glad he had published them because there was an earnestness and freshness and thought in them which were quite stirring and very valuable. Sir Benjamin and his daughter had interrupted Vaughan's sermons with a volume of Dr Thompson's (the bishop elect) Lincoln's Inn Sermons, which, the little they had read, made him rejoice in his appointment.

But December 1861 brought Henry an interesting offer of a benefice about which Sir Benjamin wrote fully to Oliver in two long letters. Lord Spencer had offered him the vicarage of Priors Marston, about five miles from Southam. Mr Hillyard, the rector of Southam, had written in most delighted and affectionate terms, wishing Henry near him again, and so the two of them had driven over to Priors Marston to investigate. They found it very pleasantly situated, with a venerable, dilapidated church, of great interest to restore; the ecclesiological instinct lay not very far below the surface in these Victorian Churchmen. The church had a capital peal of bells, there was a scattered village of 700 people, sadly neglected and much needing a pastor to interest himself about them, and a school much needing renewal. There was no home for the vicar, but Lord Spencer had promised £1,600 to be applied to build one and to increase the endowment. There were 100 acres of glebe land and certain vicarial tithes, making a stipend of altogether £230 per annum. Henry had returned home on the previous night, pleased and wanting to take his wife to see the parish. If they both liked it they would go on to see Lord Spencer at Althorp, which was fourteen miles away. Mr Hillyard had suggested that a licence of non-residence for a year, until the house was built, would probably be given by the bishop, and Henry could put a curate in to do the duty whilst he himself stayed where he was at Pendlebury. Henry and Ella had been at Claremont on the previous night, and they had held a cabinet council on the matter and were all coming round to the idea of accepting the offer. Mr Hillyard was very earnest in the matter, and Ella, Sir Benjamin thought, quite liked the prospect with the country and rides and drives and only two and a half hours from London, where they could go at any time for the day.

It seemed a delightful vista to the old father's mind, not unlike the pleasant situation of Bishop Stanley at Alderley which he had visualized for his son. But alas! at closer acquaintance the rural prospect was by no means so attractive as it had seemed at a first glance. A week later, Sir Benjamin had to report to Oliver that Henry's second visit to Priors Marston with Ella had so qualified the first impression that they had come to their conclusion without doubt. They discovered bad roads, the village was five miles from town or railway station and very retired; the only available site for building was objectionable, and any house existing was hardly suitable to their wants. It would be a year and a half before a new house could be finished, and there was no residence nearer than Southam to be found in the meantime. Nevertheless, Henry's visit to his prospective patron at Althorp had been very pleasant, and Lord and Lady Spencer had extended a cordial welcome. Lady Spencer had been very engaging, and the only other guests had been her sister and husband who had recently been married. The husband had been at Eton and Oxford, and after dinner the three young men had compared notes, setting Harrow and Cambridge against Eton and Oxford. Althorp was a fine old house, the great library overflowing into all the rooms, and there were some grand portraits. Sir Benjamin, however, thought that his family were all glad that Henry had declined the living and glad that Lord Spencer had proposed it so kindly. He had said that he would have liked to have had Henry there, but the two had parted "all right". So Henry returned to Pendlebury for a little longer. Perhaps it was well that he did not accept Priors Marston, for to have buried himself in "very retired" country might have deflected the main purposes of his life. The 1947 Crockford Clerical Directory shows Priors Marston as a vicarage in the diocese of Coventry; it still remains in the patronage of Earl Spencer and has a net income of £185 per annum with a parsonage house and a population of 414; it is held in plurality with the parish of Priors Hardwick. Meanwhile the overflowing library of Althorp has found its way to Manchester, where the munificence of a member of the commercial aristocracy has found it a home in the somewhat gloomy Gothic magnificence of the Rylands Library.

During 1862 and 1863 Henry persevered in his Pendlebury curacy, and Sir Benjamin suffered from the advancing limitations of old age. Brother Thomas was ill, too, and sometimes in great pain, but medical discipline, so Sir Benjamin thought, would scarcely trouble him, for he had had experience of it. He himself had had his training under Dr Jephson, and it so worked into a habit that it ceased to be self-denial. But increasing deafness was a sad trial. On 21 December 1862 he wrote that the Claremont household had all been to church, Henry preaching, so they said, for the Cotton Famine Relief Fund. But a mortifying increase of his deafness cut him off from much intercourse. In May 1863 he is unable to walk much. The Bishop of Orange River preached on 3 May at St John's, and he was tempted and went in the wheel chair. They had five clergymen, the bishop and two attendants, Mr Robson, the vicar, and Henry, the curate. They made quite an imposing procession in their surplices. Mr Robson read the first part of the service, the two attendant clergymen each a lesson, and Henry the remainder of the service. The church was crowded, and the sermon, so he heard, mild and good. But there were consolations in old age, notably that of seeing his sons following in the pattern of good works which he had set them. Indeed, Percival, the eldest, now a country gentleman and entirely resident on the Staffordshire property of Doveleys, gave promise of being an even more extensive church builder than his father. The irresistible urge in the Heywood family, which spread over three generations, to build churches wherever they found themselves, was now displaying itself in the second generation. In the village of Denstone near Doveleys, Percival had commissioned Mr Street to build an entire set of parochial buildings for the use of that tiny hamlet. When Sir Benjamin visited there in 1862 he found the church, schools, and parsonage quite a picture, and his admiration grew each time he saw them. The situation, the grouping, the workmanship—all, he thought, unique, and quite a country gain; they had cost much thought, and it was repaid. Percival's memorial of his mother, the baronet's dear wife, touched Sir Benjamin much, and the few words inscribed could not, he said, have been better.

In 1874 was consecrated St Augustine's, Pendlebury, which was built at enormous cost by Edward Stanley Heywood. It is one of Bodley's masterpieces, and is generally ranked with his other famous church at Hoar Cross, which it much resembles. The church is built of brick, and soars to a great height, with an unbroken roof line from east to west, and internal buttresses pierced with arches so as to form narrow processional aisles. The woodwork, glass, and interior fittings and ornaments are conceived on a lavish scale, and the building, which is set in the middle of a somewhat drab colliery area, is yet another addition to the tale of church expansion on the part of this remarkable family. Nor is this the end of the story. Another brother, Charles James, was concerned with the beginnings of Church life in the district of Pendleton, which eventually became the new parish of St Anne, Brindle Heath. Oliver was a generous benefactor to the church of St John, Pendlebury, and Arthur Henry to the church in Windermere. In the next generation the three devoted sisters, Isabel Mary, Ethelred, and Mary Monica, daughters of Sir Thomas Percival, the second baronet, were munificent donors towards the building of the Holy Angels, Pendlebury, in 1928. There, for the time being, that sort of activity on the part of the family seems to have stopped.

The year 1864 is one of significant change in the life of the Reverend Henry Robinson Heywood. He has been ordained for eight years, and the time is ripe for a living of his own. In March comes the right offer, and Sir Benjamin reports the matter to his brother Thomas in a letter of 8 March. That morning, he says, the vicar of Eccles, in a note to Henry, had offered him the incumbency of Swinton, vacant by death of Mr Broadley. Henry, apparently without hesitation had accepted it, it was what he and Ella had desired, and what they all liked. He had a good work before him, and one for which he had an especial fitness; he would enter upon it heartily and with a cordial welcome from the people. What the church was, Thomas knew—and we have also seen. There was no house for him, said Sir Benjamin; though a vicarage certainly existed then and still exists, but no doubt his father considered it neither large enough nor grand enough for his son and his growing family. The population was said to be 6,000 and the stipend £200 a year. "He will change the aspect of things," wrote Sir Benjamin, "and could not, I am sure, begin better." The father's confidence was certainly prophetic. To his eldest son, Percival, he wrote on 14 March: "Henry is our great interest now. The time and circumstances of the appointment bring Trench's lines to my mind:

'Thou cam'st not to thy place by accident,
    It is the very place God meant for thee.'"

There was a great and good work to be done; he would enter upon it heartily and with liking, and he had some special qualifications for it. Ella, too, liked it. There was a possible house which Henry was inquiring about. This presumably was the large mansion, Moorfield, at which the new vicar and his family took up their residence at the beginning, and at which he died in 1895 and she in 1928.[1] If Henry were to build, said his father to Percival, meaning presumably either house or church or both, he would need Percival's help. On that day, Henry was going to tell the gentlemen who were welcoming him so cordially that, before he accepted, he must know what their intentions were about providing a new church.

The final letter of the collection which bears upon our subject was written to Henry on 12 November of the same year, when the new vicar was firmly installed. The son had apparently been describing his new work to his father, and the father was replying. His letter had been a great pleasure to him. It was all good and valuable work. Sir Benjamin's only drawback was that Henry seemed to be running on beyond his strength, and that the curate, Mr Statham, would not be altogether the relief he hoped, the work being more than enough for both. He would be a great relief, however, in making Henry feel that all was not so dependent on himself from day to day, and it was an especial comfort that Henry liked him. "I need", concluded Sir Benjamin, "a little time to digest changes: but, as Lord Carlisle once said, I forget on what occasion, 'I would not be contumacious.'"

That perhaps might be the last word, for it is a fitting epitaph on the life of Sir Benjamin Heywood, first baronet, and real founder of the modern Heywood family. Contumacious he certainly never was, either with God or man, for a tranquil harmony with what he considered to be the will of God and with his fellow men whether in business, parliamentary, or private life was the undeviating aim of his existence. Perhaps that harmony is chiefly shown in his entirely satisfying family relationships. These extracts from his letters have illustrated the touching confidence

---

[1] The house was the property of James Bowers, proprietor of the neighbouring cotton mill and was presumably the "mill house". It had been occupied by John Longshaw before the Heywoods took possession and stood in three acres, thirty perches of land. The early deeds indicate that a dwelling-house stood there in 1761. The purchase price of the house in 1868 was £4,600, and in 1928 it was sold to a firm of speculative builders for £2,275.

which existed between the father and his children and the mutual interests extending to every phase of life which the one shared with the other. The very last printed letter in the memoir, dated 17 June 1865, shows what unbounded joy he had in the next generation which was now growing up. His grandson, Arthur, who was to be third baronet, had been staying at Claremont and had pleased his grandfather very much. The boy was thoughtful, and affectionate, and less reserved. His mechanical tastes interested Sir Benjamin. He had made him an excellent model of his intended bridge between the two woods at Doveleys, and Sir Benjamin was going to have a small engine made for him to turn his lathe. That is the end of the story, for he died two months later, on 11 August 1865.

If this brief study of the family approach to the building of Swinton Church proves anything, it is the extent to which Victorian religion was firmly entrenched in family life. It is an interesting speculation whether religion revived in the second half of the nineteenth century because family sentiment was strong, or whether family life flourished so tenderly because there had been a revival of religion. It is a fruitless speculation, for religion and family are so inextricably related that it is impossible to say which provides the antecedent cause. There is the family loyalty of the Queen, Prince Albert, and their children, so impressive to the Victorian public; there is the intermingling of the Evangelical and Catholic revivals reaping the bountiful harvest of the Victorian Church awakening. These two facts are amongst the most influential in the wide canvas of nineteenth-century social history.

But when we survey the situation in the more particular instance which these letters have revealed we see how the wealthy middle-class banking family, infiltrated and bound up with the beliefs and practices of the Tractarian revival, produced, almost inevitably, the diligent pastor and the ambitious church builder. The social trends, the religious aspirations, the architectural dilettantism of mid-Victorian England have met in a representative of a typically pious middle-class family—Henry Robinson Heywood. It now only remains to describe the actual building of the church.

5

THE BUILDING OF THE CHURCH

OUR sources for the story of the actual building of the new church at Swinton are: first, the comments on its progress given month by month in the parish magazine; second, the large volume of correspondence between the vicar and the subscribers, architect, contractor, and other persons concerned in the work, which was carefully retained by Mr Heywood, parcelled up in an old safe and which, as far as we are aware, never saw the light again until investigations were being made in connection with the eightieth anniversary of the church in 1949; and third, a rough diary which was kept by Mr Heywood in a cheap notebook from the time when a new church became a practical policy in 1866 until 1870, a year after its completion. Setting these three sets of documents side by side we can construct a picture of the building scheme at its inception and see the period piece growing day by day. Thus having traced four approaches of thought and social behaviour which converge upon this enterprise of mid-Victorian church building, we are now in a position to see the actual building in progress.

A determination to erect a more impressive and worthy building for the worship of God in Swinton than the plain brick Georgian chapel was present in Mr Heywood's mind from the time when he accepted the living in March 1864. Before he made his decision he was anxious to know the opinions of the principal gentlemen in the parish on this subject; apparently they were favourable, and he began his task with the intention of building as soon as possible. The first step was to have the chapelry legally formed into a separate parish, and this process was set in motion during the summer of 1864. In the autumn the Ecclesiastical

Commissioners signified their approval, and an Order in Council was made on 7 January 1865 and published in the *London Gazette* of 10 January. The arrangement was that Swinton should become a separate parish at the next voidance of the parent vicarage of Eccles, but progress was apparently speeded by the generous action of the Reverend J. P. Pitcairn, vicar of Eccles, who agreed to a compensation for the fees which were due to him during his lifetime from the Swinton chapelry, and after the signing of the necessary papers of 13 February 1865 Swinton received its separate identity.

Twenty months go by before we reach the next stage, when Mr Medland Taylor, the diocesan architect responsible for many buildings which the creation of the new Manchester diocese and the expansion of Church life in south Lancashire made possible, was in Swinton, measuring the old church and yard in order to make a plan of what it was possible to build on the old site. This was in October 1866, and for the rest of the year the vicar was considering carefully what might best be done. One conviction he came to at this early stage was that the diocesan architect was not of sufficient calibre for the work he proposed to do, and at the very start the name of Street comes into the vicar's head. Perhaps it was suggested by his brother, now Sir Percival Heywood, second baronet, who had recently employed Street with highly favourable results for the new church of All Saints', Denstone, with its schools and parsonage house. Heywood therefore wrote to Street inviting him to meet him when he was next in the neighbourhood, and Street replied that he would do so.

With the turn of the year the question of financial means began to exercise the vicar's mind, and by January he had resolved that he would give £3,000 of his private fortune to build a church which was to hold 900 people. As he speculated privately on the prospects, he visualized a builder's contract amounting to £6,000 and a total expenditure with all extras of £8,000. He hoped to raise another £1,000 from friends outside the parish and looked to his own flock to find the remaining £4,000. But his calculations fell very far short of what was required for the sort of grandiose church which he desired to see in Swinton, and even when Street had reduced his original plans, the final cost soared to a figure of nearly twice as much as the vicar had contemplated.

The diary begins in real earnest in February. The vicar sounded his two churchwardens, Messrs Higham and Longshaw, who both turned out to be favourable, and he therefore determined to bring the "new church" project publicly before the next meeting of his Sunday school staff. He prepared notices to that effect with the circulars convening the meeting. On 19 February he called on Mr James Atherton, a Manchester merchant and one of his richest parishioners, who lived in a large Georgian mansion known as Swinton Park. Mr Atherton seemed at first a little discouraging; he described the project as "premature" but gave the vicar a ray of hope by telling him that his only difficulty would be the *money* difficulty and that no other opposition was likely. However, after a night's meditation on the subject, Mr Atherton seems to have warmed to the prospect, and dispatched a note to Moorfield in which he promised £500 towards the scheme. This note in its fading brown ink is the first of the collection of private letters kept by Heywood relating to the building venture. Mr Atherton said that he had reflected a good deal after the conversation of the previous day, "upon the Building of a New Church at Swinton, worthy of the place, and removing the present unsightly building". He said that he had always admitted that the doing so was a mere question of *time* and *money*. The *noble* example the vicar had personally set by offering to give £3,000 towards such an object, and the confidence he had expressed in being able to raise the remaining £5,000, was most gratifying to him to hear. So, continued Mr Atherton, with much underlining, if the vicar could raise £7,500, he would, in that case, contribute £500. He knew so well the vicar's zeal, energy, and determination in all good and laudable objects, that, humanly speaking, he felt a strong confidence that his efforts would be crowned with success, and that such might be the case was the earnest wish and prayer of his, ever truly and sincerely, James Atherton. The scheme had begun to bowl along; on the following day Heywood's two curates came with their not inconsiderable mites. The Reverend A. Hudson promised £200, and the Reverend S. Faithorn Green £25.

During the next few days the vicar was sounding his own relations and others of his wealthier parishioners. He spoke to his brother Charles James Heywood at the bank, who promised to bring the subject before the other brothers. On 25 February Mr R. Knowles, a wealthy local colliery proprietor, was called upon, who though consenting to come to the public meeting declined to be drawn into any other promise. On 28 February he met Mr Fereday Smith, of Parkfield, another large mansion, who was a high official of the Bridgewater Trust; Mr Smith promised £300, but displayed an early tendency, which developed as the scheme advanced, to be somewhat angular and contrary. He said that he would much prefer a different site for the new church and wanted a building large enough to hold a thousand people. A site consisting of part of the Industrial Schools' land on the other side of the lane from the old church now appears to have been considered for the first time, and Mr Smith also wondered whether, if this were not to be had, Mr Longshaw, the churchwarden, and a local factory owner, would part with a bit of land. This controversy as to site went on for two months, until it was decided to build near the old church, on a site which was extended by the purchase of an adjacent plot from the neighbouring landowner. Meanwhile subscriptions and opinions continued to be canvassed. Mrs Heywood, the vicar's wife, promised to give £50, and Peter Holmes, a local worthy, expressed the hope—quite definitely unrealized—that there would be no pillars to intercept views. Noah Robinson, the school secretary, a man of sterling and loyal character who rendered great service both to the Church and to the local Board of Guardians, during Heywood's vicariate, was naturally cautious and conservative, and confessed to having no dislike for the old place. He does not seem, however, to have impeded the new building scheme in any way.

In the evening of 4 March was held the school committee meeting at which the vicar brought forward, for the first time at all publicly, the subject of a new church. There was no kind of opposition, and everyone was in favour of the site just opposite the existing church in the "Schools Infirmary Field". He was instructed to inquire about the possibility of getting this site and

also to call a public meeting. John Longshaw, however, had
strong contrary views and passed up a note to the vicar offering
£500 if the new church were built on the old site. At this meeting
handsome donations were announced, to be paid before Christmas, 1869; everybody was in favour of a building on an elaborate
scale, and nobody wanted the seats to be entirely "Free and Unappropriated". Heywood himself commented that in this case he
did not desire it, but as the years went by it became his great
ambition to release the church entirely from pew rents, and this,
at last, he succeeded in doing. On the following day, Mr Bowers,
another factory owner, called, promising another £15 on his
children's behalf, and suggesting that the subject of a new parsonage should be mooted, as people seemed to be in a liberal frame
of mind. On the same day the Heywood brothers promised
£1,000, and by 18 March, the day of the public meeting, the
vicar could count on promises amounting to £8,270.

Street wrote on 8 March to say that he would be at Swinton on
the following Tuesday, but made it clear that he was not prepared
to consider the matter unless he was offered the post of architect;
he would not in any way compete. The vicar thereupon wrote to
Medland Taylor, telling him not to count on being the architect.
Negotiations with the Board of Guardians proceeded daily for
the "Schools site", and at one point it appears to have been suggested that the new church should contain one aisle entirely
appropriated to the use of the Industrial Schools' children. Friends
continued to urge for the appointment of a distinguished architect; at Claremont, on 11 March, the family were pressing for a
London architect in preference to a local one, and there is a letter
from the vicar of Eccles, patron of the living, urging the same
matter. Mr Pitcairn wrote that he heartily rejoiced that there was
so favourable a prospect of a new church at Swinton, and that
Heywood had made such magnificent progress towards the
requisite funds. It would be an excellent thing if he could succeed
in erecting a goodly structure as an example to church builders of
what might and ought to be done in respect of a building dedicated for ever to the honour and glory of God. One could not
help feeling how very much depended on the architect for the

beauty and symmetry and architectural correctness of the proposed church. There had certainly been some lamentable failures
when one considered the outlay incurred. Mr Pitcairn expressed
his confidence that the builder would not let the work be stinted
in funds, and while heartily congratulating him on his success
hitherto, asked to be allowed to express an earnest hope, echoed,
he was sure by Heywood's own mind, that some first-rate
architect who really understood and entered into the spirit of
Gothic architecture (such a man, for instance, as Street of London,
who stood A.1.) might be selected to carry out his desires. What a
mighty difference, even with the same outlay, was often produced
between the designs of a really first-rate man and one below the
first rank of architects. This letter is striking testimony of the
height at which Street's reputation stood throughout the country
at this time, and Pitcairn's letter was only additional support for
the decision which was nearly formed in Heywood's mind. A
fortnight earlier he had written to Street to ask him to send some
photographs of his churches. But there was no lack of candidates
for the job, and on 12 March Heywood had interviewed another
architect called Williamson who was anxious to have it. The
brothers, Arthur and Oliver Heywood were both strongly
opposed to the idea of the new church containing an aisle for the
"pauper children".

The collected papers contain the original notice, heavily
pierced with drawing-pin holes, which was affixed to the door of
the old church calling "a public meeting in the school-room on
Monday March 18, 1867, at 7.30 p.m. to consider whether or no a
new church shall be built for the parish of Swinton, and if the
meeting shall be in favour of this proposal, then to appoint a
committee which shall be authorized to take whatever preliminary steps may be deemed needful". The notice was signed
by Henry R. Heywood, Incumbent, and John Higham and
William Longshaw, Churchwardens. At this meeting, the vicar
was in the chair, and Mr Fereday Smith proposed "that it is for
the benefit of the parish of Swinton that a church be erected".
Mr J. Bowers seconded the proposition, and it was carried
unanimously. A committee of influential local gentlemen was

elected as the building committee, and it was also resolved that the accounts be kept at Messrs Heywood's Bank; the vicar and Mr Atherton were to act as Treasurers. The enthusiasm of the meeting produced a promise of £85 10s. od. in the room; it was determined to try and raise £10,000, and the sum total then realized was £8,355 10s. od. The new church scheme was thus publicly launched, and the vicar was able to report in his April magazine of 1867 that the church was to be a large one, holding about a thousand people, that one entire half was to be free and unappropriated and the site, still undecided, was to be either that of the existing church or on the opposite side of Partington Lane, on land belonging to the Manchester Board of Guardians.

Between the public meeting on 18 March and the first committee meeting on 1 April there was a certain amount of activity. The subscribers' names were entered into a book for the first time. Mr Atherton expressed his preference for the old site, and still more money was promised, the largest sum being £100 from Mr Stuttard, another mill owner. Street's sketches arrived on 21 March, an account was opened at the bank for subscriptions on 23 March, and negotiations about the schools site continued. As a result of an interview on 26 March Heywood became convinced that he would not get the piece of land opposite the old church and on the other side of the lane at which they had been nibbling. Alternatively, the Guardians' official had mentioned the possibility of where the stoneyard was, or the Gas House field. The vicar had had conversations on the same day with Canon Tonge, one of the cathedral clergy, and others, on the architect question. They must certainly not have competition but go in for Street, Scott, or Butterfield, or else Medland Taylor or Paley. Taylor, the diocesan architect, was leaving nothing to chance, for on 30 March there arrived a great bundle of his photographs and drawings from an exhibition for the committee's inspection. On 31 March there was the good news that Richard Barton of Caldy Manor, who had married Lissey, Henry Heywood's sister, would give the communion plate, and that Mrs Henry Heywood would give £100 for a painted glass window. With the thought of

Oliver Heywood's mother, the seventeenth-century iconoclast, in mind, this was reparation indeed!

The first meeting of the building committee was held on 1 April 1867, and we are bidden by the diary to "see minutes"; unfortunately this is precisely what we cannot do, for the building committee minutes have not, so far, come to light. This is a pity, for they might be able to clear up a few points of doubt about the scheme, notably the exact extent of Street's reduction of the original plans on the grounds of economy. But the diary informs us that after much discussion, Mr Atherton proposed, and it was seconded and carried unanimously, that Mr Street be the architect. Letters of application had been read from Mr J. Medland Taylor, Mr Williamson, and Mr Gee, and a letter from Mr Beechey, the vicar of Worsley, had been read, mentioning a Mr Jackson, whose testimonials had been shown. Mr Taylor and Mr Williamson had sent plans of their works for exhibition, and the vicar showed some of Street's which had been sent to him privately. It was understood in appointing Street that he should not be communicated with until a number of details had been settled, and there was still the important question of the site to be arranged. It was clear by now that the coveted site on the Guardians' land could not be obtained, and it was agreed to negotiate with a Mr Paddison who owned the piece of land near the churchyard in order to establish an adequate site near the old church. It was understood that half the church from east to west should be free and half appropriated, and that no chairs, but benches, should be used.

The question of the land appears to have been troublesome for the next few months and was not, in fact, finally settled until 20 December. The extended churchyard site required negotiations with two parties, the Reverend W. Paddison, who was a Methodist minister, and the diocesan authorities, who were asked whether a portion of school land used in connection with an old day-school which had stood near by could be included in the new site. The last was quickly cleared up, for Burder, the diocesan solicitor, was able to inform Heywood on 17 April that the old school strip could be used for the church, as the bishop would accept the title as good. An alternative piece of land belonging to a Mr

15

Lansdale and a Mr Kershaw would have cost altogether £3,000. Paddison's land seemed to be the more reasonable proposition. On the same day some of the building committee met at the vestry to look at the plans which had been made of the adjoining plots. Shortly before 11 a.m. they went to see Paddison, and by 11.45 they had bought his plot for £1,100. An enormous price! commented Heywood; they had offered £1,000 but could not get it for less. However, this does not seem to have been the end of Paddison, for on 16 September we find that the vicar had had an interview with him and found him much agitated about the land having to be bought from him, and the money invested, and not all paid direct into his hands. A three-cornered interview between Heywood, Burder, and Whitehead, Paddison's solicitor, was the only solution, but between 20 and 30 September there was great difficulty in arranging this. Heywood was "bothering" to get the interview, but Whitehead was delaying, saying he was ill, that he would arrange sometime. It is difficult to understand what lay behind this delaying action on the part of the vendors of the land. On 21 October he went to see Paddison about the meeting which had been arranged for that afternoon, but lo! after all the bother, he was in bed! Heywood thereupon went to Manchester, intending to bring Burder and Whitehead out to see Paddison at Swinton, He wasted from 2.30 p.m. to 4 p.m. waiting for Whitehead, and then only his clerk appeared, somewhat tipsy. It was a somewhat unsatisfactory interview after all their delays and all their waiting, but the vicar had faith that it would end well. But what numberless petty bothers there were! On 22 October another meeting was arranged for the following day at Tyldesley where Whitehead's office was. After a long time he came down and the interview took place, the vicar confessing to being rather cross. By 25 November the question was still dragging on, though an end was at last in sight; the land matter had been far more troublesome than the church matter. Questions of boundary walls and a road of access for Paddison were involved, and a tenant named Cook had a business and was occupying part of the required site. The 3 December was another day of protracted negotiations, Heywood hurrying between

Swinton, Manchester, and Tyldesley to try to expedite the tiresome legal processes. The matter was becoming urgent, for the builder's contracts were to be signed on 4 December. On 14 December, after waiting a week, Heywood heard from the Manchester solicitor that the deed had arrived and had been sent to Whitehead for execution. He went in the afternoon to see Paddison about making arrangements to have the deed signed on the following Monday, but Whitehead, awkward to the last, would not agree to the arrangements. There was, however, the satisfactory news that Cook, the tenant, had got a shop and was moving; he was going to have a sale and would probably be gone before the year was out. On 19 December the notices of the sale were posted, and the sale took place on 23 December. One of these sale notices is still retained amongst the relevant papers. The vicar noted that young trees were being taken up in the churchyard on the site of the old day-school and moved down to Holy Rood, a hamlet about a mile away, where a school church had been established within the parish. The trees were to be stored there until wanted again up at Swinton. So, on 20 December, the land question was at last settled. The completion took place at Burder's office that afternoon after Heywood had been kept waiting two hours. Paddison was grasping, Whitehead exorbitant. All of them were cross. Yet Henry Robinson Heywood was very thankful, though very tired.

We may now retrace our steps to the second committee meeting on 22 April, and examine the arrangements which were being made with Street and the varying notions which the committee members had about the kind of church which was to be built. It was at this committee that it was finally decided to negotiate with Paddison for his piece of land, with the result, protracted and annoying, which has been described. There was such a talking at the committee, about all sorts of odds and ends, that the vicar did not arrive home until 10.30 p.m. But he was instructed to get in touch with Street, so that there was definite progress in that direction. Mr Atherton expressed his dislike of doors to the pews; there was argument about the height of the pews, about the width, about cushions, about what seats should be free and what not, about how much the whole job was to cost. Then there was argument about the builder's contract—some thought £7,500 was the figure to aim at—then about what the contract was to include, and about what it was not to include; in fact there was argument, so the vicar noted, about everything. Finally, tentative figures were reached; the total contract was set at £8,000, extras at £2,000, the land at £1,000. So the total estimated expenditure had now climbed to £11,000.

On 29 April Heywood called on Street at his London office and told him what was wanted. He left him a plan of the land, and Street asked for the levels. Having obtained these from Williamson, the surveyor, Heywood was in London again seeing Street for the second time on 8 May. On 2 June Street sent a rough ground plan and a north section of a suggested church, and Heywood "meditated thereupon". On 3 June there was a committee meeting in the evening to look at Street's suggestions, which, it was felt, would want some alteration, and the vicar was instructed to write to him on several points and ask for sketches. He wrote a long letter on the following day, returning his plans with suggested alterations. On 1 July Street visited Swinton for the first time since the idea of a church had been mooted. He saw the site, attended a committee meeting in the evening, and, after discussion, plans were decided upon which he was to draw out and send for the approval both of the committee and the bishop.

At this committee, for the first time, Mr Fereday Smith mooted the subject of a mortuary chapel on the site of the old church, in order to avoid bringing corpses into church. Street, who appears to have taken kindly to the suggestion, and who did, in fact, incorporate something of the same sort into his Milnrow church, proposed that it should be attached to the new church, and Heywood rather favoured the idea as being suitable for weekday services. John Knowles, of the family of colliery proprietors, suggested that the new church need not be so long if it were to contain a west gallery and two side transept galleries. Luckily, notes Heywood, Peter Higson snubbed that and other "non-ecclesiastical" suggestions. Fereday Smith, who previously had wanted low walls and a grand roof and no pillars, now changed his mind and wanted good high walls and good strong pillars "in order that our grandchildren may be able to build side galleries if they are wanted"! The grandchildren, alas, in a more secular age in the middle of the twentieth century, would rather welcome suggestions for reducing these large Victorian churches than enlarging them. But Heywood, with characteristic subtlety, thought this a grand idea, because by gratifying this hobby he got what he wanted. Mr Fereday Smith would be pleased, and the ecclesiologists would be benefited. A wonderful deal of nonsense, he commented, that church would have caused to be spoken. They had, for example, been told all about the fumes from out of coffins which their friend Fereday had said he had *seen* coming up! But Fereday, all along, was inclined to be what Sir Benjamin Heywood might have called "contumacious". He was not happy about the disposition of the appropriated and free seats in the new church. He wrote a strong letter to the vicar on 13 July, requiring that he should have the assurance of satisfaction in the matter; it seemed to him "so essential to the future well-being of the parish (especially after your day) that, I feel", he wrote, "unwilling to be a party to the building of the church unless the foregoing points be abundantly secured". Mr Smith continued to be something of a thorn in the vicar's side for some time to come.

Street's plans arrived on 22 July, and the vicar pronounced them very good. He took them to the bishop, who, it will be remembered, had exploded in a fit of episcopal fury when confronted with the Tractarian embellishments in the chancel at St John's, Higher Broughton. No doubt his lordship had mellowed a little with age, for his only criticisms were a desire for six and not seven steps up to the altar, whether as a safety measure or a counterblast to ecclesiological symbolism, we are not told; an objection to a second altar in the funeral chapel, and a preference for the reading-desk farther forward. In the evening the committee approved the plans, suggesting very slight changes in one or two points of detail. On the whole they were much approved, and Heywood returned them on the following day with a long letter to Street. Thereupon, he and his family departed for a month's holiday.

During September, on his return home, he wrote to Street's office to inquire how matters stood. The reply from Mr George Wood, who appears to have conducted most of the firm's correspondence on blue, sugar-bag paper, was that the quantities were being taken out and that the plans would then, say, in a week, be submitted to the builders. Shortly afterwards he heard again from Mr Wood that the quantities had been taken out, and that the builders wanted to see the plans and site together. Where could they have the plans in Swinton to look at for ten days? Heywood wrote back on 15 September to say that a school classroom would be available for this purpose.

There are letters written in July by Mr John Knowles and Mr Fereday Smith suggesting the names of possible contractors; these had been submitted to Street, who wrote a letter giving particulars of six tenders on 1 October 1867. It was received in Swinton on 2 October, exactly two years before the date of the consecration of the new church. It is worth examining these tenders in some detail, for a comparison of building prices between 1868 and 1953 is both interesting and instructive. The highest tender was that of Ellis and Hinchcliff at £16,750; Southron of Salford was £16,250; Clay of Audenshaw, £15,995; Neill of Strangeways (Mr R. Neill was Mayor of Manchester in 1867), £15,077; Bowden and Edwards of Chorlton-on-Medlock, £13,403 and Horsman of Wolverhampton, the successful candidate, £13,144 0. 3d. This last tender was capable of being reduced to the sum of £10,310 17s. 10d. by excluding the upper stage of the tower and the funeral chapel and calculating for the use of red stone for the external work and omitting the carving. If bricks were to be used for the foundations and the lining-out of the thickness of the walls it would add to the tender £342. If Longridge stone were to be used it would add a further sum of £920. The carving would cost £330 and the funeral chapel £741 2s. 5d.; another additional figure of £500 would make up the total amount of the tender to £13,144 0s. 3d. The lower amount, however, included a font and cover at £25, a pulpit at £60, a reredos at £120, a surplice closet at £2 10s. 0d., the altar and altar rail at £25, and four screens in the chancel at £100. These figures were placed before the committee on 7 October; it was a stormy wet night, and the vicar did not get home till 10.35 p.m. Again we are handicapped at this crucial point by the loss of the minute book, but the magazine in its general report tells us that the tender was much higher than was expected and the plans were returned to London to be reduced.

What exactly were the reductions which Street made? It is tantalizing to be unable to secure the documentary evidence which would give a final answer to this question. Local tradition asserts that there was to have been a clerestory, and that the chancel was to have been carried two bays farther east; this is possible, though we have noted that a fairly wide and shallow chancel was quite in accordance with Street's ecclesiastical ideas and with the main line of his parish church work. Our only clue to the answer to this problem lies in a letter from the architect on 9 October. His clerk writes that Mr Street, realizing that the tender was so much more than the committee had intended to lay out, had gone through the plans and reduced them generally, "both in height and also in length of chancel and transepts, with a loss of about six sittings". Street proposed asking Horsman, who had supplied the lowest tender, to look through the reduced plans and to make out an amended estimate. This arrived on 23 October and the reduced plans on 30 October. The saving effect was £1,114 5s. 2d., and a further sum of £1,260 could be subtracted by plastering the walls and by using Rainhill stone; thus the whole tender could be substantially reduced to £7,936 12s. 8d. Street wrote a personal letter to Heywood on 19 October saying that he had been altering the plans in such a way "that unless you compared the two sets of plans together you would probably hardly detect the difference". He strongly recommended the acceptance of Horsman's tender, and gave his address in Aberdeenshire where he was about to stay as at Lord Lindsay's, Dunecht, Aberdeen. A reference to his son's *Memoir* tells us that he was building a chapel and house there for the noble lord at this time. Back in London again on 28 October he wrote to say that the reduced plans would be dispatched to the bank at Manchester on the following day, and that he himself would visit Heywood at Swinton, Canon Raine at Rochdale, and York within the next day or two. He adds once again: "I do not think the church has lost much by the alterations. In fact I doubt whether you would detect them without comparing the two plans." Street met Heywood at the bank on 30 October; they examined the plans together for two or three hours.

The building committee met on 4 November, with Mr Wood from Street's office in attendance. The vicar reported in his December magazine that the members could not bring themselves to give up several of the great architectural features of the original plans, and therefore the result arrived at was to adopt chiefly the reduced plans, retaining, however, some of the main features of the first design. Though they would not get a church as beautiful as was hoped from the inspection of the original plans, yet they would have a very beautiful one nevertheless, but all the money that they could possibly collect would be required. The church was now estimated at £13,000, and the subscriptions had reached £10,337. The year 1867, said the vicar, had been occupied with preparatory work, 1868 and 1869 they must allow for building work, and in 1870, please God, they might look for a finished work.

A few details remained to be settled before the contract could be signed. On 14 November Street wrote, as has been described, desiring to alter the side elevations of the aisles from four bays to five and offering to pay for the alteration out of his own pocket. His clerk wrote on the same day to establish other points. There was no provision in the estimates for a credence, but if it was wanted it could be inserted at a cost of £5. The tower, in its truncated state, was still quite large enough for a very good peal of bells, and the windows would have sloping sills inside so that they could not be used for hats or as shelves. On 28 November, the clerk wrote that he had forwarded by rail the drawings, specification, and contract to the bank, St Ann's Street. An additional sum of £35 5s. od. had been inserted on the specification for three matters, viz. a stone carved with a cross under the east end, a bell for the vestry, and a general provision for extra depths of concrete. A meeting was arranged for the signing of the contract on 4 December at 7 p.m. at the schoolroom, Horsman the builder being present. A sum of £4,000 was mentioned in the contract as the amount of insurance. Heywood commented in his diary that all was satisfactory; there was no going back, and some little going forward. He had met Horsman accidentally at the site in the afternoon and they were still generally "downspirited" to find that it was still in such an unprepared condition and that there was so little space round about for sheds or for "teaming" (i.e. unloading) stone. But on the following day he saw "old Barlow" at work filling in a hole at the end of Church Street which ran alongside the new site, and the thought struck the vicar that he was the first man on the job, and that that was the first work done for the new church. The filling in was to make all level so that Horsman could erect some sheds there.

On the same day, the vicar was busy getting the signatures of some members of the committee who were absent on the previous night. Atherton, J. Longshaw, Hudson, and others seem to have complied willingly, but Mr Fereday Smith refused to sign the contract. He had been to consult his solicitor who recommended him not. "Just like him!" comments the vicar and adds, "*vide* letters". Mr James Atherton's letter of apology is retained; he had a dinner engagement of some standing, but appointed Heywood to sign the contract for and on his account. Mr Fereday Smith wrote by the hand of a clerk from the Bridgewater offices, Manchester, on 6 December. On the previous evening, he said, he had been so over-fatigued on arriving at home after a very heavy day's work that he could not muster courage to go through the contract which the vicar had sent him. However, having been to his solicitors that morning upon other business, he had submitted the contract to them, and had been advised not to sign. He was not previously aware that the vicar had intended to ask the committee as a body to sign the contract. When he had spoken to the vicar upon this subject many weeks previously, he had understood him to say that he intended to sign it himself and perhaps to ask one or two others who owned property in the neighbourhood to join him. Mr Smith thought that that was the eighth church on the building committee of which he had acted, but he

had never before been asked to sign any contract. The vicar
would see from the solicitor's letter which he enclosed that it was
impossible that he could sign the present one. Indeed he did not
wish to make himself liable, under any circumstances, for more
than he might from time to time promise as a subscription—and
the great amount of business that daily occupied his time made
it undesirable that he should run any unnecessary risk, however
remote, of possible litigation, as alluded to in the solicitor's letter.
His own opinion was that, according to all appearances, everything would go off smoothly, but notwithstanding that, he was
unwilling to act against his solicitors' advice, and that need not
in any way affect the progress of the church, if others chose to
run risks which he declined. How clearly are the individual characters of these mid-Victorians delineated in the fading ink of such
letters as this which have survived! "Just like him!" says the
vicar.

So we reach the new year, 1868, and in his January magazine
the vicar is able to sum up the progress made thus far. The building
contract has been signed on 4 December with Philip Horsman of
Wolverhampton. It provides for an expenditure of £10,073 7s. 8d.,
which does not include the tower above the string course at the
nave ridge line. The external walls are to be faced with Durnford
Bridge Parpoints. The internal facing is to be wrought stone
consisting of Hollington and Longridge stone. The roof is to be
slated with Bangor blue, purple, and green slates, and is to carry
ornamental ridge tiles. The nave seating is to be of pitch-pine,
and the contract includes provision for pulpit, font, reredos,
credence table at the figures previously mentioned; also £300
for the heating apparatus, £100 for chancel fittings in oak, £25
for the communion table, £20 for gas mains, and £5 for a bell in
the tower to be rung from the vestry. The contract promises
completion by 30 June 1869. The land question has been settled,
the documents signed, and the purchase money paid on 20 December. The total cost now is, builder's contract £10,000; land and
expenses £1,200; architect and clerk of works £800; organ, bell,
gas fittings, walls, gates, and labourer's work, £1,000. The total
is £13,000. To complete the tower and to furnish it with a peal

thanks him for sending a copy of the Swinton Magazine, and comments on the satisfactory statement it gave of the schools, in every way. His correspondent rejoiced with him over it and the delightfully good news he had communicated that there really was to be a new church built in Swinton. The old one was associated with the writer's happy earliest years. For as long as the writer could remember, some of them had had the treat of going once a year on the Sunday when there was a collection for the schools, to see all the children in their white frocks and caps and to hear them sing. It was quite a pleasure to the writer to send the enclosed contribution of £10 towards the building of the new church. They were only sorry they could not offer the vicar more, but they had many claims upon them. This letter is not without interest in reflecting upon the long standing popularity of the schools anniversary or schools "sermons", a notable feature, to this day, of Lancashire religious life, as well as upon the zeal with which Heywood cast his net amongst his personal friends in order to garner subscriptions large and small towards the building fund.

The first great public ceremony in connection with the new church was now in sight, and the laying of the corner-stone was fixed for 18 April. On 1 April the vicar and churchwardens met in the vestry at 3 p.m. to make the arrangements and to send out notes of invitation and tickets of admission. Nine hundred of these were dispatched, and the invited guests were requested to meet at the schoolroom at 3.30 p.m. There is a letter from Mr Fereday Smith tendering his apologies for being unable to attend the ceremony. He and his wife had deferred their departure from home until the 17th of the month in consequence of their son's not returning to Oxford till that day. They could not, however, defer going from home longer, as they were giving up the house to the painters, etc., and were anxious to get back into it by the time their daughter's vacation, which only extended to a fortnight, would be over. Under those circumstances he regretted that none of them would be able to attend the ceremony, and he therefore returned the admission cards, with thanks, as they might probably be wanted for others. He hoped that for the sake of all who would attend they would have a fine day.

The first scaffolding poles were put up on 7 April, and in the evening there was the first practice of the chants and hymns for the stone-laying. The choirs of the parish church and of the district church of Holy Rood were rehearsed by the choirmaster, Mr Dyson. The building committee met on 13 April, and the trowel and the brass plate commemorating the stone-laying were exhibited for the first time. When 18 April arrived, Mr Fereday Smith's good wishes as to the weather were gratified, for it was fine, though the east wind was cold. The ceremony was timed for 4 p.m., and shortly before that hour, the procession headed by Captain Beckton and the Swinton Volunteers left the school to march to the site. Behind the volunteers came the scholars, boys, and girls from the various schools in the parish, then the choirs of the parish church and Holy Rood. Next came the members of the building committee, the churchwardens, the clergy in their surplices, and, last, the guests and the general body of parishioners. The procession extended very nearly from the school to the site. The office for the laying of a corner-stone was read by the incumbent and his two curates, Mr Hudson and Mr Green, and the stone was laid by the vicar himself. He also read a report of the proceedings of the building committee, and addresses were delivered by James Bowers, Esq., Oliver Heywood, Esq., John Knowles, Esq., the Reverend E. H. Robson, who had been the Reverend H. R. Heywood's vicar in his curate days at St John's, Pendlebury, and the Reverend J. R. Parr. A silver trowel was presented to Mr Heywood by the subscribers, and Mr Horsman, the builder, gave an oaken mallet and level. The vicar noted that the proceedings had passed off satisfactorily, and the weather, perhaps impressed upon his memory by the length and number of the speeches, had been cold but fine. Eight or nine hundred people, he said, had been gathered round about.

The entries in the vicar's rough diary are now nearly all details of the day-to-day progress of the rapidly growing building, but the story is expanded by the collection of letters, many of them from Street's office which continue at regular intervals. Mr Fereday Smith, that indefatigable correspondent, contributes a characteristic note on 28 April. He had not, he said, been able to attend recent building committee meetings—a bad conscience, perhaps, about the affair of the signing of the contract may have kept him away from both the meetings and the stone-laying—so he wrote to inquire about the height the committee intended to carry the inside wooden panelling to protect the congregation from proximity to the cold stone walls. If it was not too late to make a suggestion, would it not be well to carry the panelling at least as high as the heads of the congregation when sitting. Our forefathers, in a great number of churches that Mr Smith had visited, seem to have had wit enough to think of this, which added materially to the comfort and health of the congregation. Too close proximity to stone, which was a good conductor of heat, was always dangerous, especially to persons who happened to have hurried on a warm day to church, for it was apt to strike a chill into them. Mr Smith did not believe that any architect of eminence would argue that panelling, either round the pillars or against the walls, would spoil the architectural effect; everything would depend upon how the panelling was treated. The day would come, even if it had not now in all cases arrived, when common sense would be held to be an essential element in artistic perfection. He questioned whether, by saving the dressing of so much stone up to a certain level, panelling would not be an economy; but possibly, all these points might have been duly considered already. Conscience may have pricked Mr Smith a little as he concluded his letter, for, he remarked, he was perhaps less entitled than some others to make suggestions at that moment, not having been a punctual attendant at the meetings, and he by no means wished to press his opinions unduly. Mr Smith, it may be remembered, was the proposer of the motion at the public meeting on 18 March 1867 that the new church should be built; his subsequent connection with the enterprise does not seem, as we have seen, to have been entirely felicitous. His project of a mortuary chapel to secure that the main church should not be contaminated by the fumes which he professed to have seen rising from the coffins never materialized; it was one of the casualties of the initial economy drive when Street had to alter his first plans. Nor, for what reason we cannot tell, was his defensive suggestion on behalf of the bald heads of the congregation successful. To this day the nave walls remain entirely of dressed stone, innocent of the desired protective panelling. Unfortunately, Mr Fereday Smith now disappears from the recorded scene, for the letter-book contains no more examples of his diverting epistolary intrusions into the building scheme.

On 7 May the stone which was to form the sills for the windows on the south side of the church was being laid on the walls ready for fixing, and the seat of the sedilia was in position. A man was also working at the outside east cross. On 8 May the first stone arch was erected over the south porch, and the keystone of that arch was then the loftiest part of the building. On 12 May the east outside cross was fixed in its place. A more personal note creeps into the diary on Sunday 17 May, with the reference to a daughter having been born to Hopcroft the foreman. Street's clerk, Mr George Wood, paid a visit on 20 May to inspect the works; Street himself was to have come but was hindered. The details of a stone credence table arrived from Street on 22 May, and on 1 June there was a new clerk of works, by name Jenkins, to replace the first clerk, who had left on 18 April. On 30 June the credence table was being erected in the new sanctuary; part of it had to be sent to Manchester for carving. The two west windows on either side of the tower, complete with their tracery, were inserted on the same day, and the vicar noted that this was the first tracery so far to be put in the church. The weather had been beautiful, fine, hot, and dry for a long time. On 3 July the credence with its carving was finished and in position.

The vicar left for his holiday about the middle of July, and returning after five weeks on 17 August he found the north side of the church much progressed, with its windows being put in; three were already in position. Work was proceeding on the north arches and pillars and was well advanced. All had gone well whilst the vicar was away. On Friday 4 September work was being done on the south arcade of the nave, all was progressing steadily and well, and the vestry, to all appearances, was ready for its roof. On the 17th they were still going on with the south side arches, the tracery of the east window in the north chancel aisle was in, and the outside wall of the north aisle was only about eighteen inches short of its full height. They were beginning to put in the windows of the south side at the west end nearest the porch.

The July magazine had contained a subscription list reaching now the figure of £11,107 15s. 3d., and the August magazine carried a biographical notice of George Edmund Street extracted from the *Illustrated London News* which has been previously referred to. In September an extract from the *Rochdale Pilot* was quoted, describing the laying of the corner-stone of a new church at Milnrow near Rochdale on 15 August. This church had also been designed by Street, and was to cost £10,000 plus the furnishings. It was to accommodate 1,100 people without galleries. The account gave a detailed list of gifts which had been made to the Milnrow Church, and the vicar expressed the hope that such generosity would be emulated in Swinton. Although the corner-stone had been laid later than at Swinton, the Milnrow Church was completed and consecrated some months earlier. In the October magazine the vicar gave directions to intending donors of stained-glass windows. Only first-rate work was to be allowed in the new church and those who intended to present windows must consult the vicar before they approached any artist in the matter. Even this scarcely seems to have been an adequate safeguard, but so greatly have notions of taste and colour and draughtsmanship altered as regards stained glass that the contemporary work of Clayton and Bell, and even Kempe, is more criticized than admired in these days.

October 1868 brings us to a point twelve months before the consecration of the church. On the 5th Mr Wood was visiting Swinton again, and the workmen were busy on the south windows and the walls over the south arches. The wooden frame for the chancel arch was being put up, and the woodwork for the vestry roof prepared. At the district church of Holy Rood they were having a farewell tea-party for the Reverend A. Hudson, the curate who had been a liberal subscriber to the new church fund at the start and who had been appointed vicar of the new church of Holy Trinity, Bingley.

16

On 9 October they were busy on the chancel arch, and on the 19th and 20th on the vestry chimneys, which now, in their stack of three, stood up as a little pinnacle. Nearly all the windows on the south side were finished, leaving then only the great east and west windows to do. The 30 October saw the appearance of a roof for the first time, when roofing began on the north-chancel aisle, and on 3 November Mr St Aubyn, the new and third clerk of works, arrived on the job. Street visited the work on 14 November, but the vicar was absent at the time; when he returned on the 20th he found the rafters installed on the north and south chancel aisles and work proceeding on the chancel rafters. All the windows were in except those at the east and west, but there was no roof on the vestry yet. Mr St Aubyn was preparing drawings of how the glass was to be arranged in the windows. There is a reference on this day to the "tragic end of John Cook that we had to do with in site arrangements". What this end was we are not told, but the former tenant of the new church site was brought home in his coffin that evening. There was very nearly another tragedy on the building itself on 12 December, when a man called Mather of Barton tumbled off the east end of the church. It was the first accident that had occurred on the site, but luckily the man was not much hurt, and the vicar wrote to Mr Connell, the vicar of Barton, on 14 December, asking him to look after Mather. The east window tracery was being put in on 9 December, the north-aisle principals were now up, and on 28 December the vicar noticed for the first time some slates piled up in a corner.

It was apparently about the end of 1868 that it began to be felt that it would be a pity to leave the tower in an unfinished condition. Amongst the relevant papers is included a petition signed by thirty-one local gentlemen, urging that this work should be proceeded with immediately. It is addressed to the churchwardens of St Peter's Church, Swinton, and says:

We, the undersigned parishioners of Swinton, regarding with regret the fact that the funds at present available for the erection of the new church are not sufficient to complete the tower also, are anxious that the churchwardens of St. Peter's Church, Swinton, should call a public meeting at an early opportunity to ascertain the feelings of the parishioners on the subject and see what can be done in the matter.

Mr Atherton, the treasurer of the building fund who had been an early and generous subscriber to the new church, does not seem to have been very keen on the subject of the tower. He summarizes the financial situation in a letter to the vicar on 7 December and points out that £1,665 needs still to be raised to complete everything required except the tower and the bells. Instead of trying to raise funds for the tower and bells, which would probably cost £2,250 to £2,400, he would suggest that the committee throw all their interest and influence into raising the sum of £1,665; towards such an object, if agreed upon, he would contribute £100.

The vicar discussed the situation in his December magazine. No doubt, he said, it would cost less money and cause less confusion to complete the fabric then, rather than to bring masons and sheds and so forth on to the ground at some future time. No doubt the church would look short of a very important part of itself until it got its tower, but, for all that, they had never yet ventured to hope that it would get that, its completion, for some years to come. He wanted to state that he, for his part, was not going to *beg* now for the tower, but if anyone chose to offer for the tower, their offers would be thankfully accepted. The matter must be decided, one way or another, before the year was out. A thousand pounds, promised by Christmas, would probably justify the committee in telling Mr Horsman to go on. The decision to proceed was apparently made, for in the April magazine following, when the tower fund is mentioned for the first time, a sum of £790 has been promised, the Reverend H. R. Heywood heading the list with a subscription of £300. At the end of 1868, £11,335 12s. 11½d. had been promised towards the original appeal, of which £9,000 had been paid. The teachers and scholars of the Church Sunday-school, who were going to give the reredos at a cost of £120, were reminded that towards that sum £41 had now been given. The teachers and scholars of Holy Rood school, who were going to give the font at £25, had now paid £5. Spiritual advance, in good Tractarian style, was also keeping pace with the building operations, for at the end of 1868 it was announced that in future there would be Morning Prayer in church at 10.30 a.m. on every festival and saint's day and that there would be an evening service with a sermon every Wednesday at 7.15 p.m.

The first entries in 1869 deal with the slating of the church. It was a long and tedious business, and was interrupted by many delays which seem to have irritated the vicar a good deal. The diaper patterning of the vari-coloured slates may have been the cause of the delay, and frequently we find that the slaters were held up for want of proper material. They arrived on 13 January and began first on the south side of the south chancel aisle; on the 15th they reached the north side. The vicar was in London on the 19th conferring with the architect and also with the firm of Hill about the organ. On the 20th, the day on which the top stone, the cross at the east end of the nave was set up, he was with Warner arranging about a bell. The masons had a flag flying on the 21st in honour of the top stone and as a hint to the committee to provide a recognition of their services. On his return from London on the 22nd the vicar saw this top stone, the first gable end cross that had been put up, for the first time and noted that the vestries were now roofed in. On 28 January Warner's man from London was in Swinton to see about the bell; a bell would be all right in the temporary place in the unfinished tower, but they would only be able to chime it. The masons who had not hoisted their flag in vain were rewarded on 6 February; everybody on the works was given 2s. 6d. in lieu of a supper, in honour of the top stone. By 16 February all the west-window tracery was in place. Distinguished visitors began to come to inspect the new church, now assuming something like its final shape; Canon Marsden was there from the cathedral on the 16th, and on the 17th came Sir Thomas Percival Heywood, the vicar's elder brother, who admired everything, the west window particularly.

March was a month of aggravating delay because of the shortage of green slates, and the vicar complained that the progress on the building had of late been very slow. On 4 March Street visited in the morning, and on the 11th the tenor bell was cast in

London. "Delay, delay," bewailed the vicar on 15 March. "Slates will not come. Nothing has been getting on lately except the tower." However, on the 24th, a fresh consignment of slates, in the shape of one cart-load, appeared. There had been a long and useless delay and they were weary of seeing no "getting on". Now for the slaters! The 26 March was Good Friday, and the slaters began again. It was unfortunate that they should come and begin, only to be stopped; "but", said the vicar, "they must not slate to-day." On Easter Tuesday they were putting the ridge tiles on the roof of the nave, and the green slates were nearly all used up again. Another delay, the vicar supposed! Mr Hudson, the former curate, paid a visit on that day, inspecting the tower which had now reached the height of the nave. On 31 March the slaters were stopped again!

On 1 April a visit from Street was expected, to make a survey of the tower and to report whether it was safe to go on. Some supposed very slight settlements had been pointed out to the vicar. In a mining area the danger of subsidence is something for which watch must be continually kept and, in fact, corrective repairs have regularly been effected on this church because of this trouble during the last eighty years. Street, however, did not arrive, as expected, but a load of iron gutters and pipes made their first appearance. On the 9th, the cross for the gable end of the chancel arrived from Wolverhampton, but it was broken when it was received, so it had to be returned to be cut anew. On Saturday the 10th the tower was finished according to the terms of the original contract, namely, to the roof line. On this day they were grubbing up a big root just at the entrance to the place where the heating apparatus would be accommodated. Horsman, the builder, in a letter of 24 February had contracted to construct a heating chamber with flues, chimney, steps leading to the chamber, and a low wall adjoining the steps for £120 extra. Hopes were held out that slating would recommence at the beginning of the next week, but the vicar feared that it was a vain hope.

Street paid his next visit to Swinton on 15 April, and was present all morning examining the tower to see if it was fit to be proceeded with. A reversed arch was to be put under the south tower window where a weakness showed, but no further work was to be done on raising the tower for a month, anyhow. The carver was also on the site getting sketches from Street, and some more green slates arrived. Not enough, but some, said the vicar. The slaters now were to come on the following Monday. On Monday 19 April the vicar noted that there was something more like life; the slaters had returned, and he hoped that they would finish now. The plasterers were expected on Thursday, and the carvers on the following day. Carving began in the nave on Wednesday 21 April.

It is worthwhile to pause in the narrative at this point, and to give a little attention to the carver and the cost of his work. The carving of the capitals of the nave piers is one of the most beautiful details of the work in Swinton Church, and we are fortunate in possessing a letter which gives us the information we would wish to have. The carver was Mr T. Earp[1] of 49 Kennington Road, Lambeth, South, and he was responsible for the work both at Swinton and Milnrow. One has sometimes wondered, when viewing the work of medieval carvers in old churches and cathedrals, who the craftsman was and what he was paid; it is interesting to be able to answer such questions for a mid-Victorian church. In a list of estimates given on 28 October 1868 Mr Earp quotes these figures: six clustered capitals in the nave, £45; four responds in the nave, £16; two capitals to the chancel arch, £16; two capitals to the chancel aisles, £12; two bosses £1; four bosses in the nave £2; thirty exterior bosses £12; six "gurgoyles" in the tower £10. The total bill for this extensive estimate of carving in a large church thus reaches the modest sum of £114.

In the magazine of April 1869 the vicar states these detailed costs of carving, and invites individual donors to make themselves reponsible for them. In a private note on Earp's estimate and also in the magazine we are given the names of the people who responded. Mrs Lansdale, Mrs Heywood, Mr N. Robinson, Mr J. Clough, Mr Bowers, Mrs Gibson, and the Reverend

---

[1] A reference to him in the guide book of Holy Trinity, Hastings, where he worked, describes him as the greatest stone carver in England of his time.

S. F. Green. In the same magazine, Messrs Warner's estimate for a peal of eight bells is also given, and amounts to £774 13s. od., with a chiming apparatus costing £60 extra. Already four of the bells have been promised, the tenor by the Vicar at £161 14s. 6d., No. 7 by Mrs T. Knowles at £126 1s. 6d., No. 6 by R. Knowles, Esq., at £107 14s. od., and No. 5 by C. J. Heywood, Esq., at £93 19s. od. In the May magazine the vicar is reported as having given £1 10s. od. for carving at the credence table, and donors are still required for two more capitals in the nave and one on the chancel arch. The subscription list for the church stands at £12,149 2s. 5½d. and the tower fund at £945. Mr Street's award of the diploma as foreign member of the Imperial and Royal Academy of the Fine Arts at Vienna is reported, together with the *Architect* comment on his work.

We return now to the vicar's diary to observe the last stages in the building of the church. On Saturday 15 May Mr Wood was in Swinton inspecting the work, carving was going on on the north capitals, and plastering, but nothing else. The tower work was at a standstill. "Slack!" commented the vicar. On Tuesday the 18th he went to see the bishop in the afternoon about the consecration of the church which was planned for 2 October. He wrote also to the Bishop of Peterborough to invite him to come and preach on the great occasion, but the bishop declined. On the 19th the stone cross was erected on the outside of the east end of the chancel. On 7 June the vicar saw the first signs of the heating apparatus, and the work of fixing it began. Street was present in Swinton again on the 15th, inspecting the tower, and pronounced that after inserting some more rings in it, the work might proceed. Lighting arrangements were now coming under discussion, work on the brick-work of the heating chamber was going on, and the carver was at work on the piers on the south side. On this visit, the vicar instructed Street to design an altar cloth. On the 28th some of the glass for the windows arrived and was unpacked. In his June magazine the vicar had announced to his people the hope that the new church might be consecrated on Saturday 2 October.

On 9 July the vicar saw for the first time that some of the seating had arrived; it was stored up against the south wall of the nave.

The men who were installing the gas and heating systems were at work. On the 30th work was proceeding again on the tower, and enormous slabs of stone were being hoisted up which were to be set in place on the following Monday. So next week, the vicar congratulated himself, they might have the pleasure of seeing the tower work going forward again after a three months' stoppage. The joiners were fitting together the wood flooring and the pews, the carver had reached the chancel end of the church, and all was ready for tiling the vestries. Men were still at work on the windows. The vicar was now away for three weeks, and on his return on 26 August found the tower progressing; it had reached the bottom of the clock faces. The seats were mostly in their places, the tiling was well advanced. Work had begun on the reredos, and the inside carving was finished. They were beginning to construct the floor for the seats in the chancel, and new ridge tiles crowned the nave. The 23 September is the last entry in the diary before the consecration of the church. The chancel gas corona was put up, and there was gas in the church for the first time. Going in to look after the evening service in the old church, the vicar found men at work on the reredos. The super altar had been put up on that day, the joiner was panelling the vestry, but the organ had not yet arrived.

In July, the Reverend Sidney Faithorn Green, curate, accepted the rectory of St John's, Miles Platting, in the gift of the vicar's brother, Sir T. P. Heywood. He had apparently been a great strength to his vicar, especially during the arduous adventure of building the new church, and Heywood was loath to lose him. He spoke of the loss to Swinton as being very great and widely felt; Mr Green left with the good wishes of everyone, and it was pleasant to recollect that Miles Platting was only about six miles from Swinton. After the customary farewell tea-parties, Mr Green received "a very handsome time-piece" and "a very beautiful silver inkstand". He ministered for the last time in Swinton on 5 September and communicated a large number of parishioners, "many of whom not only then received the Holy Communion at Mr. Green's hands for the last time, but received it for the last time in the Old Church". He began his new duties at Miles Platting on 12 September. It would have surprised many of his friends, old and new, had they known that twelve years later he would be languishing in a cell in Lancaster Castle. He was condemned under the Public Worship Regulation Act in Lord Penzance's court on eleven charges: (1) the mixed chalice; (2) lighted candles; (3) unlawful vestments; (4) kneeling during the prayer of consecration; (5) elevation of paten and cup; (6) placing the alms on the credence instead of allowing them to remain on the Holy Table; (7) using the sign of the cross towards the congregation; (8) consecrating so as to prevent the people from seeing him break the bread or take the cup in his hand; (9) unlawfully, and in a ceremonial manner, and as part of the service, raising the cup; (10) a large cross of brass on the Holy Table, or on a ledge immediately above the same and appearing to form part thereof; (11) a baldachino. He was condemned in 1879, and for contempt of court was imprisoned in Lancaster Castle from 19 March 1881 to 4 November 1882. His release was secured only by his resignation of the benefice. Throughout the twenty months of his imprisonment Sir T. P. Heywood and his brother, the vicar of Swinton, were exploring every avenue to procure his release, and numerous indignation meetings were held on his behalf in different parts of the country. After leaving prison the Reverend S. F. Green was invited to preach at Swinton, and, in spite of rumours of some local opposition to his appearing in the pulpit of the church, he was received with an enthusiastic welcome on the part of a huge congregation.

The July magazine gave the twenty-second subscription list to the new church fund which now stood at £12,181 7s. 2½d. and the tower fund at £1,056; £1,250 more was still needed for the tower and nearly £900 for the church; donors were still invited for three carved capitals in the church and the thirty bosses and six "gurgoyles" outside. In the August magazine there is a note which reflects upon the health of Dr Prince Lee, the diocesan bishop, and a list of preachers who are to take part in the opening of the church. In the September magazine, with the church fund at £12,224 10s. 4d. and the tower fund at £1,068 9s. 8d., it is announced that the last service in the old church will be on the evening of the Feast of St Michael and All Angels. In the October magazine the arrangements for the consecration, with the names of visiting preachers, were given in full; £800 was still wanted for the church and £1,200 for the tower. The vicar had had various disappointments in his arrangements for visiting preachers. The Bishops of Oxford and Colombo both found that they could not preach at any of the services, nor could the Rev. A. Broadley, presumably the son of a former vicar of Swinton. The Bishops of Chester, Peterborough, Lichfield, and Rochester had also been invited but declined. The Deans of Ely, Chichester, and Chester similarly said no. The thanks of the whole parish, said the vicar, were due to Canon Hillyard of Southam for his untiring and un-wearying exertions to provide his old curate with help and them with profit at that long looked for time. Those preachers who had been good enough to say they would come, would, the vicar was sure, meet with a hearty welcome. Some of them came hundreds of miles to meet the parishioners of Swinton; surely every parishioner of Swinton would go as far as the church to meet them.

On Saturday afternoon, 2 October 1869, at 3.30 p.m., the new church was consecrated by Dr Prince Lee, the Lord Bishop of Manchester. He died on 24 December, so this must have been one of his last official appearances. The vicar reported that there was a large gathering of clergy, parishioners, and visitors. Evening Prayer was read by the vicar, and the two lessons by his two former curates, the Reverend A. Hudson and the Reverend S. F. Green. The Archdeacon of Manchester preached an excellent sermon. The first sermon that had been preached in the old church had been printed and published at the request of the con-gregation; that sermon after a lapse of seventy-eight years was interesting to possess. Would not the archdeacon's sermon, asked the vicar, be interesting to read and possess, both then and there-after? The collection after the service amounted to £144 10s. 0d. On Sunday the 3rd there were three services, and in the morning, at 10.30, Canon Hillyard, Mr Heywood's former rector, was the preacher. There were many communicants, and the offering amounted to £40 0s. 11d. In the afternoon the sermon was preached by the vicar himself, after which the sum of £19 12s. 10d. was collected. At the evening service, when the Reverend Prebendary Mackarness, Bishop-elect of Oxford, preached, there was a crowded congregation. The collection was £20 6s. 2d., making the amount for the day £79 19s. 11d. There was daily morning prayer throughout the whole of the week following, while on the Wednesday there was a full evening service, with a sermon by the vicar again—a poor substitute, he interpolated, for the Reverend G. Body, who was to have been the preacher. The collection was £12 18s. 3d. On Sunday 10 October the consecration and opening services were completed. Holy Communion was celebrated at 7.30 a.m., the offertory being £2 15s. 3½d. Morning Prayer was at 10.30, when the Bishop of Winchester's eldest son, the Reverend J. M. Sumner, preached. The collection was £34 4s. 8½d. In the afternoon the patron of the living of Swinton, the Reverend J. P. Pitcairn, vicar of Eccles, was the preacher. The collection was £7 10s. 10d. In the evening the Reverend W. Walsham How—a well-known name—preached an excellent sermon to a very large congregation. The collection afterwards amounted to £20 18s. 9¾d., bringing the total of the day's collections to £65 9s. 7¾d. and the total of all the collections during the opening services to £302 17s. 9¾d.

Had he said much of the collections, concluded the vicar in his account of this memorable week, perhaps a trifle conscience-stricken? Had he said little of the prayers? It was because he could measure, and had to measure, the value of money; it was because he could not measure the value—so much was it greater—of the prayers. God grant that they might have been, and yet might be, heard. God grant that that church might be a treasure more priceless than gold to many souls. God grant that in the Great Day of his appearing, that church might have been the means—under his blessing—of presenting before him many who should not be ashamed, but who having waited for him and having looked for him here below, should have found that "House of God" to them "The Gate of Heaven".

* * * *

This moving peroration is, of course, not quite the end of the story of the building of the period piece, for the tower still remained to be finished, and there was still a little unfortunate wrangling on the subject of money payments to Mr Horsman and Mr Street. In August 1870 Mr Street was complaining of the building committee's dealing too rigorously with him, but no bones appear to have been broken on the subject. Mr Horsman wrote his last letter on 30 July expressing his satisfaction at the settlement of his account. He was unwell and able to do but little business, hence his accounts were not supervised by himself. He was very sorry not to have come up when everything was completed, but he hoped that all was to the vicar's satisfaction, as he had instructed Green, the foreman, not to leave until it was so.

The December magazine contained the first two baptisms performed in the new church on 3 October, the first two weddings on 20 November, and the first funeral on 16 November. The deed substituting the new church for the old, and transferring from the old to the new all its appropriate rights and functions, was sealed by the Ecclesiastical Commissioners on 4 November, and a copy received and placed in the church safe on the morning of Sunday 14 November. We may now return to the vicar's private diary to trace the progress that remains, to completing the tower and to the demolition of the old church.

The entries which finished before the consecration of the new church on 23 September do not start again until March 1870, on which day, being a Saturday, at 5 p.m., Mr Longshaw, Mr Higham, and others met the vicar and the curate, Mr Laurie, at the old church, to arrange for its closure. It was rather a melancholy job, thought the vicar, although the poor old church was very forlorn now. On 29 March, between 9 and 10 a.m., the vicar and his church officers were arranging the road around the old church in order to have everything convenient for the sale. The petition for the faculty to demolish had been affixed to the church door on the previous Sunday, and a copy had remained there all the week. On 31 March they were stripping off the ivy from the old church.

On 6 April, a very fine day, the interior fittings of the church were sold. On 10 April which was Palm Sunday, the bell was used in the afternoon for the last time. There was an evening service, but no bell was rung, as the ringer could not get into the old church. On Monday the 11th Mr Bowers, the factory owner, bought the bell, the clock, and the turret, and Mr Laurie, the curate, the cross. The sale was over at 3.20 p.m., and by the time of evening service, the cross, the bell, and the clock were all down. On 13 April, being Wednesday in Holy Week, the top stone of the tower of the new church was laid by Hugh Sumner Heywood, the vicar's young son, in much rain. Mr Laurie, the curate, Mrs Heywood, his mother, and Noah Robinson watched the lad do it. There was a certain poignancy in this little event, for a year later Hugh Heywood died, at the age of eleven, and the beautiful Kempe window representing the Paradise hymn of St Bernard of Cluny, and fixed in the east end of the north chancel aisle, was given in his memory by his uncle Oliver Heywood and his wife.

On Wednesday 4 May during the evening service, the east end of the old church was pulled down with a rush; the vicar heard it while he was reading a lesson in the new church. A month later, after being away, the vicar returned on Saturday 4 June to find all traces of the old church gone. On the following Monday he heard the bells for the first time. The very first tinkle he heard was during early morning prayer, but afterwards he tolled the bells himself and had the tenor bell rung up. Now they were beginning to pull down the temporary partition inside the church between the nave and the tower. On Friday 18 June the bells were first practised on, and there was chiming on four bells under the instruction of a teacher from Pendlebury. On Thursday 30 June the last scaffolding pole which stood in the corner by the belfry door was taken down in the presence of Noah Robinson and the vicar. On Sunday 3 July was the tower and bell opening with the new bishop, Dr Fraser, present in the afternoon, and on Monday the 4th Green, the foreman, departed. On 5 July 1870 came the final clearance of Horsman from the parish. "Now", concluded the vicar, "we are left and have only to *pay*." The final entry in the diary is on Tuesday 20 December 1870: "Scaffold being put up for the E. window. Man here, but not glass."

The magazine entries for the next couple of years round off the story of the building of the church; they are largely a continuous record of gifts for its decoration and embellishment. Indeed, the stream of such generosity has scarcely dried up during the last eighty years, and now, in the middle of the twentieth century, it is as full flowing as ever. The February 1870 magazine has the notice of the gift of three stained-glass windows by Messrs Clayton and Bell at a cost of £158, £146, and £59. In April £500 is reported as collected for the new organ, and £105 10s. 0d. for the carving inside and outside the church. In May Mr Street is designing a very handsome oak lectern, an eagle, which Mr Noah Robinson has been good enough to give to the church. In June it is mentioned that in gallery No. 9 at the Royal Academy will be found a drawing of Swinton New Church and in the *Builder* of 7 May a short notice of this and another of Mr Street's churches. The church fund now stands at £13,371 13s. 2¾d. and the tower fund at £1,108 10s. 11d. The vicar appeals for renewed generosity, and offers £350 himself towards the required balance. On 30 June Dr Fraser, the new Bishop of Manchester, dedicated the tower and bells, and another £100 was raised at the collections at three services. September records the gift of alms boxes and a surplice cupboard, and Mr Bayley, the curate, has promised a bell costing £65, and Sunday school teachers and scholars another bell at £60. The November magazine prints the figure of £700 in heavy type, as the sum now wanted to pay off everything connected with the church building accounts. In December the donor of the pulpit, unnamed, has given falls and drapings which impart warmth and colour to the stone-work and also a complete edition of the works of Baxter in twenty-three volumes, which would no doubt impart an air of scholarship to the vicarage in which they were to be lodged.

In January 1871 Mr Higham has given two very handsome cloth coverings for the desks in front of the clergymen's seats, helping to give warmth and colour to the chancel. The sum of £400 is the balance now required for the building fund. The clock and bell from the old church are installed and doing duty at Mr Bowers's mill. The clock, says the vicar, does duty as before, but the bell has now no Sunday work, but has to be awake at 5.30 on all other mornings in the week. The new east window by Clayton and Bell, given by the vicar's brother, Charles James Heywood, was in its place and completed by New Year's Day. In September 1871 it was reported that all moneys due on account of the church and tower were now paid, and that a complete statement of accounts would be given in the October magazine. Before we examine these final accounts, we may look at one or two notes by the vicar. The marble cross on white alabaster ground for the centre of the reredos was still in the vestry; the effects of the anti-Tractarian demonstration which had a little marred the consecration of the new church, were still unrepaired, but, although the exact date is not apparent, it was not long afterwards that the cross appeared in its appropriate place above the middle of the altar. Two more stained-glass windows were promised—one by Mr and Mrs Oliver Heywood, and one by Mr and Mrs Charles J. Heywood—the clock fund was growing, and £200 more was mentioned as required to complete the organ. The vicar hoped that sometime in the future two open iron screens would be erected on the north and south sides of the chancel, and that there would be two low walls at the entrance to the chancel. A cover or canopy for the font, and screens for the two western doors would also be desirable, and sometime or other the churchyard would need a more suitable wall and better gates, at least one of which ought to be a lych-gate. Needless to say, all these desiderata were given in time. Eight bells were rung for the first time on Easter Day 1872, a wall designed by Street was erected round the churchyard, but the lych-gate had to wait until after the First World War, when it was built as a memorial to the fallen. The tower clock was formally set going at noon on 17 September 1874. Amongst the rich gifts which have been lavished on the church in more recent years, mention may be made of a handsome set of communion plate in silver gilt, studded with semi-precious stones, a bishop's chair, and a processional cross. The windows of the church are now filled with a notable array of stained glass, which furnishes an interesting guide book to the development of that art over the last eighty years. Beginning with Kempe and Clayton and Bell, who were Street's contemporaries, it ranges through Burne Jones, Morris and Co., and Frampton, to the Whalls of the present century. A fine window by Miss Joan Howson, an eminent contemporary artist, is the last of the series, and brings the story of embellishment up to 1953. The advancing usages of Tractarian Churchmanship, with its increasing emphasis on daily services, made desirable the provision of a Lady Chapel, and this was created out of the north chancel aisle in memory of a curate of the church who was killed in the First World War. Riddel posts and curtains have been added to give dignity to the high altar. Apart from these trimmings, no structural alterations have been made in Street's church; architecturally it remains as he planned it, a magnificent specimen of Victorian Gothic. It has been fortunate in the affectionate treatment it has received from the generations which followed its building, who, luckily, were not sufficiently sophisticated to despise the architecture of the period and to attempt to improve upon it.

The final accounts given in the magazine of October 1871 enable us to give a satisfactory and detailed answer to the question: "What did a Victorian period piece cost, and who paid for it?" Let us attempt an answer to this fascinating question. The Receipts and Expenditure sides of the balance sheet show a figure of £17,922 12s. 11d. An analysis of the credit side gives us 208 individual items, mostly personal subscriptions, though they include a few amounts such as "Incorporated Church Building Society, £60", "Exhibition, 1869, £32 1s. 7d." These items amount to £16,931 14s. 0d.; in addition there is a sum of £990 18s. 11d. made up of church and school collections and sundry cards and boxes, bringing the total up to the £17,922 12s. 11d. There were four subscriptions of over a thousand pounds. The largest amount was from the vicar, who gave £4,651 4s. 9d.; the second from his father, Sir Benjamin Heywood, Bt., who gave £1,100; the third from his brother, Charles James Heywood, who gave £1,061; and the fourth from J. Bowers, Esq., the local mill owner, who gave £1,031. Mr Atherton of Swinton House, the lay treasurer of the fund and the parishioner of whom we heard first in the building scheme, was not far behind with £950. There was one subscription of over £700, one over £600 and two over £500. The sale of the old church brought £410 10s. 3d. Next come three amounts of over £300 and three over £200. Seventeen subscribers gave between £100 and £200, three between £70 and £80, and the Church Building Society, £60. Six subscriptions of £50 or over include one of £50 from G. E. Street, Esq., the amount promised for altering the side elevations of the design from four windows to five. There were three subscriptions of over £40 and three above £30. In the next range of £20 and over there are twelve subscriptions, one of £18, one of £17, and sixteen between £10 and £15. The smaller amounts run into the larger numbers, two of £8, four of £7, six of £6, thirty-one of £5, four of £4, nine of £3, thirteen of £2, and thirty-five of sums between £1 and £2. There were fifteen amounts between 10s. and £1, and ten smaller than 10s. The last two details on the list are of two subscriptions of 2s. 6d. Besides these 208 subscriptions it is obvious that the £990 18s. 11d. from sundry collections, cards, and boxes must represent the pence and shillings of hundreds of unnamed humbler folk and children. There is the clearest evidence that the Reverend H. R. Heywood associated with himself, his family, and his wealthy friends a tremendous number of his poorer parishioners. Items in the detailed list like "Chaseley Servants, £6 0s. 0d.", "Industrial Schools Servants £1 5s. 0d.", "Vicarage Box, £1 4s. 8½d.", "Two Wesleyans, 5s. 0d.", tell their own tale of the extensiveness of this community effort. We remember Heywood's appeal that not fathers and heads of families only must build the church, but sons and daughters, children and servants. An analysis of this subscription list abundantly establishes our contention that the building of the period piece was an exciting social adventure undertaken by all sections of the community. Rich and poor combined to erect a great building, which was not only a worshipping but also a social and recreational focus in a neighbourhood, the Christian answer of all classes, led by the wealthy and privileged both cleric and lay, to the mid-Victorian problem of social wretchedness and boredom.

17

The receipts side of the balance sheet gives a complete answer to the question as to who paid for the church. Let us now answer the question as to its exact cost. That may best be done by reproducing in its entirety the expenditure side of the accounts. The furnishing costs are of considerable interest, and architects may like to note how much Street was paid in the middle of the nineteenth century for designing one of his larger churches.

EXPENDITURE

	£ s. d.	£ s. d.
Faculty to pull down old church . .	10 12 10	
Gilbody—Sale of old church . . .	25 19 0	
Trowel for Corner Stone . . .	10 13 0	
		47 4 10
Land, Law Expenses connected therewith, fencing, flagging, paths, etc. . .		1,430 4 3
P. Horsman—Contract, Extras . .	12,232 19 1	
Architect	718 0 0	
Clerk of Works	276 8 4	
Heating Apparatus . . .	226 0 0	
Gas Fittings	218 17 0	
Reredos	195 13 0	
Rugs, Hassocks, Coverings . .	137 8 11	
Carving	119 10 0	
Pulpit	114 0 0	
Sundries	98 0 0	
Lectern	34 0 0	
Legal Expenses	29 0 0	
Altar Cloth and Cover . . .	24 19 2	
Safe	15 0 0	
Lightning Conductor . . .	14 4 0	
Alms Boxes	13 10 6	
		14,467 10 0
Four Bells & Frame for eight . .	529 19 0	
Four Stained Glass Windows . .	832 11 0	
Organ	500 0 0	
Holy Communion Plate & Box .	81 10 0	
Choir Surplices	33 13 10	
		1,977 13 10
TOTAL		17,922 12 11

The story of the building of our Victorian period piece is now complete. It is not, however, the end of the tale of achievement of the enterprising Tractarian vicar. He lived for twenty-six years after the consecration of the church, and it is evident as one turns the pages of the magazines, that for the rest of his lifetime he gave his people little rest in their task of strengthening and expanding the Church in an industrial area where the population continued to grow. Before the new parish church was paid for there were appeals for more money for school churches on the outlying fringes of his large parish—Holy Rood in the Hazelhurst district, Wardley on the Walkden Road, St Stephen's in the Valley district. A new cemetery was established, under the management of a Burial Board elected by a parish vestry meeting, when the churchyard was filled up. The entire church was made free of pew rents, and an assured sum of £50 a year was promised by the congregation, to compensate for the vicar's loss of income. The parish church schools were seven times enlarged, and together it was estimated that over £40,000 was spent during Heywood's incumbency on church and school buildings in the parish.

Honours came to him in the last years of his life. He succeeded Canon Pitcairn as rural dean of Eccles, he was made an honorary canon of Manchester Cathedral, and was elected by the clergy as one of their proctors in the Convocation of York. A volume of his sermons, published in 1896 by Longmans, Green and Co., includes sermons preached in Manchester Cathedral in 1891, Chester Cathedral in 1892, and the Royal Military Chapel, Wellington Barracks, in 1894. There are also some of the addresses delivered when he was a special Lent preacher in St Paul's Cathedral in 1892, 1893, and 1894. But his extensive labours in a large parish had aged him prematurely. In 1893 he had told his brother Sir Percival that if he could have the slightest leading to another and lighter sphere of work he would follow it, for he was tired. But the leading did not come, and he worked on and died as vicar of Swinton on 12 March 1895 at the age of sixty-two. There were unprecedented scenes of acclamation and respect when he was buried in the churchyard, very many friends, eighty of his brother clergy, and thousands of his people surrounded the grave. "Who will be found to carry on the really gigantic work at Swinton I cannot think", wrote the elder brother whose own end came in 1897.

So he died and left to a strangely different world his Victorian period piece. To those who came after him he bequeathed a very deep affection for the church which he built; whether he was able to inculcate as deep a love for the Lord of the Church is a more doubtful matter. That is a question of which the answer is known only to One whose eye penetrates more deeply than the recognizable sources of historical data. If he did not so succeed it was not from any fault of his, for the mainspring of all his busy activity was a very consistent faith in a God whom he had learnt to know from that mingling of Protestant and Catholic traditions in which he was reared. It is unlikely that such great churches as he and Street left us will ever be built again. It is with consternation that one realizes that the mid-twentieth-century answer to similar problems of the movement and regrouping of industrial populations is a pre-fabricated building with stage at one end and curtained altar at the other, costing nine or ten thousand pounds. Yet with such equipment as this the spiritual task of the mid-twentieth century is the same as that of the mid-Victorians. The Churchman of the atomic age is heir also to the great and moving traditions of revealed religion throughout the centuries. It is his task as it was that of his Victorian ancestors to implement them in the idiom of his own time.

BIBLIOGRAPHY

NOTE. Books on Victoriana are, of course, innumerable. The following are those to which I am especially indebted in preparing *Victorian Period Piece*.

1. THE SOCIAL APPROACH

PRINTED WORKS

Benson, A.C., and Viscount Esher (editors), *The Letters of Queen Victoria*, 3 vols. Murray, 1908.

Bolitho, H., *Victoria and Albert*. Cobden-Sanderson, 1938.

Christie, O. F., *The Transition from Aristocracy*. Seeley, Service & Co., 1927.

Disraeli, B., *Coningsby*. Everyman ed., 1948.

Falk, B., *The Bridgewater Millions*. Hutchinson, 1942.

Hart-Davis, H. V., *History of Wardley Hall, Lancashire*. Sherratt & Hughes, Manchester and London, 1908.

Holland, P., *Recollections of Old Swinton*. Swinton, 1914.

Marriott, J. A. R., *Queen Victoria and Her Ministers*. Murray, 1933.

Price, W. R., and Moorman, M., *Anna Maria Philips, A Memoir*. C. H. Barker, Manchester, 1949.

Proctor, R. W., *Memorials of Manchester Streets*. Sutcliffe, Manchester, 1874.

Reeve, H. (editor), *The Greville Memoirs*, 8 vols. Longmans, Green & Co., 1875.

Waugh, Edwin, *Sketches of Lancashire Life*. Simpkin, Marshall & Co., 1857.

Wingfield-Stratford, E., *The Victorian Tragedy*. Routledge & Sons, Ltd., 1930.

Woodforde, J., *The Diary of a Country Parson*, edited by John Beresford, 5 vols. Oxford University Press, 1924.

MISCELLANEOUS SOURCES

Heywood, T., *Sir Benjamin Heywood, A Memoir*. Printed for private circulation by Thomas Fargie, 20 Cross Street, Manchester, c. 1866.

Papers, contemporary letters, cuttings, etc., relating to the building of
Swinton Church, collected by the Reverend J. S. Leatherbarrow.

Papers relating to the building of Milnrow Church, Rochdale, collected by the Reverend J. Raines, F.S.A., kindly lent by the
present incumbent, the Reverend G. Wilson.

2. THE RELIGIOUS APPROACH

PRINTED WORKS

Addleshaw, G. W. O., and Etchells, F., *The Architectural Setting of
Anglican Worship*. Faber & Faber, 1948.

Armstrong, H. B. J. (editor), *A Norfolk Diary: The Reverend Benjamin
J. Armstrong*. Harrap, 1949.

Benson, A. C., and Viscount Esher (editors), *The Letters of Queen
Victoria*, 3 vols. Murray, 1908.

Broadley, R., Various works.

Brontë, P., *A Sermon preached in the Church of Haworth, Sept. 12, 1824*.
R. Brown, Haworth, 1885.

Buckingham, Duke of, *Memoirs of the Court of George IV*, 2 vols.
Hurst & Blackett, 1859.

Christie, O. F. (editor), *The Diary of the Reverend William Jones,
1777–1821*. Brentano's, 1929.

Elliott-Binns, L. E., *Religion in the Victorian Era*. Lutterworth, 1936.

Faber. G., *Oxford Apostles*. Faber & Faber, 1933.

Fellowes, E., *Sayings and Doings of the Lord Bishop of Manchester in
the Administrations of his Diocese, etc*. Joseph Masters, London,
1852.

Holland, *Recollections of Old Swinton*. Swinton, 1914.

Manchester Diocesan Directory, 1953.

Plomer, W. (editor), *Kilvert's Diary*. Jonathan Cape, 1944.

Reeve, H. (editor), *The Greville Memoirs*, 8 vols. Longmans, Green
& Co., 1875.

Webb, B., *My Apprenticeship*, 2 vols. Pelican Books, 1938.

Whiffen, M., *Stuart and Georgian Churches outside London*. Batsford,
1947.

Woodforde, J., *The Diary of a Country Parson*. O.U.P., 1924.

MISCELLANEOUS SOURCES

Collected and bound copies of the parish magazines of Prestwich and
Swinton.

Heywood, H. R., Private Papers, printed Sermons, etc.
Miscellaneous bound tracts contemporary with the early Oxford Movement.
Milnrow Papers.
Notitia Cestriensis, Rt. Reverend Francis Gastrell, D.D., Lord Bishop of Chester, edited for the Chetham Society by Canon Raines, 1850. Chetham Society (Old Series), No. 21.
Swinton Church Papers.

3. THE ARCHITECTURAL APPROACH

PRINTED WORKS

Clarke, B. F. L., *Church Builders of the Nineteenth Century.* S.P.C.K., 1938.
Clark, K., *The Gothic Revival: An Essay in the History of Taste.* Constable, 1929.
Dickins, L., and Stanton, M. (editors), *An Eighteenth Century Correspondence: To Sanderson Miller, Esq.* Murray, 1910.
Eastlake, C. L., *A History of the Gothic Revival.* Long, 1872.
Goodhart-Rendel, H. S., *English Architecture since the Regency.* Constable, 1953.
Hibbert, S. (later Hibbert-Ware), *History of the Foundations in Manchester,* 3 vols. Agnew & Zanetti, 1830.
Overton, J. H., *The English Church in the Nineteenth Century.* Longmans, Green & Co., 1894.
Street, A. E., *Memoir of George Edmund Street, R.A.* Murray, 1888.
The Torrington Diaries of the Hon. John Byng, 3 vols. Eyre & Spottiswoode, 1934.
Whiffen, M., *Stuart and Georgian Churches outside London.* Batsford, 1942.

MISCELLANEOUS SOURCES

Notes on the Churches of Lancashire, Sir Stephen R. Glynne, Bart., edited for the Chetham Society by the Reverend J. A. Atkinson, 1893. Chetham Society (New Series), No. 27.
Swinton Church Papers.
Swinton Parish Magazines.
Thomas Taylor, Regency Architect, Leeds, by Frank Beckwith. Publications of the Thoresby Society, 1946. Monographs I. No. 94, 1949.

4. THE FAMILY APPROACH

PRINTED WORKS

Grindon, L. H., *Manchester Banks and Bankers*. Manchester, 1877.
Halley, R., *Lancashire: its Puritanism and Nonconformity*. Manchester, 1869.
Hammond, J. L., and B., *The Bleak Age*. Pelican Books, 1949.
Love and Barton, *Manchester as it is*. Manchester, 1839.
Turner, J. H. (editor), *Oliver Heywood's Diaries, etc.*, 4 vols. A. B. Bayes, 1882.

MISCELLANEOUS SOURCES

Heywood, T., *Sir Benjamin Heywood, A Memoir*. Printed for private circulation by Thomas Fargie, Manchester, *c.* 1866.
Leatherbarrow, J. S., *The Lancashire Elizabethan Recusants*. Chetham Society (New Series), No. 110, 1947.
Memoir of the Reverend Oliver Heywood, B.A. Idle. Printed by John Vint, 1827.
Reminiscences, Letters and Journals of Thomas Percival Heywood, Baronet, arranged by his daughter. Printed for private circulation by Thomas Fargie, Manchester, 1899.

5. THE BUILDING OF THE CHURCH

MISCELLANEOUS SOURCES

Heywood, H. R., Manuscript Diary kept during the period of the building of the church.
Swinton Church Papers.
Swinton Parish Magazines.

INDEX